THE CHANGING
OF THE

KRISTIAN COATES ULRICHSEN
(*Editor*)

The Changing Security Dynamics of the Persian Gulf

جامعة جورجتاون قطر
GEORGETOWN UNIVERSITY QATAR

Center *for* International *and* Regional Studies

HURST & COMPANY, LONDON

Published in Collaboration with Center for International and Regional Studies, Georgetown University–Qatar

First published in the United Kingdom in 2017 by
C. Hurst & Co. (Publishers) Ltd.,
41 Great Russell Street, London, WC1B 3PL
© Kristian Coates Ulrichsen and the Contributors, 2017
All rights reserved.

Printed in India

The right of Kristian Coates Ulrichsen and the Contributors to be identified as the authors of this publication is asserted by them in accordance with the Copyright, Designs and Patents Act, 1988.

A Cataloguing-in-Publication data record for this book is available from the British Library.

ISBN: 9781849048422

This book is printed using paper from registered sustainable and managed sources.

www.hurstpublishers.com

CONTENTS

ACKNOWLEDGMENTS

This book is the result of a two-year research initiative undertaken by the Center for International and Regional Studies (CIRS) at Georgetown University in Qatar. Directed by Mehran Kamrava, the project was developed and supported by the CIRS team: Zahra Babar, Suzi Mirgani, Elizabeth Wanucha, Barb Gillis, Dionysis Markakis, and Haya Al Noaimi. Special thanks go to Justin Gengler and Ole Wæver, who enriched the working group meetings with their contributions. Finally, grateful acknowledgment goes to the Qatar Foundation for its support of research and other scholarly endeavors.

LIST OF CONTRIBUTORS

Khalid Almezaini is an Assistant Professor at Qatar University where he teaches International Relations of the Gulf States and Security of the Gulf. Before joining Qatar University, Almezaini taught Middle East Politics at the universities of Cambridge, Exeter and Edinburgh. He completed his PhD at the University of Exeter. Almezaini's research interests range from International Relations of the Middle East states to foreign aid and foreign policies of the Gulf states. He is also interested in the political economy and security of the Gulf States. Almezaini is the author of *Politics of Aid: Foreign Aid Programs of the Arab Gulf States*, published 2016.

Alanoud Alsharekh is a Research Associate at the London Middle East Institute at SOAS, and has held senior consultative and teaching positions in academic, governmental and non-governmental institutions in the Arabian Gulf and abroad. Her research won the Arab Prize for best publication in a foreign journal in 2014, and includes books such as *The Gulf Family: Kinship Policies and Modernity* (Saqi Books, 2007) and *Popular Culture and Political Identity in the Arab Gulf States* (Saqi Books, 2012). Alsharekh was awarded the knighthood of the National Order of Merit by the French Government in 2016 for her dedication to improving women rights in the region.

Gawdat Bahgat is professor of National Security Affairs at the National Defense University's Near East South Asia Center for Strategic Studies. His areas of expertise include energy security, proliferation of weapons of mass destruction, political economy, and US foreign policy. Bahgat has published eleven books and more than 200 articles in scholarly journals.

Kristian Coates Ulrichsen is Fellow for the Middle East at Rice University's Baker Institute for Public Policy and Associate Fellow at the Royal Institute of International Affairs (Chatham House). His research focuses on the international relations and international political economy of the Persian Gulf as well as the reformulation of regional security structures. Coates Ulrichsen is the author of six books, including Insecure Gulf: *The End of Certainty and the Transition to the Post-Oil Era* (2011), *Qatar and the Arab Spring* (2014), and *The First World War in the Middle East* (2014), all published by Hurst.

Nader Entessar is Professor and Chair of the Department of Political Science and Criminal Justice at the University of South Alabama. He specializes in foreign and security issues in the Persian Gulf region as well as ethnic politics in the Middle East. He is the author of numerous articles in academic journals in the United States, Europe and the Middle East. His most recent books are *Iran Nuclear Negotiations: Accord and Détente since the Geneva Agreement of 2013* (Rowman & Littlefield, 2015), and *Iran Nuclear Accord and the Re-Making of the Middle East* (Rowman and Littlefield, 2017).

Joseph A. Kéchichian is Senior Fellow at the King Faisal Center for Research & Islamic Studies in Riyadh, Sa'udi Arabia, and a Senior Writer with the Dubai-based *Gulf News*. He served as the Honorary Consul of the Sultanate of Oman in Los Angeles, California between 2006 and 2011. Kéchichian received his doctorate in Foreign Affairs from the University of Virginia in 1985. In the summer of 1989, he was a Hoover Fellow at Stanford University. Between 1990 and 1996, he labored at the Santa Monica-based RAND Corporation as an Associate Political Scientist, and was a lecturer at the University of California in Los Angeles. His latest books include *From Alliance to Union: Challenges Facing Gulf Cooperation Council States in the Twenty-First Century*, Brighton, Chicago, Toronto: Sussex Academic Press, 2016; *'Iffat Al Thunayan: An Arabian Queen*, Brighton: Sussex Academic Press, 2015; and *Legal and Political Reforms in Sa'udi Arabia*, London: Routledge, 2013.

Dionysis Markakis is a lecturer in International Relations at Queen Mary University of London. A Post-Doctoral Research Associate at the Center for International and Regional Studies (CIRS), Georgetown University in Qatar, he holds a PhD from the London School of Economics and Political Science (LSE). His recent book is *US Diplomacy Promotion in the Middle East: The Pursuit of Hegemony* (Routledge, 2015).

Toby Matthiesen is a Senior Research Fellow in the International Relations of the Middle East at the Middle East Centre, St. Antony's College, University of Oxford. He was previously a Research Fellow at Pembroke College, Cambridge, and at the London School of Economics and Political Science and gained his doctorate from the School of Oriental and African Studies (SOAS). He is the author of *Sectarian Gulf: Bahrain, Saudi Arabia, and the Arab Spring That Wasn't* (Stanford University Press, 2013), and *The Other Saudis: Shiism, Dissent and Sectarianism* (Cambridge University Press, 2015). His current research focuses on the Sunni-Shia divide and the legacies of the Cold War in the Middle East.

Marc Valeri is Senior Lecturer in Political Economy of the Middle East and Director of the Centre for Gulf Studies at the University of Exeter. He is the author of *Oman: Politics and Society in the Qaboos State* (Hurst, 2009) and co-editor of *Business Politics in the Middle East* (Hurst, 2013).

Nussaibah Younis is a nonresident senior fellow with the Atlantic Council's Rafik Hariri Center for the Middle East. She is a Middle East expert who specializes in Iraqi politics and the Islamic State of Iraq and al-Sham (ISIS). Younis is the author of *Invasion to ISIS: Iraq, State Weakness and Foreign Policy* (Hurst, 2015). Before joining the Atlantic Council, she was senior research associate at the Project on Middle East Democracy, a research and advocacy group based in Washington DC, where she directed research programs as well as conducted her own research. Younis was previously an international security program research fellow at the Belfer Center for Science and International Affairs at the Harvard Kennedy School. Younis is a regular commentator on Middle East affairs, and she has given numerous TV and radio interviews on the BBC, Voice of America, and Al Jazeera among others. She has published op-eds in the *New York Times*, the *Wall Street Journal*, and *The Guardian*.

1

INTRODUCTION

Kristian Coates Ulrichsen

The political and economic upheaval triggered by the 'Arab Spring' uprisings of 2011 has underscored the vulnerability of states across the Middle East and North Africa to the intersection of domestic pressures and external shocks. The initial phase of the uprisings has given way to a series of messy and uncertain transitions that has ignited violence both within and across states and left societies deeply fractured. Although the bulk of the protests occurred outside the Persian Gulf, with the notable exception of Bahrain and the partial exception of Kuwait, Persian Gulf states were at the forefront of the political, economic, and security response across the region. The greater role of Gulf Cooperation Council (GCC) states, in particular, is consistent with broader changes to the architecture of world politics in which contemporary power and influence are increasingly diffused and distributed among a far wider variety of often-competing state and non-state actors. And yet, the dramatic decline in world oil prices since June 2014 has heightened fiscal stresses in all Persian Gulf economies and called into question the redistributive political economies that have, in part, underpinned sociopolitical stability over the past four decades. Moreover, the Saudi-led campaign in Yemen that started in

March 2015 demonstrated nothing less than the militarisation of GCC defence policy and a direct escalation of the regional struggle with Iran, hitherto carried out largely through proxy actors in local battlegrounds.

The contradictory trends of the volatile 'post-Arab Spring' landscape form both the backdrop to and the focus of this volume on the changing security dynamics of the Persian Gulf, defined as the six GCC states plus Iraq and Iran. The Persian Gulf has long been a zone of instability as the region experienced three major interstate conflicts between 1980 and 2003 and the subsequent civil conflict in Iraq, as well as two prolonged diplomatic crises between Qatar and Saudi Arabia, Bahrain, and the United Arab Emirates (UAE) in 2014 and 2017. While the legacies of the Iran–Iraq War (September 1980–August 1988) and the Iraqi occupation of Kuwait (August 1990–February 1991) were relatively contained, the same is not true of the US-led invasion and subsequent occupation of Iraq (March 2003 onward). The chaotic aftermath of the eight-year occupation of Iraq had a lasting impact on regional security structures as it altered the balance of power in the Persian Gulf, empowered non-state actors in Iraq, and deepened internal fissures along ethnic and sectarian fault-lines across the wider region. One of the greatest changes in Persian Gulf security dynamics since 2003 has been the shift from interstate war towards violent conflict within states driven primarily by non-state groups that nevertheless operate in a rigorously transnational sphere.

Iran constituted another recurring flashpoint of regional and international tensions for much of the same period as the three interstate Persian Gulf wars. The clerical leadership in Iran consolidated political control following the revolution that toppled the Shah, Mohammad Reza Pahlavi, in January 1979, and was seen as a particular threat to security both by the Gulf Arab monarchies and the United States. Gulf Arab states viewed with alarm the initial attempts by elements in Iran to 'export' their revolutionary zeal to neighbouring states and suspected successive post-revolutionary Iran of 'meddling' in regional conflicts through the support of non-state actors such as Hezbollah and Hamas. For two generations of US policymakers, the memories of the 444-day hostage crisis between November 1979 and January 1981 have coloured American perceptions of Iran. In much the same way, Iranian perspectives of US policy are often seen through the prism of the 1953 'coup' that removed the Prime Minister, Mohammad Mossadegh, and reinstated the Shah.[1] Mutual tensions converged in the decade-long nuclear crisis that began with opposition allegations of a clandestine Iranian nuclear programme and peaked during the presidencies of George W. Bush (2001–09) and Mahmoud Ahmadinejad (2005–13).

Further from the Persian Gulf, the radicalisation of sizeable elements of the Arab Spring protest movements added a further layer of instability and insecurity, most notably in the spiralling civil wars in Libya and Syria after 2011. Both conflicts drew in a multitude of regional actors, state and non-state alike, and evolved into complex proxy wars between 'secular' and Islamist factions in Libya and among a plethora of Gulf Arab and Iranian-backed groups in Syria. The conflicts in Syria and Libya ramified across large swathes of the Middle East and North Africa, greatly increased sectarian violence in post-occupation Iraq, and contributed to a wider geopolitical picture of deep division and protracted levels of intercommunal violence. The United States and the European Union arguably intervened too hastily in Libya and too slowly in Syria as the shadow of Iraq loomed large over policymakers. As a previous collection of essays published by the Center for International and Regional Studies at Georgetown University in Qatar put it in 2014, 'the final chapter of the Arab Spring has yet to be written'.[2]

New sources of insecurity: national, regional, international

Three unrelated developments since mid-2014 nevertheless have redirected the forces of change and upheaval in dangerously destabilising new ways and each injects potent new sources of uncertainty into national, regional, and international security structures. The first is the startling rise to prominence and power of the so-called Islamic State of Iraq and Syria (ISIS), which culminated in the defeat of al-Qaeda's affiliate, Jabhat al-Nusra, in a series of battles for control of the Syria–Iraq border region in late 2013 and early 2014 and the rapid occupation of large swathes of western and northern Iraqi territory in June 2014. Extensive research into the origins of ISIS by German newspaper *Der Spiegel* has traced the organisation's roots to the Sunni insurgency that followed the ousting of Saddam Hussein in 2003.[3] Members of ISIS themselves have recounted how many of the group's eventual leadership first met while in US detention at Camp Bucca in southern Iraq in 2004. Their number included Abu Bakr al-Baghdadi, the emir of ISIS, who had been arrested by US forces in Falluja in February 2004 after establishing one of the many militant groups that composed the escalating Sunni revolt against the US presence in Iraq.[4] Meanwhile, domestic developments in Iran (since June 2013) and in Saudi Arabia (since January 2015) have underscored the rapidity of change in the regional and international posture of both states, as a 'post-Ahmadinejad' Iran re-engaged with world powers and Saudi Arabia under King Salman developed a far more assertive—but unpredictable and even volatile—set of foreign policies.

It was against this backdrop of greater volatility in regional security structures that GCC states became more visible and proactive participants in regional and international politics during the 2000s and early 2010s. Led by Qatar, the UAE, and, to a lesser extent, Saudi Arabia, the emergence of GCC states as regional powers with a growing international reach predated the Arab Spring but accelerated and acquired a potent new dimension once the initial shock of the upheaval had subsided. GCC states took the lead in responding to the political and economic challenges triggered by the Arab Spring. The scope and scale of Persian Gulf states' assistance to Egypt have provided a clear example of the practical and policy implications of this process in action, as first Qatar and latterly Saudi Arabia and the UAE backed different sides in the post-Mubarak maelstrom of Egyptian politics. The Egyptian example also has illustrated how Gulf states are not impartial actors that do not take sides in choosing how and to whom to provide aid. Policies instead have been indelibly linked to particular political currents rather than being tied to outcomes such as reforms of governance or improvements in transparency.

Over the four years since 2011, the GCC states therefore aligned their growing capabilities (in the political, economic, and security arenas) with a far more expansive policy intent, with the intensification of military operations in Yemen since 2015 being the most visible manifestation of the muscular new approach to regional security. Engaging with an assertive and interventionist GCC across the Middle East and North Africa has become a feature of the regional landscape and caused periodic friction with the United States as President Barack Obama's administration engaged in the most high-level and comprehensive negotiations with Iran since the 1979 revolution. The combination of Iran's ongoing international rehabilitation and the outbreak of the GCC-led conflict in Yemen in 2015, coupled with the sharp drop in international oil prices, reinforces the notion that regional stability and security in the Persian Gulf are in a state of considerable uncertainty.

The second source of uncertainty—which, like the threat from ISIS, also dates from mid-2014—is the accelerated urgency of far-reaching economic and subsidy reform as Persian Gulf economies were hit hard by the collapse and sustained low level of oil prices. Although all six of the GCC states and Iran have made significant attempts to diversify their economies over the past two decades with varying degrees of success, they remain heavily reliant, both directly and indirectly, upon revenues from oil and, in Qatar's case, gas. In most cases, oil revenues account for between 80 and 90% of total government revenues, and from 24% of total GDP in Bahrain and 30% in the UAE, to 36 and 38% in Qatar and Oman, 46% in Saudi Arabia, and 56.6% in Kuwait in 2014.[5] In the one exception, Dubai, where oil accounts for about 5% of GDP, the emirate suffered the indignity of being 'bailed out' by its oil-rich neighbouring emirate, Abu Dhabi, with US$20 billion in 2009 after the bursting of the speculative real estate bubble and the drying up of easy credit precipitated a short but very sharp debt crisis.[6]

As a result, total government revenues still correlate closely with oil revenues, leaving GCC economies highly vulnerable to external shocks and sources of volatility in international oil markets, over which they have little control. Government revenues in Oman thus fell by 35.9% in the first nine months of 2015 on the back of a 45.5% decline in oil revenues (although spending itself only contracted by 1.8%),[7] while in Qatar the value of hydrocarbon exports plunged 40.5% year-on-year between July 2014 and July 2015.[8] Kuwait, meanwhile, recorded a 45.2% year-on-year fall in government revenues for the first eight months of the 2015–16 fiscal year and a near-identical 46.1% drop in oil revenues over the same period.[9] Saudi oil income fell by 23% in 2015 just as government spending rose at the start of the year after King Salman took the throne and major combat operations commenced in Yemen, contributing to the record $98 billion budget deficit for the year.[10]

The challenge for Gulf officials is how to reformulate a ruling 'bargain' that has broadly underpinned sociopolitical stability for decades but no longer appears economically sustainable. Until 2014, the prevailing hope in the region was that this 'moment of truth' was more of a medium-range issue than an urgent short-term one, and that politically sensitive reductions in current spending could be avoided or minimised by cutbacks in capital expenditures instead. Moreover, the regional political upheaval of the previous five years illustrated how the instinctive response of many GCC governments was to intensify populist short-term measures intended to blunt or pre-empt the social and economic roots of potential or actual political tension. Total state spending in the six GCC states rose by 20 per cent in 2011 as governments responded to the outbreak of the Arab Spring with welfare packages and other benefits.[11]

Such policies succeeded in preserving political structures and domestic stability (for the most part) in 2011, but had the unintended consequence, as political economist Steffen Hertog has noted, of creating 'a ratchet effect that demands ever larger outlays during every political crisis' because 'expectations are easy to raise but difficult to curb'.[12] The measures taken in 2011 to blunt the impact of the wider political unrest were overwhelmingly short-term in nature and encompassed cash handouts (Bahrain and Kuwait), creating thousands of additional new jobs in already saturated public sectors (Bahrain, Saudi Arabia, and Oman), and raising workers' wages and benefits (Oman, Qatar, Saudi Arabia, and the UAE). And yet, the packages also created a contagious expectation from many citizens in GCC states of additional government largesse, as demonstrated in January 2011 when, shortly after Kuwait's Emir announced the Gulf's first handout worth $4 billion, Qatari nationals demanded that their own government follow suit. Despite the fact that Qatar has the highest per capita GDP in the world, a local English-language newspaper in Doha, *The Peninsula*, reported that the announcement 'has led to huge excitement in the Qatari community', with many Qataris suggesting publicly that their government 'should announce a similar or even more attractive "gift package" for its people'.[13]

One of the few direct and, as a result, most contentious policy responses to target all Persian Gulf residents, whether national or expatriate, has been the launching of long overdue reform of subsidy programmes, which—in energy alone—were estimated to have cost Saudi Arabia $107 billion in 2015.[14] At the time of writing, all GCC states except Kuwait have taken action to scale back fuel subsidies, with the UAE being the first to do so in August 2015. Prices for gasoline have risen by as much as 100% in Saudi Arabia, 57% in Bahrain, 33% in Qatar, and 20% in Oman since 2015, while those for diesel have gone up by 200% in Saudi Arabia, 106% in Kuwait, 52% in Qatar, and 31% in Bahrain, albeit from very low starting points.[15] Bahrain also removed subsidies on meat prices, expressed its intent to phase out power and water subsidies, and raised industrial gas use prices, as has Oman.[16] Elsewhere, water bills in Saudi Arabia surged by up to 2,000% in some cases following the introduction of new rates in December 2015, prompting a parallel surge in complaints to the country's consultative Shura Council and the sacking of the Minister of Electricity and Water in April 2016 for the 'unsatisfactory' implementation of the tariffs.[17]

In Iran, a shake-up of fuel subsidies took place earlier than in GCC states and was announced in 2010 as part of the Five-Year Development Plan for 2010–15. Although the plan initially was hailed for its boldness in tackling subsidy reform head-on, subsequent implementation was hampered by poor data availability, lack of widespread political backing, and a tripling in the price of gasoline and basic food items, which perversely increased (rather than decreased) low-income families' dependence on government handouts, in the form of the direct cash payments that had been introduced in 2010 to offset the impact of the lifting of fuel subsidies.[18] As a result, the government of President Hassan Rouhani has struggled to move to the second phase of the reforms, which would invest the surplus generated by the lifting of fuel subsidies into job creation schemes, the health care sector, and public transportation, and, as Iran approached a presidential election in 2017, he found little political support for scaling back the cash payments introduced by former President Mahmoud Ahmadinejad in 2010, even in the face of rapidly rising fiscal pressures.[19]

And yet, Moody's has forecast that the spate of fuel price rises will only lead to savings equivalent to about 1 per cent of GDP and, as such, will do little more than dent the overall size of the fiscal deficits facing the GCC states.[20] The broader political sensitivity of tampering with one of the key mechanisms of wealth redistribution from the state to its citizenry has been evident most strongly in Kuwait and Bahrain, the two GCC states with the most vocal and activist parliamentary bodies. Bahrain softened the blow of the meat price increases by compensating citizens for the additional costs, while in Kuwait lawmakers amended a government proposal that would have included Kuwaiti citizens in planned increases to water and electricity charges so that they would apply only to residents of apartment buildings (which are overwhelmingly populated by expatriates) as well as corporate users.[21] Later in 2016, the Kuwaiti government resigned and the Emir called early elections, which resulted in the return of the political opposition en masse to the National Assembly, rather than confront parliamentarians directly over fuel subsidy reform.[22]

It will not be easy for officials in any Persian Gulf state to make further and deeper cuts that really begin to impact on citizens rather than expatriates or corporations, but sooner or later nationals will inevitably start to feel the pain if governments are to make credible inroads into economic reform. The sacking of the Saudi Minister of Electricity and Water was thus a warning of the political pitfalls that lie ahead for the policymakers entrusted with pushing through unpopular decisions. What evidence that does exist suggests that subsidy reform remains a highly sensitive issue that could rapidly become politicised if it is mishandled or if it is seen to progress too far too fast. In its annual survey of youth opinion across the Arab world, Dubai-based ASDA'A Burson-Marsteller found that 93 per cent of respondents in Bahrain, 92 per cent in Oman and Qatar, and 86 per cent in Saudi Arabia were in favour of continuing subsidies.[23] That same month (April 2016), a survey in Kuwait illustrated the strength of attachment to the notion of the government as provider of both welfare and employment for its citizenry, as government statistics showed that fully 58 per cent of unemployed Kuwaitis preferred to remain jobless and wait for a government position to open up rather than take a job in the private sector.[24]

Officials in Persian Gulf states additionally remain mindful that previous attempts in other regional states to scale back subsidies and raise prices of basic utilities and foodstuffs have provoked violent backlashes in numerous instances. In July 2005, dozens were killed and hundreds injured in disturbances across Yemen that mobilised more than 100,000 people against government plans to reduce fuel subsidies and increase the price of benzene by 86 per cent and diesel by 165 per cent.[25] Seven years later, an increase in gasoline prices in Jordan sparked days of rioting and labour strikes throughout the country, notwithstanding even the addition of a compensation package that would have provided poorer households with a $100 credit per person per year.[26] Going further back in time, reductions in food subsidies caused widespread unrest in Egypt in 1977 (when protesters mocked President Anwar Sadat with slogans such as 'Wain al-futur, ya batal al-'ubur?' ('Hero of the crossing, where's our breakfast?')), Morocco in 1981, Tunisia in 1984, and Algeria in 1988.[27] These lessons from the past will form an inevitable backdrop to policy formulation as the assertive new leadership of Saudi Arabia, led by the youthful Crown Prince Muhammad bin Salman Al Saud, attempts to transform economic—but not political—structures through Saudi Vision 2030, and rulers of other states attempt to wean their populations away from the redistributive mechanisms of wealth that have underpinned regional political economies since the 1970s.

While the rise of ISIS represents a regional form of insecurity and the challenge of low oil prices a domestic challenge, the third source of volatility is the election of Donald Trump as President of the United States, committed to a vague and undefined 'America First' approach to international affairs. Trump's unexpected victory in the electoral college, after Hillary Clinton won nearly three million more votes in the November 2016 election, presented US allies, partners, and foes alike with a dramatic turning point in US domestic and foreign policy priorities, due in part to the incoherence of President Trump's messaging during the long presidential campaign and the volatility of his early weeks and months in office. While officials in GCC states were glad to see the back of the Obama administration and welcomed Trump's initial opposition to the

Joint Comprehensive Plan of Action (JCPOA) agreed by the Obama administration and other world powers in 2015, the tenets of US policymaking towards
the Persian Gulf were far from clear as this volume went to press in 2017.

Irrespective of any policy responses to specific issues that may arise during
the Trump presidency, the arrival of an unpredictable and aggressively populist president in the White House inevitably calls into question the role of the
United States in the Middle East and the Persian Gulf. Although rulers in
GCC states expressed great anger at an interview given by President Barack
Obama in April 2016 which appeared to refer disparagingly to Persian Gulf
leaders as 'free riders', President Trump has expressed his own opposition to
free riding in characteristically blunter terms. For the first time since the enun-
ciation of the Carter Doctrine in 1980, which signalled the centrality of the
Persian Gulf to US national security, the willingness of the US government to
underwrite most of the costs of that security architecture is in doubt.
Moreover, emotive issues such as the so-called Muslim ban called for by
Trump as candidate and enacted by him in part as President, risk giving suc-
cour to radical extremist groups such as ISIS and damaging by association
traditional US political and security partners in the GCC. Certainly, the reckless and inflammatory language used by President Trump in his Tweets in
support of the Saudi and Emirati actions against Qatar in June 2017 offered
an early indication of the unpredictability likely to dominate US policy
toward the region during his presidency, while the gap that opened up
between the White House and the State Department/Pentagon hinted at the
inconsistency in approach across different parts of the US government.

It is this state of flux, in which all the different 'parts' (state and non-state
alike) are moving simultaneously, that forms the context of this volume of
essays, which examine in depth how regional notions of what security is and
to whom it is applied have evolved. As the conduct of foreign and security
policies has become increasingly proactive, rather than reactive, among the
GCC states, and Saudi Arabia and the UAE remain heavily involved in a
thinly disguised proxy war directed against perceived Iranian 'meddling' in
Yemen, understanding the motivations and objectives behind policymaking
on both shores of the Persian Gulf has never been more urgent or timely.
Moreover, the intensely transnational nature of the threats to regional and
international security posed by organisations such as ISIS has placed the GCC
states and Iraq in the cross hairs of the global response and sharpened the
policy dilemmas facing officials who seek to balance domestic considerations
against international pressure to take firm and resolute action. Finally, Iran's

re-emergence into the international community adds a further set of uncertainties as internal struggles between advocates of a 'moderate' and 'hardline' approach to politics remain unresolved (just as they do in the United States), and European business leaders queue up to make commercial inroads into the largest untapped market in the broader Middle East.

Security in flux

Since the 1980s, the concept of 'what security is' has undergone a transformative shift as the end of the Cold War led to a scholarly widening and deepening of security studies, which moved the discipline far beyond a 'traditional' military and state-centric focus. This occurred simultaneously with the great acceleration of the processes of globalisation, which themselves injected powerful new dimensions into international security studies.[28] Globalising flows, in particular, created 'an interpenetration of foreign and domestic ("intermestic") issues such that national governments increasingly operate in spaces defined by the intersection of internal and external security'.[29] Globalisation also contributed to an increase both in the scale and the velocity of risk as threats and challenges to security—such as global terrorism—crossed national boundaries at ever-greater speed. Mary Kaldor and Joseph Stiglitz noted, for example, that attempts to deprive international terrorist organisations such as al-Qaeda 'of a homeland in one country does little good' as 'it quickly shifts its base of operations elsewhere'.[30]

As part of the deepening and widening of security studies, a constructivist approach to international relations has gained ground over the past two decades. This studies the role of beliefs and norms as social constructs that shape approaches to questions of power and security. Constructivism emphasises the importance of local agency in exploring the factors that motivate policymakers to reach and implement the decisions they take. Analysing 'how people act' addresses one of the central deficiencies of the broader international relations literature, namely a neglect of the human dimension in contemporary world politics.[31] Constructivist approaches ascribe value to the location and distribution of nodes of power within society as well as the relationships between knowledge, power, and interests. The evolution of a position of 'national interest' on any one issue thus represents the outcome of an intersubjective process that combines ideational and material factors and is fluid rather than fixed over time.[32]

Distinguishing between security as discourse and security as material threat also enhances the study of 'securitisation'. This refers to the processes by which issues become constructed as threats to security, and by whom and for what reason. If an issue is successfully securitised, and accepted as such by the relevant audience, the principal actor feels empowered to take extraordinary measures to combat it. These exceed the rules-based systems that otherwise regulate the conduct of normal behaviour, and demonstrate the importance of agency in defining and shaping responses to particular issues.[33] At a macro-level, the global 'war on terror' represented a successful example of securitisation. It enabled the United States to bypass international norms and structures after 11 September 2001 to combat the perceived threat from al-Qaeda-linked terrorism.[34]

A closer examination of the processes of securitisation in the Gulf ties the region into the broader world group of developing states, and embeds the study of regional security issues within the realm of comparative politics. This forms part of Keith Krause's identification of a 'security problematic' in contemporary world politics in general, and in the post-Cold War period in particular. This arises out of the fact that perceived threats to security can be ideational as well as material, and can be tied to the survival not of the state but of a particular referent group. In these instances, the idea of security is critical, and the ideational affiliation of the security of the state with the security of its citizens cannot be automatically assumed to be the case.[35] In this taxonomy, the internal and external dimensions of security become intertwined as regimes seek security against possible contestation from within their own societies as much as against external aggression from neighbouring states. The Gulf states' external security alignments, both bilaterally with the United States and multilaterally through the creation of the GCC, meet this requirement by reinforcing regime security against internal dissent as well as foreign threats.[36]

Internationally, the shift in the concept of security began during the Cold War but accelerated sharply following its ending in 1989 and during the period of accelerated globalisation that followed in the 1990s and 2000s, particularly as regional security dynamics in Latin America and Eastern Europe themselves underwent rapid and significant change.[37] The reconceptualisation of what security 'is' and 'does' has overseen a broadening and deepening of the global security agenda to encompass new and emerging threats that are increasingly longer-term and non-conventional in nature, and embed the study of security problems firmly within the broader political and socio-economic context of development. Barry Buzan and Lene Hansen have noted how the 'widening and deepening' of international security studies occurred as 'the disappearance of the Cold War had changed both the questions on the security agenda and the actors who could engage them'.[38] The widening and deepening approach to security expanded the security agenda to encompass a wider array of socio-economic and environmental factors and extended the object of reference beyond that of the state.[39]

The reconceptualisation of security has been intertwined with the great intensification of global interconnectedness and the stretching of power and authority across multiple layers of global governance.[40] A distinct form of 'global politics' evolved in the 1990s and 2000s which took account of the great acceleration of global interconnections and states' engagement within relentlessly transnational frameworks and issues. The confluence of these trends prompted a major reassessment of the concept of national and global security, and their relationship to each other. Mary Kaldor and Joseph Stiglitz have argued that 'globalization has increased the scale and velocity of risk' and heightened the need for global solutions to problems that routinely cross national boundaries and operate at a multitude of supra- and sub-state levels.[41] And yet, as David Held observes, 'the paradox of our times' is that 'the collective issues we must grapple with are of growing extensity and intensity, yet the means for addressing these are weak and incomplete'.[42]

At the heart of this collective action problem, in security just as in global governance, is the difficulty of designing policy responses to complex and interconnected challenges that transcend resilient boundaries of national sovereignty. This challenge has been visibly illustrated in the air campaigns launched by the US and selected Western and Middle Eastern allies in 2014 in an attempt to contain the spread of ISIS. The effectiveness of the anti-ISIS measures has been blunted by the fact that the two strands of the air campaign had to work under very different operational environments in Iraq and in Syria against a foe whose territorial authority made no such distinction. The British House of Commons, for example, voted overwhelmingly in September 2014 in favour of participation in the US-led air strikes on ISIS targets in Iraq yet remained aside from the air campaign against ISIS in Syria for lack of parliamentary support for any such engagement, having been defeated on such a motion in August 2013.[43] It was only after the deadly terrorist attacks in Paris on 13 November 2015 changed the political calculus in Britain (as in Europe) that Prime Minister David Cameron felt he had sufficient political support among UK parliamentarians to win a renewed vote for military intervention in Syria, albeit against ISIS rather than the Assad regime, as initially proposed in 2013.[44]

Debates on security in the Persian Gulf have, however, remained heavily dependent on realist and neorealist considerations of the balance of power and balance of threat in terms of the actual formulation of domestic and regional security policies both by state officials (on both coasts of the Persian Gulf) and by most observers of Persian Gulf security affairs. Although voluminous, the literature on Persian Gulf security studies (as with foreign policy studies and international relations) has, as Fred Lawson argued forcefully, been 'framed in terms of concepts and methodologies that lag far behind the times in each field' and thus have little useful contribution to a scholarly understanding of the actual dynamics of foreign and security policymaking and interstate interaction in the Persian Gulf—that is, how security works in the region in practice.[45]

Balance of threat theory, as developed by Stephen Walt, held that states would determine and modify alliances based on their threat perception from other states, which itself was a function of aggregate strength, geographical proximity, offensive capabilities, and offensive intentions. Aspects of this are clearly discernible in the Arab Gulf states' creation of the Gulf Cooperation Council in May 1981 as a defensive response to the perceived threats to regional security posed by the Iranian Revolution and the outbreak of the Iran–Iraq War. After several years and several failed proposals to form a regional grouping, the GCC suddenly came together in the space of three months between February and May 1981. Emirati political scientist Abdulkhaleq Abdulla has aptly described how 'such extraordinary speed is practically unheard of in the history of regional integration and is particularly uncharacteristic of the rulers of the six Arab Gulf states whose normal tendency is to procrastinate on a decision with potential ramifications for their sovereignty'.[46] The GCC formed a part of the balance of power in the Persian Gulf alongside Iraq and Iran in an uneasy triangular relationship that was itself fluid, fragile, unstable, and, in the aftermath of the 2003 occupation of Iraq—which cemented the United States as part of the regional balance of power—artificial.[47]

Balance of power and balance of threat assessments continue to feature high on national and regional security agendas in the Persian Gulf, as evidenced by the Saudi- and UAE-led coalition that intervened militarily in Yemen in March 2015 to prevent the further empowerment of Houthi rebels backed ostensibly (in their view) by Iran. Yet, the enduring dynamic between the Arab Gulf states and Iran illustrates the importance of integrating constructivist approaches to security that focus on narratives and identities in shaping and reshaping policy agendas. As we have already noted, a constructivist approach focuses on the decisions made by policymakers and the environment within which they must operate. It locates and identifies the agency in analysing how and why issues become securitised or not and takes security both as a social construct and a material threat, building upon work by scholars such as Alexander Wendt and Richard Price,[48] who emphasise the importance of beliefs and norms in shaping state behaviour, and of what Christian Reus-Smit has labelled the role of 'human action in contemporary world politics'.[49] This is particularly important in the case of the Arab Gulf states, in which the conduct of foreign and security affairs is restricted to a tightly drawn circle of senior members of the ruling family and their closest advisers, and in Iraq and Iran, where foreign policy represents the outcome of sets of overlapping political influences.[50]

Scholars of the Persian Gulf thus confront a paradox whereby regional security agendas often follow the remorseless assessment of balance of power considerations even as decision-making structures remain highly personalised and open to intersubjective interpretation. During the presidency of Mahmoud Ahmadinejad (2005–13), senior Iranian officials on several occasions made inflammatory remarks about the Arab Gulf states, such as those by Iran's Deputy Foreign Minister, Manouchehr Mohammadi, who in June 2008 referred to the next crisis in the Persian Gulf as being the 'crisis of legitimacy of the monarchies and traditional systems, which considering current circumstances cannot survive'.[51] Seven years later, comments by Saudi Arabia's new Foreign Minister, Adil al-Jubayr, in October 2015 made clear the enduring 'war of words' over perceptions of Iranian activity among Arab Gulf policymakers. Al-Jubayr, who succeeded the veteran Saud al-Faisal Al Saud in April 2015, struck a belligerent tone when he accused Iran of 'meddling' in Syria and Yemen and stated, somewhat hyperbolically, that 'Saudi Arabia and its people are the target of continuous aggression' from Iran.[52]

With this in mind, it was unsurprising how policymakers in the Arab Gulf states responded to the initial spread of the regional upheaval to GCC states by attributing the protests to external interference rather than as the product of domestic political or socio-economic factors. Initially, they targeted Iran, particularly as the uprising in Bahrain and the demonstrations in the Eastern Province of Saudi Arabia were largely Shi'a protests. Thus, in April 2011, Bahrain's Foreign Minister, Sheikh Khalid bin Ahmed Al Khalifa, claimed, 'We have never seen such a sustained campaign from Iran on Bahrain and the Gulf as we've seen in the past two months.'[53] Five months later, the report on the uprising published by the Bahrain Independent Commission on Inquiry (BICI) found no evidence of any Iranian role in the unrest, despite months of Bahraini government claims to the contrary.[54]

Studying the dynamics of regional security in the Persian Gulf through the examination of identities and beliefs (both real and perceived) held by key actors therefore casts a light on how officials decide which issues become securitised and subsequently acted upon. The importance of viewing security (and policy) through such a lens was noted in a journal article in 2009 on Iran's nuclear ambitions by Shahram Chubin of the Carnegie Endowment for International Peace, who observed: 'there has been an inflation of the Iranian threat, which is poorly understood and often exaggerated. Depicting Iran as a military threat obscures the real political threat the country poses to its region; Iran's regional behavior has been neglected and overshadowed by the contentious nuclear issue. However, it is precisely Iran's behavior and goals which feed concerns about its nuclear ambitions.'[55] This is as important in 2017 as it ever has been, as the region is once again host to a number of conflict zones that illustrate the interlinked aspects of local, regional, and international security. The escalation in the Syrian conflict since 2011, the emergence of ISIS in 2013, and the outbreak of the Yemen war in 2015 all thrust contrasting interpretations of regional stability to the forefront of policy responses to the interlinked crises of security in the Persian Gulf. Perception of developments has thus played, and will continue to play, a major role in determining the make-up of security agendas in all Persian Gulf states in a post-Arab Spring era of heightened volatility and greater political uncertainty. Engaging in depth with local and regional debates is vital therefore, both from a scholarly and a policy viewpoint, to understanding the changing dynamics of Persian Gulf security when even the 'facts on the ground' are themselves the subject of acute contestation and geopolitical friction.

Against the backdrop of the new threats to regional security posed by the rise of non-state actors and the post-2011 political and economic upheaval, the election of Hassan Rouhani, a man widely viewed as a 'moderate', as President of Iran greatly altered the course of international and, with it, regional politics. Rouhani's election victory in June 2013 was followed in November by a breakthrough in five secret rounds of dialogue between Iran and the United States, which represented the outcome of Omani efforts in 2012 and 2013 to reduce regional tensions and seek a diplomatic resolution to points of potential conflict.[56] Months of subsequent negotiations between Iran and the international community (represented by the P5+1 group of states) culminated in a Joint Comprehensive Plan of Action (JCPOA) signed in July 2015. Under the terms of the JCPOA, Iran agreed to heavy restrictions on its uranium enrichment and intense monitoring and verification of its nuclear programme to preclude any risk of militarisation or proliferation. The nuclear agreement illustrated a very different multilateral approach to addressing flashpoints of regional tension through international diplomacy rather than by the use of force, as had occurred with the invasion and occupation of Iraq in 2003.

And yet, the regional response to the Iran deal reflected the differences in approach between the Obama administration, which viewed the agreement in terms of non-proliferation, and GCC states, which focused instead on their perceived view of Iranian 'meddling' in regional conflicts. Paradoxically, the international agreement with Iran was followed by an escalation in the regional conflict in Yemen as both Saudi Arabia and the UAE redoubled their efforts to inflict a decisive military defeat on Houthi rebels firmly backed—in the perception of security policy hawks in positions of leadership in both Riyadh and Abu Dhabi—by Iran. The Yemen campaign—which itself was launched only days prior to the expiry of an initial deadline for agreement between Iran and the P5+1 in March 2015—confirmed the view of many in GCC capitals who saw the primary threat from Iran not in Tehran's nuclear programme but in Iran's support for militant non-state actors such as Hezbollah and, so they believed, the Houthi rebels in Yemen. As such, it was perhaps no coincidence that the nuclear agreement was followed within days by an intensification in the GCC-led coalition's military effort that culminated in the liberation of Aden from Houthi control. In addition to the Saudi-led air strikes and training, the Yemeni forces were assisted also by Special Forces from the UAE, one of whom was killed in action.[57] Several weeks later, on 4 September 2015, 52 soldiers from the UAE were killed in a missile attack on their base in Yemen. For a country whose first military fatality only came in March 2014, some 43 years after independence, such a death toll was both unprecedented and profoundly shocking.[58]

A powerful and unsettling new set of security dynamics has thus risen to the top of national and regional agendas as GCC states deploy 'hard' military assets in unprecedented ways while Iran re-engages with the international system. The scale of Emirati and Saudi casualties in the Yemen campaign has changed the discourse on security and conflict in both countries and led to the rise of a 'cult of martyrdom' in the UAE in particular. The country observed its first 'Martyrs Day' on 30 November 2015 amid efforts by officials and commentators to identify and affirm a link between war, national identity, and wider state-building projects.[59] In the immediate aftermath of the deaths of the 52 UAE soldiers in Yemen, the Emirati journalist Ayesha Almazroui suggested that 'Recent events are contributing to the development of national identity' while the veteran Lebanese commentator Rami Khouri noted, more sanguinely, that 'the war in Yemen is a rite of passage' for members of the GCC, 'who are asserting their power and the maturity of their statehood by launching a war against a weaker neighbor'.[60]

Aside from the choice of terminology, in which conflict fatalities are labelled routinely as 'martyrs' and their deaths cast in the context of a national sacrifice, the militarisation of GCC security policy is a qualitatively new development that will inject new sources of instability into the regional security architecture. The rapid growth of sectarian identity politics has lent a dangerous edge to the mobilisation of national resources to counter the rise of non-state actors and transnational threats in the Persian Gulf. Tensions between Saudi Arabia and Iran have spilled over in numerous regional and international forums, including the Vienna talks in October 2015, which sought a resolution of the Syrian crisis, and the OPEC summit in the same city two months later.[61] The danger facing all stakeholders in Persian Gulf security is that the threshold for an accidental escalation of tension into outright conflict is lower than it has been for many years and may not survive many more trigger points, such as the stampede in Mecca that killed more than a thousand people, including hundreds of Iranians attending the hajj in September 2015. Similarly, the visceral deterioration of relations between Saudi Arabia and Iran culminated in the cutting of diplomatic ties in January 2016 following the execution in Saudi Arabia of the prominent Shi'a cleric Nimr Baqir al-Nimr and the storming of Saudi diplomatic missions in Iran. Prospects for negotiated settlements of the conflicts in Yemen and Syria became the first casualty of the spiralling bilateral tension between the two 'superpowers' in the Persian Gulf and put paid to months of patient diplomatic spadework by international mediators.

About the volume

The speed and scale of developments across the Arab world since 2011 mean there is an urgent need for a comprehensive, critical, and fresh perspective on the evolution of regional security dynamics in the Persian Gulf. Analysing the region as a whole, rather than through a GCC-centric or Iranian-focused approach, draws out the narratives and identities that play off each other and feed into the construction of security agendas at both the national and regional levels. Coming from a wide variety of backgrounds, the ten contributors to this volume adopt a comprehensive and holistic approach to key dimensions of regional security as well as to the issues that feed into security policymaking at its various levels. The chapters combine thematic and regional-level analyses of critical issues with case studies that chart the evolution of national-level trends and include the security implications of such issues as political succession and the evolution of state–business relations. Interwoven throughout are the internal and external aspects of security that are heavily enmeshed not only within the 'new' non-state actors and transnational threats but also among the technologically supercharged 'public sphere', which has, as Marc Lynch has documented, 'radically reshaped the way information, ideas, and opinions flow through Arab society'.[62]

Following on from this introductory chapter, I examine in chapter 2 the myriad linkages between domestic and regional security and how these are evolving across the Persian Gulf. The Persian Gulf noticeably did not share in the evolution of security structures that took place in other world regions such as Eastern Europe or Latin America during the 1980s and 1990s. Instead, the fallout from the US-led invasion and occupation of Iraq in 2003 and policy responses to the Arab Spring in 2011 led to the growth of what I label a 'geopolitical straitjacket' which contributed to the rise of sectarian identity politics and the emergence of the dangerous new threat from ISIS. My chapter details the policy dilemmas that ISIS presents to policymakers in GCC states, who face the additional pressure of having to take sensitive decisions against the backdrop of a potentially prolonged period of low oil prices and fiscal stress.

In chapter 3, Toby Matthiesen examines the ways in which GCC states, notably Saudi Arabia, Qatar, the UAE, and Kuwait, have sought to influence the political and economic pathways of transition in North Africa since 2011. Matthiesen details how GCC states' foreign policies have shifted away from 'petrodollar diplomacy' towards an unprecedented form of direct activism in the regional maelstrom of the 'post-Arab Spring' landscape. Such policies are intended to increase the GCC states' symbolic capital, military strength, and regional hegemony, but Matthiesen warns that the 'new Gulf interventionism' also carries severe risks, not least by linking the GCC states' security to the stability of a range of authoritarian regimes with domestic and regional security policy agendas of their own. Matthiesen charts, in particular, the impact of social polarisation arising from the region-wide crackdown on the Muslim Brotherhood as well as the vulnerability of the 'open-ended commitments' made to North African states in an era of comparative austerity.

Gawdat Bahgat explores the changing landscape of global energy and its economic and security implications for Persian Gulf states in chapter 4.

Bahgat puts the 'shale revolution' in North America into the context of broader US strategic interests in the Gulf and the wider Middle East, and assesses the implications of the divergent trajectories whereby the United States has become less dependent on imported Persian Gulf oil while China has moved in the opposite direction. Bahgat analyses also the strategic implications for Persian Gulf producers of long-term trends such as the growing drive for energy efficiencies, rising concerns about greenhouse gas emissions, and increasing diversity of the global energy mix. Bahgat ends by assessing how the post-2014 volatility in international oil prices presents both a set of challenges and opportunities for Persian Gulf producers, who continue to utilise energy interdependency to underpin their security and strategic relationships with international partners.

The state of the 'oligarchic pact' and the relationship between political and business actors in Abu Dhabi, Bahrain, and Oman are analysed by Marc Valeri in chapter 5. Valeri examines the evolution of state–business relations in these three case studies through the prism of greater ruling family involvement in the business and private sectors. This, Valeri argues, signifies an important shift away from the initial relationship between ruling and business elites that developed after the influx of large-scale oil revenues in the 1960s and 1970s. The 'unprecedented intrusion of ruling family members in the private sector' over recent years is likely to have major implications for the social contract between ruler and ruled and, by extension, for domestic stability as the traditional 'rentier bargain' breaks down. Valeri's choice of Abu Dhabi, Bahrain, and Oman enables him to draw out common themes from the study of three very different political economies and provide comparative analysis of the nature and impact of the structural shift in the relations between ruling and business elites in favour of the former.

Dionysis Markakis broadens the focus in chapter 6 to assess whether (and how) India is developing into a rising power in the Persian Gulf. Markakis approaches India's reconnection with the region in terms of 'middle power theory' and disaggregates the dominant economic, sociocultural, and military drivers of Indian policies in the Persian Gulf. Markakis suggests that India is still attempting to carve out its niche in the international system and that multiple factors lie behind its hesitance to engage proactively in regional and world affairs. These include the strong element of multilateral alignment that runs through Indian foreign policy as well as domestic institutional weaknesses within the structure of the Indian government itself. Remarkably, India, with a population that exceeds one billion people, has the same number of diplomats as Singapore, a country of five million. Thus, for Markakis, a primary challenge for Indian policymakers is how to outline a more proactive, rather than reactive, approach to foreign policy and the conception and exercise of power. The longstanding and multifaceted relationship between India and the Persian Gulf makes the region an area where India could be expected to develop a more assertive approach, fuelled in part by India's growing dependence on the Persian Gulf for commerce and energy.

In chapter 7, Nussaibah Younis examines the collective action dilemma at the heart of GCC states' security policies in the light of the startling rise of ISIS. Younis documents the internal disarray among GCC states in the months prior to the ISIS takeover of Mosul and declaration of a Caliphate in June 2014, as the fallout from the differing responses to the Arab Spring continued to reverberate throughout the region. Yet, while the early shock provided by the ISIS advance in Iraq compelled GCC rulers to put aside their differences temporarily and revisit stalled plans for a shared defence architecture, Younis argues that their commitment to the multinational anti-ISIS coalition proved short-lived. Instead, GCC scepticism about the limited US role in tackling ISIS and opposition to Iran's perceived role of interference in regional flashpoints combined to refocus the renewal of GCC security cooperation on countering Iranian influence in the Persian Gulf rather than supporting the international fight against ISIS in Iraq and in Syria.

The turbulent relationship between Iran and Saudi Arabia since the pivotal year of 1979—the year of both the Iranian Revolution and significant domestic turmoil in Saudi Arabia—is analysed by Nader Entessar in chapter 8. Entessar examines how the very different foreign policy objectives of the two regional powers in the Persian Gulf have evolved over the three and a half decades since 1979. Entessar's chapter contains a wide-ranging overview of the national interests and motivations, levels of threat perception and military balance, and changing domestic and foreign policy contexts that feed into the regional roles of Saudi Arabia and Iran, and underscores the point that the projection (and degree) of influence of each is not static but fluctuates as domestic, regional, and global political and strategic circumstances themselves shift. Entessar offers guarded optimism that the 'diplomacy deficit' that has greatly exacerbated volatility and insecurity in the Persian Gulf can be gradually bridged through greater bilateral contact and the realisation that a zero-sum approach to regional security is ultimately unattainable.

Succession dynamics have come to prominence in Saudi Arabia since the accession of King Salman to the throne in January 2015 and the acceleration of the generational handover of eventual power to the grandsons of 'Abdul 'Aziz Al Saud. Joseph A. Kéchichian examines the politics of Saudi succession in chapter 9 and offers an in-depth perspective on the new actors that will reshape Saudi leadership in the years and decades ahead. He analyses the momentous changes in the Saudi policy landscape unveiled during the early months of King Salman's reign and assesses the unprecedented replacement of the Crown Prince in April 2015 in the context of the (seemingly) decisive resolution of the generational transition question, which had become a parlour game for analysts and commentators alike. At a time when succession issues are again rising to the surface (in Kuwait and Oman), Kéchichian's chapter provides a timely case study of the interaction between the mechanisms and dynamics that enabled the ruling families in GCC states to defy renewed predictions of their fragility and confirmed them as the great survivors of Middle East politics.

From Saudi Arabia, the focus shifts to Kuwait, to a critical analysis of the youth-led protests that shook Kuwaiti politics in 2011 and 2012 and threatened for a time to flare out of control. Alanoud Alsharekh analyses the multiple roots of youth dissatisfaction with the political and economic status quo in Kuwait and explores the intersection of youth-led demands for change with the broader pressure points that led Kuwait from one political crisis to another after 2006. Alsharekh documents how both the Kuwaiti government and the established political opposition failed to capitalise on the emergence of the politically active new youth movement. The rise of youth-led groups that break the mould of established political systems has implications for all other GCC states and also for Iran, and Alsharekh's concluding observations on the difficulties in assimilating the region's youthful population into existing power-sharing mechanisms—as well as labour market structures—hold great comparative significance for future stability and sustainable growth.

The volume ends with a chapter by Khalid Almezaini that examines the transformation of UAE foreign policy since 2011 as the country moved far beyond traditional understandings of small state behaviour and combined elements of soft and hard power in a hawkish and interventionist approach to regional insecurity. With the UAE deeply involved in the GCC-led military campaign in Yemen and in the struggle to shape the political transitions in the North African states that experienced regime change in 2011, Almezaini uses theoretical and empirical analyses to highlight the threat perceptions and policy drivers that illustrate how and why officials in the UAE changed course and broke free of the structural constraints that normally govern the actions of small states. Almezaini demonstrates that the shifts in the UAE's external posture reflected a combination of internal and external pressures as domestic concerns over the perceived threat to stability posed by the Muslim Brotherhood meshed with the rapidly changing regional context after the Arab Spring.

2

LINKS BETWEEN DOMESTIC AND REGIONAL SECURITY

Kristian Coates Ulrichsen

Internal and external dimensions of security have become inextricably linked to debates as well as policy responses to domestic and regional security threats and challenges in Gulf Cooperation Council (GCC) states and in Iraq and Iran, with the growth of the Islamic State of Iraq and Syria (ISIS) only the latest, if by some distance the most extreme, manifestation of the trend. Regional and global developments in the 1990s and 2000s eroded the thin marker between the national and international spheres of policy in a region already heavily penetrated by supra- and sub-state ideational and material processes. The outbreak of the Arab Spring in 2011 and regional responses to the broader political upheaval across the Middle East and North Africa gave urgency to the porous relationship between internal and external security. Yet, as this chapter will illustrate, the challenge facing officials and regimes in the Gulf is that there appear to be no easy answers to the set of profound political, economic, and security questions that have been triggered by the Arab Spring and the rise of ISIS. Instead, the rapid growth of ISIS has rekindled memories of past contestations of regime authority by radical Islamist groups, particularly in Saudi Arabia, yet with regional and even global amplifications of the new and online media and social networking.

There are four parts to this chapter. The opening section focuses on the deeper transitions under way in regional and global security as wars between states gradually gave way to conflicts within societies as primary causes of instability, and the very concept of 'security' itself was broadened and deepened. It also charts the growth of volatile new non-state, transnational threats such as al-Qaeda in the 1990s and, a decade later, its regional offshoot, al-Qaeda in the Arabian Peninsula. Their rise took place against the backdrop of the fallout from the 2003 US-led invasion and subsequent occupation of Iraq. The second section describes the 'geopolitical straitjacket' that arose when Gulf policies to counter the perceived rise of Iranian and Shiite influence in the region became a liability following the rapid growth of ISIS in 2014. The third section examines how the rise of ISIS presents a dangerous new security threat to the GCC states by transcending national boundaries and interlinking the domestic and regional dimensions in ways that defy easy responses. The chapter ends with a fourth section that analyses the international dimension to regional security in the light of the GCC campaign in Yemen, which started in March 2015.

Persian Gulf security in transition

The Gulf remains an extremely volatile sub-region of the Middle East with multiple and interlinking threats to internal and external security alike. It did not share in the transformation of security that occurred in Latin America and Eastern Europe in the 1980s and the 1990s. In both these regions, the emergence of new concepts of cooperative security was associated with a shift away from realist approaches predicated largely on a zero-sum notion of 'national security'. No such comparative shift took place in the Gulf, which instead experienced three major inter-state wars based on regional balance-of-power considerations in the period between 1980 and 2003.[1] And yet, each of the three conflicts—the Iran–Iraq War of 1980–88, the Iraqi invasion of Kuwait and the subsequent Gulf war in 1990–91, and the US-led invasion of Iraq in 2003 and its violent aftermath—illustrated how threats to security operated at the transnational and intercultural, as well as traditional inter-state, levels.[2]

The three Gulf wars decisively altered the positioning of the GCC states vis-à-vis Iran and Iraq, and accelerated their integration into the Western military and security umbrella. Significantly, they led also to the gradual meshing of US and Gulf states' strategic objectives into an interlocking relationship founded upon shared interests in regional stability. While the United States only acquired large-scale basing rights in the aftermath of the Iraqi invasion of Kuwait in August 1990, developments between 1986 and 1988 introduced a sizeable external naval force into the Gulf for the first time since Britain's 1971 military withdrawal from the region. The internationalisation of Gulf waters after 1986 occurred as the United States, the United Kingdom, France, Italy, and the Soviet Union all sent warships to conduct convoy operations that protected Kuwaiti re-flagged and chartered vessels during the 'Tanker War' phase of the Iran–Iraq War. By the end of the conflict in August 1988, there were 82 Western vessels, including 33 combat ships, in the Gulf and adjacent waters, along with 23 Soviet ships, minesweepers, and support vessels.[3]

While the international response to the Tanker War was significant, it was the legacy of decisions taken between August 1990 and February 1991 that subsequently exerted the decisive influence on the evolution of Gulf security architecture. The permanent—and increasingly visible—presence of US troops and bases in the Arabian Peninsula led to a growing divergence between political and public opinion as the American military footprint deepened throughout the 1990s. The joint defence agreements signed between the US and Gulf partners shortly after the liberation of Kuwait proved inadequate to deter Saddam Hussein and were hastily reassessed in October 1994 after the Iraqi President massed two Republican Guard divisions near the Kuwaiti border. In response to this act, the Clinton administration in Washington DC expanded its naval and military assets in GCC states as part of the 'dual containment' approach to Iraq and Iran.[4]

Part of the subsequent backlash in Gulf societies arose as a result of the growing influence of Islamism as a social and political force in all GCC states. It also reflected greater popular scepticism of US motives and perceptions of regional threats, particularly after the election of the reformist Mohammad Khatami as President of Iran in 1997. Khatami's election was greeted with cautious optimism in GCC capitals and by efforts to normalise relations between the Gulf states and Iran.[5] The emerging gap between regime and public opinion over foreign and security policies opened up a space for oppositional voices to register their discontent at what the Kuwaiti sociologist Ali al-Tarrah labelled the 'smothering embrace' of the US military presence in the Gulf.[6] In Qatar, too, the close official rapport between Qatari and US military and defence interests was not universally acclaimed. Shortly after 9/11, Muhammad al-Musfir, a professor of political science at Qatar

University, bluntly told Mary Ann Weaver of *National Geographic* that 'Your military is a very provocative element, and it's not just my students who are saying this. Go to the suq. Go downtown. Go to any café. The attitude is decidedly anti-American.'[7]

Such ambivalence was most evident among Islamists in the Gulf, although it also encompassed secular and nationalist strands of opinion as well. Most notably, it provided the background to Osama bin Laden's notorious declaration of 'Jihad against Jews and Crusaders' on 23 February 1998. In this proclamation, the dissident ex-Saudi founder of al-Qaeda stated menacingly that 'for over seven years the United States has been occupying the lands of Islam in the holiest of places, the Arabian Peninsula, plundering its riches, dictating to its rulers, humiliating its peoples, terrorizing its neighbors, and turning the bases in the Peninsula into a spearhead with which to fight the neighbouring Muslim peoples'.[8] This statement represented an existential threat to the ideational and moral legitimacy of the Gulf monarchies and was especially potent in Saudi Arabia. Moreover, the advent of the Internet and Arab satellite television channels from the mid-1990s greatly facilitated the spread of oppositional messages and provided new forums for discussion and mobilisation. Although the King Fahd University of Petroleum and Minerals was the first Saudi institution to connect to the Internet as early as 1993 and Saudi Aramco followed suit in 1995, it was only in January 1999 that public access became widely available through commercial providers.[9]

Globalising pressures also played a significant role in creating an enabling environment for the expression and overspill of popular frustration in the early stages of the Arab Spring in 2011. The appearance of a form of 'global politics' occurred alongside the revolution in information and communication technologies (ICT). This created new forms of private, public, and increasingly virtual spaces in which to mobilise, organise and channel societal demands.[10] Political bloggers were active during the parliamentary elections in Bahrain in 2006 and Kuwait in 2008 and 2009, while online youth networks were important organisers of the 'Orange movement' that secured important changes to the electoral process in Kuwait in 2006. Social networking sites such as Facebook and Twitter, and encrypted communications technologies such as Skype and BlackBerry Messenger, emerged as forums for debate, coordination, and unregulated exchanges.[11]

In addition, Qatar-based Al-Jazeera's coverage of the Egyptian uprising spread transformative images of largely peaceful demonstrations defying political suppression and refusing to submit to the security regimes that had kept authoritarian leaders in power. This was immediately evident in Bahrain, where cafes that usually showed Lebanese music videos instead aired non-stop footage from the enormous demonstrations in Cairo's Tahrir Square.[12] These new forms of media and communication had the greatest impact on a youthful generation, in the Gulf states as elsewhere, who were among the most technology savvy with some of the highest rates of smartphone penetration in the world. Their synthesis eroded the system of controls and filters constructed by ministries of information and official government media outlets. Significantly, they constituted social as well as technological phenomena as powerful agents of social change and political empowerment.[13]

A major theme of the twenty-first century security landscape, particularly in the Middle East, has been the deep-rooted presence of non-state groups, in many cases (but not exclusively) violent in nature, and the rapid growth of transnational threats at both the sub-state and the supra-state levels. Together, these trends accelerated the hollowing out of the state in large parts of the Middle East and laid the foundation for the resurgence of identity politics in the states that experienced 'regime change' from Iraq (in 2003) onwards and the sudden collapse of longstanding regimes in 2011. Joel Migdal has documented how the rise of non-state actors has transformed the regional power dynamics in the Middle East, challenged state authority, and made national boundaries far more porous. This occurred as the 'core Arab states', such as Egypt, Syria, and Iraq, became weakened by mounting domestic challenges and the impact of regional and international conflicts in the 1980s and 1990s.[14] Moreover, the backdrop of state weakness, fragmentation, and even failure in much of the GCC's broader hinterland provided the conditions for the intensification of such groups' operations both before and especially after the political upheaval of the Arab Spring.[15]

The rise of oppositional movements that benefited from the spread of new information and communication technology highlighted how the internal and external dimensions of security in the Gulf states were interconnected and bound together in the 2000s as never before.[16] The threat this posed both to regional and global security became dramatically clear when Gulf nationals made up seventeen of the nineteen airplane hijackers on 11 September 2001.[17] The attacks on New York and Washington DC indicated the myriad linkages between globalisation and security in an era of intensely transnational and increasingly non-state threats.[18] Al-Qaeda's exploitation of globalising flows of finance and people as it prepared and executed the attacks illustrated the dark side of global interconnections. It also underscored how a profoundly 'regressive' form of globalisation existed, as organisations mobilised across states and within societies to compete with 'progressive' (and more conventional) global civil society groups in the new spaces opened up by globalising processes.[19]

The impact of globalising changes around the turn of the millennium also accelerated the rise of new forms of 'imagined communities' which both tapped into and fuelled the growing awareness of 'Islamic issues'.[20] For Saudi Arabia, in particular, its leaders' projection of pan-Islamism as a tool of regime legitimacy exposed them to contestation on the same grounds as Saudi militants who travelled abroad to participate in jihad in places as diverse as Afghanistan, Bosnia, Chechnya, and Kashmir. This threat was amplified after the mid-1990s as the Arab satellite television channels broadcast daily footage of Muslims suffering elsewhere in the world. The Norwegian academic, Thomas Hegghammer, cites a Saudi official responding to the 2003 upsurge of terrorist activity in the kingdom, who acknowledged, 'We encouraged our young men to fight for Islam in Afghanistan. We encouraged our young men to fight for Islam in Bosnia and Chechnya. We encouraged our young men to fight for Islam in Palestine.'[21]

In 2002–03, the emergence of al-Qaeda in the Arabian Peninsula (AQAP) and the fallout from the US-led invasion and subsequent occupation of Iraq demonstrated how non-state violence was replacing inter-state conflict as the primary threat to regional security and stability in the Gulf. The declared AQAP objective of forcing the withdrawal of Western forces and influences from the Arabian Peninsula was directed at the core of the Gulf states' domestic and international political economy. Attacks on Western targets and compounds as well as operations such as the failed February 2006 assault on the Abqaiq oil-processing facility were aimed at the heart of the social and commercial contracts binding GCC regimes to their societies and to the international system. The choice of Abqaiq was audacious as the facility is situated close to the massive Ghawar oilfield, and up to two-thirds of Saudi oil production passes through it en route to the Ras Tanura refinery and export terminal, itself the largest offshore oil-loading facility in the world.[22]

Shortly afterwards, the international security expert, Paul Rogers, noted that al-Qaeda quickly claimed responsibility for the operation as 'part of the project to rid the Arabian Peninsula of the infidels' and intended to stop the 'pillage of oil wealth' from Muslims.[23] For Rogers, the adoption of such economic targets meant that 'the key lesson here is that determined and dedicated insurgents have a capacity to damage the economy of a country that far outweighs their numbers ... the Abqaiq attack is a sharp reminder of what the

Al-Qaeda movement could do if it chose to take this route.'[24] Although AQAP was dismantled within Saudi Arabia by a series of concerted counter-terrorism measures, the January 2009 reconstitution of the organisation in Yemen revived the threat to Saudi Arabia from violent non-state actors and suggested to Saudi policymakers that their deradicalisation and rehabilitation programmes might only have displaced, rather than defeated, the threat from radical jihadism. The second iteration of AQAP encompassed a number of Saudi veterans of the rehabilitation programmes who absconded later to Yemen and developed subsequently one of the most dangerous 'offshoots' of al-Qaeda, as it demonstrated both the intent and the capability to undertake attacks against Saudi Arabia and further afield. These included an attempt to assassinate the head of counter-terrorism in Saudi Arabia (and, as of 2015, the Crown Prince), Muhammad bin Nayif Al Saud in August 2009 and the abortive effort to bring down a Northwestern airliner over Detroit on Christmas Day 2009. Both attacks only narrowly failed, as did a subsequent plot to detonate two bombs hidden in printer cartridges on US-bound aircraft in October 2010. Memories of the Abqaiq incident were also rekindled by the arrest in 2010 of three AQAP cells, totalling 113 militants (including 58 Saudis and 52 Yemenis), who allegedly were planning suicide assaults on oil facilities in Saudi Arabia.[25]

In addition to the growth of pan-Islamism as a mobilising tool, the 2000s witnessed also a gradual rise in sectarian politics, which was especially pronounced across the majority of the six GCC states. In part due to the mismanagement of the occupation and administration of post-Saddam Iraq, the growth of sectarian identities deepened another fissure in Gulf societies, which undermined the prospect of reaching consensus on critical regional issues. Sectarian tension, along with ethnic and tribal divisions, differences between citizens and expatriates, and between different classes of citizens themselves, all heighten Gulf states' vulnerability to the politicisation of internal fault-lines. Any breakdown of social cohesion would jeopardise the web of social relationships that bind together the many different communities and groups within the highly stratified Gulf polities. Were this to happen it would also erode regime credibility and societal confidence in the 'social contract' between state and society, based around the redistribution of goods and services in lieu of extensive participatory mechanisms.[26]

Recent scholarship on the evolution of sectarian identities and politics in the Gulf has emphasised the role of governments in ascribing to religion problems that instead have their roots in political and economic issues.[27] This

29

builds on Toby Matthiesen's introduction of the label 'sectarian identity entrepreneurs', who represent 'an amalgam of political, religious, social, and economic elites who all used sectarianism to further their personal aims'.[28] And yet, while the initial impulse to 'sectarianise' was a top-down process it gradually morphed into a bottom-up phenomenon that escaped the capacity of elites to control, as the second half of this chapter details. Indeed, as Justin Gengler has pointed out, the growth of sectarian rhetoric, particularly but not only in Iraq since 2003 and in Bahrain since 2011, has awakened 'transnational Sunni Islamist movements' to counter the 'Shia activism and regional Iranian interference' in Gulf (and Iraqi) polities.[29]

Iraq: a geopolitical straitjacket

Contemporaneous developments in Iraq have underscored further the growing capacity of non-state actors and transnational pressures to destabilise state structures even if the GCC states notably remained largely untouched by any direct spillover from Iraq's multiple local conflicts. Thus, the impact on regional stability of the third Gulf war in (and after) 2003 differed qualitatively from that of its two predecessors, between 1980 and 1991, which primarily were inter-state in nature. The major difference in 2003 was the dynamic interplay between domestic actors and regional and international events in a globalised arena of difficult-to-regulate flows of people, finance, information, and ideas. And yet, until the emergence of ISIS in 2013–14, the Gulf states not only avoided the worst overspill of conflict from the third Gulf war, which began in 2003, but also ensured that the destabilising flows actually ran in the opposite direction into Iraq.[30]

Governments in the six GCC states all gave varying levels of political logistical assistance to the US-led invasion of Iraq in 2003. The Gulf states' role as administrative facilitators left them vulnerable to considerable levels of domestic opposition, with up to 97 per cent of Saudis opposed to any cooperation with an American attack. Anti-war demonstrations occurred in other Gulf States as well, with those in Bahrain particularly well attended and prolonged. Policymakers in the GCC were therefore put in the awkward position of having to balance their security ties with the United States against high levels of popular opposition to the invasion. This security dilemma prompted many Gulf rulers to distance themselves publicly from the United States while privately offering greater encouragement and support to the effort to oust Saddam Hussein's regime.[31]

The elevated levels of public anger at US actions in Iraq formed part of a broader chorus of anger at the George W. Bush administration's Middle East policies more generally. In March 2007, King 'Abdullah of Saudi Arabia went as far as to denounce the 'illegitimate foreign occupation' of Iraq in an unprecedented public display of anger at the kingdom's primary security partner. In this environment, the GCC states might have expected significant blowback due to both their geographical proximity to Iraq and their leaders' military and political ties with Washington. This, we should note, did not happen, as the Gulf states implemented a range of hard security measures that ensured they remained relatively immune to the cross-border overspill of the multiple indices of human insecurity, such as sectarian conflict, terrorism attacks, and flows of refugees and displaced persons, which impacted on Syria and Jordan far more.[32]

Instead, the destabilising flows of men and money ran largely in the opposite direction, from the GCC into Iraq. Between 1,500 and 3,000 Saudi militants joined the Sunni insurgency and constituted a significant proportion (up to 60 per cent) of the total number of foreign fighters in Iraq.[33] In Kuwait, members of two organisations of radical militants—the Peninsula Lions and the Mujahideen of Kuwait—also channelled fighters to the insurgency and mounted a number of attacks on US forces in Kuwait itself. Notably, the emergence of such groups—both in Kuwait and in Saudi Arabia—took the security services by surprise. Kuwait's Interior Minister (and, since 2006, Crown Prince), Sheikh Nawaf al-Ahmad Al Sabah, linked the growth of the Peninsula Lions to the militant al-Haramain Brigade in Saudi Arabia and went so far as to allege that 'Initial investigations have proved that the financing of the terrorist elements came from outside the country, specifically from one of the neighboring brotherly countries'.[34]

Such observations fed into broader concerns over the role of Gulf-based individuals and organisations in terror-financing networks. After 9/11, but prior to the invasion of Iraq, an independent task force set up by the Council on Foreign Relations to examine the issue concluded bluntly that 'for years, individuals and charities based in Saudi Arabia have been the most important source of funds for Al Qaeda. And for years, Saudi officials have turned a blind eye to this problem.'[35] Four years later, the Iraq Study Group appointed by the US Congress in 2006 to assess the worsening violence and civil war in the country observed that 'funding for the Sunni insurgency comes from private individuals within Saudi Arabia and the Gulf States'.[36] Particular attention was focused on the activities of the Saudi-based International Islamic Relief

Organisation (IIRO), a transnational Muslim humanitarian group, owing to its operations in Falluja and other insurgent strongholds and its exclusion from Saudi charitable regulations.[37] Later, in 2008, the US Treasury ordered the assets of a Kuwaiti charity—the Revival of Islamic Heritage Society—to be frozen owing to its alleged links with al-Qaeda, to a chorus of disapproval among Kuwaiti politicians.[38]

With the direct threat from Iraq contained, regional discourse in the Gulf focused instead on the geopolitical and strategic implications of post-occupation Iraq for the balance of regional power. This revolved around GCC leaders' securitisation of their conclusion that the removal of Tehran's main counterweight in the Persian Gulf resulted directly and indirectly in the expansion of Iranian influence in Iraq. The Sunni regimes in the Gulf repeatedly expressed varying levels of alarm at the empowerment of Iraqi Shia Muslims, which they feared could stoke unrest or greater political demands from their own Shiite communities. As early as February 2003, the Saudi Foreign Minister, Prince Saud al-Faisal Al Saud, warned President Bush that he would be 'solving one problem and creating five more' if Saddam Hussein was removed by force. In 2005, he added that the United States was 'handing the whole country over to Iran without reason'. Saudi policy thus focused on preventing certain scenarios, such as the disintegration of Iraq or the complete disempowerment of its Sunni communities, by supporting Sunni Islamist movements within Iraq.[39]

The sectarian lens therefore constituted a powerful filter through which GCC ruling elites viewed developments in Iraq, especially as sectarian violence spiralled between 2005 and 2007. Officials deeply distrusted the government led by Nouri al-Maliki, who they suspected was an Iranian proxy and an ideational threat to their own conservative polities. This had significant implications in framing GCC states' policy toward Iraq, generating a self-fulfilling prophecy as the Gulf states' reluctance to expand their political and economic engagement with Baghdad actually enabled Iran to take the lead in many reconstruction and development projects. Thus, while investment from Kuwait and the UAE increased, notably in Iraqi Kurdistan, Saudi Arabia still had not (by 2014) posted a resident ambassador in Baghdad. Notably, too, the Emir of Kuwait was the only GCC head of state to attend the Arab League Summit that took place in Baghdad in March 2012.[40]

In the aftermath of the final withdrawal of US troops in December 2011, the threat posed by Iraq to Kuwait and its GCC partners was one of a weak state struggling to assert political authority and a monopoly of the use of force over the panoply of non-state groups still operating in the country. This differed significantly from the challenge of a 'strong' Iraq under Saddam Hussein, but ties between Iraq and the GCC struggled to revive during the premiership of Iraqi Prime Minister Maliki (2006–14). In addition to the aforementioned Gulf scepticism at Maliki's leadership, which intensified as Maliki's authoritarian tendencies became more apparent, the Iraqi government itself harboured anger and resentment at the GCC states' role in fuelling the insurgency that gathered pace after 2003. The ill feeling on both sides ultimately magnified the vulnerability of the Gulf monarchies to the threat from ISIS as it emerged as a destructive regional force in 2014.[41]

The Islamic State threat to the Gulf

In late 2013 and early 2014, ISIS prevailed in a series of violent confrontations with other rebel groups along the Syria–Iraq boundary, and in June 2014 swept eastwards into Iraq where the group routed the Iraqi Army and overran Iraq's second largest city, Mosul. ISIS emerged from the radical maelstrom of the post-2003 occupation of Iraq as former political and military leaders of the ousted Ba'ath party made common cause with radical militants such as Abu Musab al-Zarqawi.[42] Following the defeat of a precursor group, Islamic State in Iraq, by the Sahwa (Awakening) movement of Sunni tribal forces in Anbar province in 2006–07, ISIS was reduced to a rump organisation until it moved into areas of northern and eastern Syria in 2013. In October 2013, ISIS seized the city of Raqqa, which had fallen to the Syrian opposition in March, and used the city as a springboard for the expansion of territory along the strategic corridor that connected its wings in Syria and Iraq. Having established itself as the dominant force in the Syrian opposition, by the time the ISIS leader Abu Bakr al-Baghdadi declared the creation of a Caliphate on 29 June 2014, the group had captured a third of Syria and a quarter of Iraq and controlled an area larger than the size of Great Britain.[43]

The ISIS threat to the Gulf states grew rapidly in 2014 as the region, and particularly Saudi Arabia, confronted a virulent new non-state threat, nearly a decade after AQAP was banished to Yemen, and new flows of recruits and networks of financing and support from within Gulf societies. Whereas AQAP specifically targeted Western interests in the Gulf states, ISIS focused on territorial consolidation in, and resource extraction from, the areas under its control in Iraq and Syria. The Gulf states' subsequent participation in the US-led air campaign against ISIS targets in Iraq and Syria posed a security dilemma for officials forced to balance their security relationship with the US against the threat of backlash from domestic ISIS sympathisers.[44]

Having spent much of the period after the 2003 invasion lamenting the plight of Iraq's Sunni communities and most of 2012 and 2013 channelling support to various Sunni rebel groups in Syria, Gulf officials found themselves caught in a geopolitical straitjacket in 2014. The balancing act was especially acute in Kuwait, which US officials had for several years after 2011 identified as a centre of funding and other forms of material assistance for participants in Syria's civil war. However, unlike in Qatar or Saudi Arabia, where support for Syria largely flowed in one direction towards (different) groups of Sunni fighters, prominent figures among Kuwait's Sunni and Shi'a communities provided high-profile support to both the opposition and the Assad regime. This interaction between domestic politics and external events underscored Kuwait's vulnerability to regional fissures—as during the Iran–Iraq War of the 1980s—and contributed to an upsurge in sectarian rhetoric and intercommunal tension after 2011.[45]

Whereas in Kuwait the threat of blowback came primarily from the fact that members of both communities backed opposite sides in Syria, Bahrain and Saudi Arabia were vulnerable to the extremist sectarian narratives propagated by ISIS. These played on the sharp growth in sectarian tensions in both countries, as officials attributed the Arab Spring protests in 2011 to largely Iranian (and Shi'a) interference. The risk of direct sectarian blowback was most visible and acute in Bahrain, where the Sunni ruling family and security forces crushed a largely Shi'a-led uprising in 2011, which left the country divided along sectarian lines.[46] In September 2014, an ISIS video featured a former official of the Ministry of Interior denouncing Bahrain's decision to join the US-led air strikes on ISIS and calling on officers in the security services to defect, while another Bahraini from the same influential Sunni al-Binali tribe with close ties to the ruling Al Khalifa family emerged as one of the most senior clerics within the ISIS Caliphate in northern Iraq.[47] Bahraini government unease at the potential danger from within the security forces was evident in their reluctance to take action against IS sympathisers even in the face of public expressions of support for the group. This included acknowledgement by government officials that 'the threat is real, the issue is very serious. These are people from within the security services, from the police and the military.'[48]

GCC states also faced a deeper challenge both internally from networks of ISIS cells and externally from the flow of Gulf nationals to the ISIS battlefronts in Iraq and Syria and, in some cases, their return to the Gulf states with the intention of carrying out attacks. Risk of blowback has, moreover, been amplified in Saudi Arabia and Bahrain owing to the rise in sectarian identity politics and social polarisation that has taken place in both countries in recent years. The uncovering of several organised ISIS-linked cells and groups in Saudi Arabia in 2014 illustrated the growing challenge to internal security in the Gulf. In May 2014, 59 Saudis were among 62 arrested in the first discovery of a terrorist network attributed to ISIS. The group had allegedly been plotting assassinations and other attacks within Saudi Arabia. Four months later, in September, 88 people, including 84 Saudis, were arrested for terrorist recruiting and planning attacks both inside Saudi Arabia and abroad. A trend that caused alarm among Saudi officials was the discovery that between half and two-thirds of those detained had previously been arrested on terror-related charges, although the lack of due process and the proclivity of officials to label as 'terrorism' most forms of political opposition mean such figures are unreliable at best. Nevertheless, they called into question the effectiveness of the high-profile deradicalisation and rehabilitation programme set up by Prince Muhammad bin Nayif Al Saud in the aftermath of the May 2003 AQAP bombings of residential compounds in Riyadh.[49]

A spate of attacks in GCC states since mid-2014 attributed to ISIS indicates that the organisation poses a multifaceted threat to internal security from both opportunistic attacks and carefully planned mass-casualty events. A series of 'copycat' attacks in Saudi Arabia and one in Abu Dhabi in late 2014 suggested initially that the ISIS threat arose primarily from 'lone wolf' operations. Two shootings involving American employees of the defence contractor Vinnell left one dead and another wounded in Riyadh in November 2014, while two more employees were wounded in the oil-rich Eastern Province in January 2015.[50] Also in November 2014, supporters of ISIS claimed responsibility for the shooting of a Danish national in the Eastern Province, while a Canadian was stabbed in a random attack at a shopping mall the same month.[51] Most disturbingly, an American teacher was brutally murdered in an upscale shopping mall in Abu Dhabi in December 2014, weeks after the US Embassy in the UAE warned of jihadi threats to attack Americans in the country. Although there was no evidence that the separate attacks were linked either to each other or to broader networks of ISIS cells, they constituted an emerging pattern that rattled expatriates and Gulf security services alike.[52]

Moving beyond the initial 'lone wolf' attacks and beginning with an assault that killed eight Shi'a worshippers in the Eastern Province in November 2014 by a cell that had pledged loyalty to the ISIS leader al-Baghdadi and that was

in frequent communication with ISIS in Iraq, a series of increasingly sophis-
ticated, coordinated, and mass-casualty attacks highlighted further the risk to
internal security from radicalised militants operating within Gulf societies.
Just as three Saudis were behind the November attack, four Saudis carried out
an audacious suicide bombing that killed the commander of Saudi Arabia's
border operations in January 2015 after re-entering the kingdom from Iraq's
volatile Anbar province.[53] In May 2015, an ISIS affiliate that called itself the
Wilayat Najd (Najd Province) carried out suicide bombings at Shi'a mosques
in the Eastern Province cities of Qatif and Dammam over two consecutive
Friday prayers, which left 22 and 4 dead, respectively.[54] The same affiliate also
claimed responsibility for the suicide bombing of the Imam al-Sadiq mosque
in Kuwait City in June 2015, which killed 27 people. Carried out by a Saudi
citizen who transited through Bahrain on his way to Kuwait, the attack was
designed to cause maximum damage to intercommunal relations in Kuwait,
as it targeted the centre of the Hasawi community of Kuwaiti Shi'a. Also
known as Shaykhis, the Hasawi originally emigrated from the al-Hasa region
of Saudi Arabia's Eastern Province in the late-nineteenth and early-twentieth
centuries, in part to escape endemic marginalisation and discrimination.[55]
Further attacks took place against Saudi Shi'a communities in the Eastern
Province in October 2015 and January 2016, with the October 2015 attack
being claimed by a self-declared ISIS offshoot that provocatively called itself
Wilayat al-Bahrain (Bahrain Province) in another attempt to play on and
enlarge sectarian fault-lines.[56]

The growing evidence that ISIS-affiliated cells possessed both the capability
and the intent to undertake terrorist attacks inside GCC states indicates the
difficulties facing political and security policymakers in Gulf states. More
worrying than any actual number of arrests made is the possibility that militant groups such as ISIS might tap into a broader latent feeling of strategic
sympathy with the re-empowerment of Sunnism in Iraq and Syria, particularly
as sectarian tension across the region soared with the successive crises of the
Syrian civil war after 2011, the conflict in Yemen from 2015, and the Saudi–
Iran rupture in 2016. Evidence in support of such an eventuality may be found
in the platform given to radical preachers and fundraisers in Gulf states
between 2011 and 2014, when controls belatedly began to be imposed. An
investigation into Gulf funding for Syrian rebel groups conducted by Abu
Dhabi's *The National* newspaper in 2013 described Kuwait as the 'back office
of logistical support' for such groups.[57] This occurred as supporters of the various rebel groups took advantage of Kuwait's lax terror-financing and money-

laundering laws to raise and transfer funds to Syria with little official oversight. For this reason, money collected privately in other Gulf states, such as the UAE or Qatar, often would be sent to Kuwait for onward transmission to recipients in Syria often through third-party intermediaries in Turkey or Iran (owing to the tightening of regulations in other Gulf states on direct financial transfers to Syria).[58]

The irruption of ISIS onto the regional security landscape in 2014 prompted a range of belated policy responses at both the national and international levels. US concern at the apparent lack of control over charitable giving and private fundraising in Kuwait manifested itself in a blunt statement in March 2014 by Treasury Undersecretary David Cohen that Kuwait had become 'the epicentre of fundraising for terror groups in Syria' and noted more generally that a new financial tracking unit set up by the Kuwaiti government to investigate suspicious financial transactions and money laundering was still not operational.[59] Moreover, Kuwait's Justice and Endowments Minister, Nayef al-Ajmi, resigned in May 2014 after being named by Cohen as having a history of 'promoting terrorism', and after his ministry came under suspicion for allowing non-profit organisations and charities to collect donations for the Syrian people at mosques in Kuwait, which Cohen argued was 'a measure we believe can be easily exploited by Kuwait-based terrorist fundraisers'.[60] US Treasury officials turned their focus on Qatar also and described 'Abdulrahman al-Nuaimi, a former president of the Qatar Football Association and a founding member of the government-backed Sheikh Eid bin Muhammad al-Thani Charitable Foundation, as a major financier of al-Qaeda and its regional affiliates. Al-Nuaimi had for many years advised the Qatari ruling family on its charitable giving, but stood accused of pursuing a dual role, promoting humanitarian causes and civil rights on the one hand while simultaneously supporting extremist groups and acting as an interlocutor between al-Qaeda and Qatar-based donors on the other hand.[61]

To be sure, much of the support extended from the Gulf States to Syria was not intended for ISIS specifically nor did it necessarily end up in the hands of militant organisations. It nevertheless remains a challenge for GCC officials to establish with any accuracy the 'end-user' of the chains linking the GCC with the range of groups operating along the Syria–Iraq border. ISIS has demonstrated an ability to recruit among disaffected pockets of Muslims worldwide and raise revenues from areas under its control. These have given the organisation a degree of strategic depth and operational autonomy that has proved resilient against months of US-led air strikes in Iraq and Syria and illustrated the weakness of hard security responses. The ISIS 'narrative' also taps into longer memories of violent Islamist contestation of monarchical power in Saudi Arabia, dating back to the creation of the modern kingdom in the 1920s.[62] Technocratic responses taken by GCC states, such as the placing of ISIS (along with the Muslim Brotherhood) on lists of proscribed terror groups, as well as other measures such as the construction of elaborate boundary defences, struggle to address the softer ideological appeal of Sunni extremism among significant elements of Gulf societies.[63] This was reflected in an (admittedly unofficial) survey of Saudis on social media which found that 92 per cent of respondents believed the ideology of ISIS to be 'consistent with the values of Islam and the *sharia*'. The challenge for ruling elites in the Gulf has been, and remains, that, in the absence of formal opinion polls and legal outlets for the expression of political discontent, there is no accurate gauge for the level of societal support for such extremism.[64]

The international dimension

This final section brings in the international dimension to the evolving domestic and regional security landscape in the Gulf. In 2014, the GCC states partnered with the United States in a loose coalition that began a campaign of air strikes against ISIS targets in Iraq and in Syria. The following March, the GCC states, led by Saudi Arabia, launched a military campaign against Houthi rebels in Yemen whom they suspected of being supported by Iran. The development of assertive regional policies did not take place in a vacuum but rather occurred against the backdrop of rising uncertainty in the GCC about the future role of the United States in the Middle East arising from the Obama administration's 'pivot toward Asia'.[65] US relations with GCC partners came under unprecedented strain over the course of the Obama presidency. Beginning with the withdrawal of US support for embattled Egyptian President Hosni Mubarak at the start of the Arab Spring and continuing with (muted) American criticism over the security response in Bahrain as the Al Khalifa ruling family restored order with GCC support, officials in the GCC states began to question US motives as never before. As early as May 2011, the influential Saudi foreign policy commentator, Nawaf Obaid, wrote of a 'tectonic' shift in the US–Saudi relationship and lamented that 'Washington has shown itself in recent months to be an unwilling and unreliable partner' against the supposed regional threat from Iran. In a sign of the growing autonomy of Saudi and other Gulf states' policy calculations, Obaid warned that 'in areas in which Saudi national security or strategic interests are at stake, the Kingdom will pursue its own agenda.'[66]

As Gulf states' frustrations with US policy toward the Arab Spring mounted, declaratory and policy pronouncements became shriller. The failure to take military action against the Assad regime in Syria following the 21 August 2013 use of chemical weapons in Ghouta was greeted with dismay in GCC capitals, as were the signs of a rapprochement between the United States and Iran following the election of Hassan Rouhani as President in June 2013. Saudi Arabia's decision that October to turn down one of the ten rotating, non-permanent seats on the United Nations Security Council weeks after snubbing the annual meeting of the UN General Assembly revealed the depth of regional alarm at the direction of US policy in the Middle East. Shortly after the November 2013 breakthrough at Geneva, which produced an interim agreement on Iran's nuclear programme, the former Saudi Ambassador to the United States, Prince Turki al-Faisal Al Saud, told an audience at the European Council on Foreign Relations (ECFR), 'How we feel is that we weren't part of the discussions at all, in some cases we were—I would go so far as to say we were lied to, things were hidden from us.'[67]

Although US–Gulf relations improved somewhat with the shared threat from ISIS, cooperation in the air campaign in Iraq and Syria in late 2014, as well as logistical and intelligence cooperation in the air strikes against the Houthi positions in Yemen in 2015, the Gulf states will continue to adopt more assertive and autonomous regional positions in the immediate future. This reflects the deep scepticism of Gulf officials towards the Obama administration's lengthy negotiations with Tehran, which began in 2013 and continued through to the conclusion of the framework agreement in March 2015, 'Adoption Day' in July 2015, and 'Implementation Day' in January 2016.

In addition to the Saudi anger at the Iranian nuclear negotiations in Geneva and the rupture in diplomatic relations in January 2016, policymakers in GCC capitals also accused Iran of an escalating intervention in Yemen following the rapid assertion of Houthi rebel control in 2014. Yemen highlighted the different perceptions of Iran that divided officials in Riyadh and Abu Dhabi from their counterparts in Washington DC: the former viewed Iran as a destabilising 'meddler' in regional conflict zones while the latter viewed President Rouhani as a man they could do business with to defuse the longstanding standoff over Iran's nuclear programme and international isolation. These tensions and the diverging views on how to view the unfolding disintegration of the Yemeni government peaked following the Houthi takeover of

Sanaʻa in late 2014 and the ousting of embattled Yemeni President Hadi on the same day in January 2015 as the death of King ʻAbdullah of Saudi Arabia. After Hadi escaped to the southern port city of Aden and re-established a base of control there, a further Houthi advance in March 2015 threatened to over-run Aden and entrench Houthi—and, in GCC eyes, Iranian—power in Yemen. This led to Saudi Arabia and nine other Arab states, including every Gulf State except Oman—to launch air strikes on Houthi strongholds in Yemen in Operation Decisive Storm, as the proxy struggle for influence between Iran and Saudi Arabia escalated into outright regional conflict.[68]

The conflict in Yemen highlighted the new assertiveness in GCC policies, as the Gulf states acted collectively in a bid to secure regional interests, how-ever narrowly defined. It constituted an important evolution in regional secu-rity structures as the locus of decision-making shifted to (Arab) Gulf capitals rather than external partners in Washington DC or, earlier, in London. Significantly, the Yemen operation marked the first use of the joint military command that was created by the GCC in November 2014, alongside joint naval and police forces.[69] However, GCC officials do not currently possess a viable alternative to the US-led security guarantee that continues to underpin regional stability, and struggled to make significant military progress in Yemen despite months of intense air strikes and the deployment of increasing num-bers of ground forces, which consisted both of GCC nationals and, more murkily, of South American (and Australian-led) 'mercenaries'.[70] Furthermore, the longer the military campaign in Yemen has continued, the greater has been the private criticism of GCC actions from policymakers in Washington DC, who question openly whether the Saudi-led coalition has realistic military and political objectives in Yemen, not to mention the tools of power and statecraft to achieve them.[71]

Thus, the challenge for policymakers in the Gulf states is that they find themselves caught between two paradoxical trajectories: more able to project their influence and shape changing global institutions and structures, while susceptible to domestic contestation arising from the interlinking of local discontent with regional and international pressures. The global emergence of the Gulf states and the new challenges posed by the Arab Spring therefore constitute two diverging trends for the contemporary Gulf. On the one hand there are the broader shifts in geo-economic power and the rebalancing of the global order towards multiple centres of political and economic influence, while on the other there is the new sense of vulnerability that stability may be more elusive than previously imagined. This has on occasion caused great mistrust and suspicion in the highly charged 'post-Arab Spring' atmosphere as the GCC states became more assertive in the international arena and gaps opened up between established and emergent regional players. Syria offers a salutary example of the difficulties that arise when the international community is divided and when regional and international actors pursue unilateral policies that follow competing or even contradictory lines.

3

RENTING THE CASBAH

GULF STATES' FOREIGN POLICY TOWARDS NORTH AFRICA SINCE THE ARAB UPRISINGS

Toby Matthiesen

This chapter deals with the relations between countries of the Gulf Cooperation Council (GCC) and the three North African countries that saw mass uprisings (Tunisia, Egypt, and Libya) since 2011. Morocco[1] and Algeria,[2] which survived the Arab uprisings with their political systems intact, will not be discussed in this chapter because the persistence of the old regimes either ensured unanimous Gulf support (Morocco) or limited opportunities for Gulf involvement (Algeria). Indeed, the chapter will look at the ways in which various Gulf states, above all Qatar, the United Arab Emirates (UAE), Saudi Arabia, and, to a lesser extent, Kuwait, have tried to influence the political transitions in Tunisia, Egypt, and Libya.[3] It argues that the period since 2011 has witnessed a profound shift in the foreign policies of the GCC states from petrodollar diplomacy to direct involvement in politics and even military intervention.

This topic has received some attention in the media and in country-specific case studies of the Arab uprisings. A number of works have looked at the changing GCC foreign policies since 2011, but, with a few exceptions, the recent role of the GCC countries in North Africa has not been studied in depth.[4] By involving themselves so forcefully in the internal affairs of North African states, GCC actors not only have deployed an unprecedented measure of 'hard' power alongside more usual 'softer' forms of influence, but also have inserted themselves in the turbulent maelstrom of the post-Arab Spring transition process. In addition to close association with the volatility of political processes they cannot fully control, the ongoing financial commitment to securing the range of GCC states' interests in North Africa constitutes a new form of potential insecurity in an age of comparative austerity, when ruling elites in the Gulf are trying to cut back on the welfare state and introduce new forms of revenue-raising from their population, including citizens.

For countries that have for centuries relied on alliances with great powers, mostly the United Kingdom and the United States, for their external and at times internal security, this new interventionist foreign policy of the GCC is a striking shift. And while in the eyes of Gulf decision-makers their interventions contribute to state security, it is not certain that this will be the long-term outcome of these interventions, especially given the highly volatile and polarised political, security, and economic situation in North Africa. In essence, this new politics of interventionism has contributed to the regional security dilemma, whereby any state's loss of influence in a corner of the Arab world leads to an increase in influence for rival forces. Of course, this has in some ways also previously been the case, but what is new is that this regional security dilemma is now fought out between different Gulf states with a large amount of resources (mainly Saudi Arabia, Qatar, and the UAE, as well as Iran). This has changed the nature of Arab politics and the international relations of the region.

Over decades, a system of Arab politics had emerged that was shaped by negotiations, interactions, and debates about Arabism between Arab political leaders.[5] This system became increasingly replaced by an Arab regional system in which most Arab states (except Syria, Iraq, and Algeria) have come under the strong influence of oil-rich countries of the Gulf. The financial survival of many Arab states is to varying degrees dependent on Gulf aid. Unlike in previous decades, however, Gulf interests in Arab politics are now not just pursued with money and diplomacy. Instead, the region has witnessed material military support and even the direct involvement of Gulf militaries, so far mainly

Special Forces and air power, in North Africa, Syria, Iraq, Bahrain, and Yemen. In addition, the struggle over influence in the Arab world is not just fought against non-Arab regional countries such as Iran, Turkey, and Israel, but also increasingly between GCC countries (as illustrated by the rift between Qatar and other GCC member states in 2014).

The Gulf states' responses to the Arab uprisings

If anyone was in need of more proof regarding the scale of the Gulf states' ambitions in North Africa, the Egypt Economic Development Conference held in March 2015 in ousted President Hosni Mubarak's favourite holiday resort, Sharm el-Sheikh, provided it. The conference was intended as a show of support for former General and now President 'Abdel Fattah al-Sisi and to demonstrate that Egypt was 'back on track'. Several Gulf states had been decisive in shaping the future of the three North African countries that saw mass uprisings in 2011 (Tunisia, Egypt, and Libya). But that a small Gulf state, the UAE, would more or less single-handedly announce it would plan and build a new administrative capital for the Arab world's most populous country, a large part of which would be named after a former ruler of the UAE, was unprecedented.[6]

Cairo faces huge problems in terms of traffic, urban development, and over-population, and the new capital is partly intended to ease some of these problems, or at least make life easier for diplomats and bureaucrats, who are supposed to live and work in the new city. But the symbolism of how the new US$45 billion capital, which is supposed to house millions of people, was announced is striking. Kuwait, the UAE, and Saudi Arabia, the countries that had pledged funds to Egypt immediately after the coup that brought Sisi to power in July 2013, pledged $4 billion each at the start of the conference. Most of the funds are intended to be invested in projects while $3 billion will be deposited in Egypt's Central Bank.[7]

Crucially, Qatar, which in 2012 had supported former President Mohammed Morsi and the Muslim Brotherhood, and at that time had deposited $2 billion in Egypt's Central Bank, did not pledge any funds in 2015. Over the period from 2011 to 2013, Qatari support to Egypt was estimated at a total of $8 billion. After the coup that toppled Morsi and brought Sisi to power, the new Egyptian government went as far as returning the $2 billion that Qatar had previously deposited in the Central Bank.[8]

This brief episode highlights some of the most crucial dynamics that shaped the international relations of the Middle East after 2011, dynamics that also have a profound impact on Gulf security, if not in the short term then in the medium to long term. Firstly, the Gulf states have become much more proactive players on the regional scene. The collapse of the 'old' strong states of the MENA region (Iraq, Syria, Egypt, and Libya) has opened up new opportunities for the GCC. The GCC states were therefore (together with non-Arab regional states such as Turkey, Iran, and Israel) the main militarily and economically powerful regional states that in 2011 were in a position to react quickly and influence the developments within the 'uprising states' in a direction that they perceived to be in their interest.

This new interventionism of the GCC, or the 'Gulf moment', as it has been termed by some in the region, has turned the GCC states into more prominent diplomatic, political, and military actors on the regional and international stage.[9] But with increasing exposure come new risks. As relatively small states, the GCC countries started to get involved in highly complex conflicts hundreds if not thousands of kilometres away. Their involvement therefore led to new problems and issues, as well as threats from people, movements, and states that the GCC states had alienated during their foreign policy adventures. In some ways, then, the new interventionism, which was in part intended to increase the security of the Gulf states (and the egos of some Gulf leaders), did not resolve the security dilemma. On the contrary, it rekindled old enmities and created new ones: briefly Gaddafi, then Iran, the Syrian regime, the Muslim Brotherhood, the Islamic State, Shi'a militias aligned with Iran, and the Houthi movement in Yemen, to name but a few.

Rumours of assassination plots of Gulf leaders, of planned attacks by various groups within the GCC, a rise in Shi'a militancy in Bahrain and the Saudi Eastern Province, and Islamic State attacks in Saudi Arabia and on Saudi border posts are all in part the results of this new interventionist foreign policy. The Houthi movement, against which Saudi Arabia started to wage war in late March 2015, is but one group that was alienated by Saudi and wider GCC policies. In many ways, the (brief) empowerment of the Houthi movement and the general political upheaval in Yemen are a function of Saudi Arabia's policies in Yemen. It appears that the wars waged against the Houthi movement in the second half of the 2000s by the Yemeni army, and particularly the direct military campaign by Saudi Arabia against the Houthis in 2009–10, achieved the opposite of their intended objectives. The Saudis not only failed to crush the movement but instead radicalised it and militarised it even further, and also reinforced the anti-Saudi outlook of the Houthis.[10]

The Muslim Brotherhood and polarisation in the Gulf

The GCC involvement in Bahrain, Iraq, and Syria can be viewed through a sectarian lens, in that the GCC states saw an opportunity to counter Iran, the Maliki government in Iraq, and the Assad regime in Syria by exploiting grievances among many Sunnis in Iraq and Syria against institutionalised discrimination, as well as fears amongst Sunni elites at Shiʿa demands for reform and political participation in Bahrain. Geopolitics did play a role, as did very tangible security concerns and the threat of a newly empowered Shiʿa-dominated Iraq on the northern borders of the GCC, but it seems that identity, and in particular sectarian identity, did play a crucial role in shaping GCC foreign policy towards transformations in the Mashreq (the Arab world east of Egypt) and the wider Arabian Peninsula.[11]

However, the GCC involvement in the Maghreb cannot be seen in this light, although the idea that Iran could possibly find allies among the countries in transition (and in particular the Morsi government) was a factor. In addition, a perception that Shiʿa proselytising was intensifying in Egypt connected these two arenas of the Arab world in the view of GCC elites. But the most important divisions in the Maghreb are between the old regimes and revolutionary forces, and between secularists and Islamists, as all key actors are Sunnis (or Copts in the case of Egypt). This is perhaps the reason why, whereas all the GCC states (with the partial exception of Kuwait and Oman, in part due to their mixed sectarian composition) contributed to the sectarianisation of the conflicts in the Mashreq, there were fundamental disagreements between these states as to what the future of the Maghreb should look like. And so in the case of the Maghreb, the new interventionism of the GCC has led to profound difficulties within the council.

The rivalry between Qatar, on the one hand, and the UAE and Saudi Arabia (plus Bahrain), on the other, shaped the regional politics of the Middle East in the period from 2011 until 2015. This period of division has to a certain extent been less prominent after the leadership transitions in both Qatar and Saudi Arabia but will likely remain a factor. The rivalry has played out particularly forcefully in Egypt and Libya, where the two camps support opposing sides in a civil war. It also had an impact in Tunisia, albeit less so than in Egypt and Libya. In many ways, Tunisia became the only success story of the Arab uprisings in view of the limited amount of political violence and several non-violent transitions of power brought about by the ballot box.

The Pharaohs of Arabia: The Gulf states in Egypt

Egypt had for a long time been the most important Arab country, and had under the presidency of Gamal 'Abdel Nasser in the 1950s and 1960s been the main rival to Saudi influence in the region, a rivalry that was dubbed the 'Arab Cold War' because it was also related to superpower competition.[12] Arab nationalism in its various forms had found many supporters across the Gulf. Millions of Arabs came of age listening to the Cairo-based Sawt al-Arab radio station, which ridiculed Arab monarchs and called for the overthrow of the Al Saud ruling family. Present-day Saudi decision-makers had lived through that period and remember this Egyptian challenge. So, perhaps, the main reason for getting involved so heavily in Egypt was the fear that a newly empowered Egypt, particularly one championing a rival ideology such as that espoused by the Muslim Brotherhood, could once again emerge and challenge Saudi–GCC dominance in the region, and could also find support among people in the Gulf. Hence, the political projects that were tested in Egypt from January 2011 until the summer of 2013, both the early Arab Spring protests with their emphasis on freedom, human rights, and dignity, and the political project of the Muslim Brotherhood, were completely anathema to Gulf rulers. If Egypt had become a more or less functioning democracy with a decent economic performance, this would have created a dangerous precedent for Gulf rulers. At the same time, it would have been equally troublesome for Gulf rulers had the Muslim Brotherhood solidified its power, and been able to reshape the regional alliance system and support other Muslim Brotherhood branches across the region, including in the Gulf.

The Muslim Brotherhood is probably the only organised movement that could pose a serious threat to the Gulf monarchies as a whole. Having said that, however, the Gulf regimes also do have a long history of interaction with the Muslim Brotherhood, and in some cases the post-2011 anti-Muslim Brotherhood propaganda paints a very ahistorical picture of the relations between the Brotherhood and the Gulf states, and of the history of migration and economic cooperation that has strengthened the Muslim Brotherhood over the last few decades. Of all the GCC states, only Qatar emerged publicly as a backer of the Muslim Brotherhood after 2011. This is partly the result of Qatari attempts to shape a distinct foreign policy and open up to dissidents and opposition activists from the region, many but not all of whom are Islamists, over recent decades. The Egyptian cleric Yusuf al-Qaradawi, widely seen as the spiritual guide of the global Muslim Brotherhood movement, has long been based in Qatar, teaching at Qatar University and becoming a household figure in the Arab world through his regular show on Al-Jazeera. So when many of the Muslim Brotherhood branches started to become involved in the uprisings across the region, it was not an ad hoc decision by Qatar to support them. Rather, this was a continuation of a long-term policy, and the Qataris no doubt sought to reap some of the benefits for their long support of these groups and individuals.[13]

Saudi Arabia itself also has a long history of harbouring Muslim Brotherhood exiles and supporters who fled Nasser's or Hafez al-Assad's crackdown on them. They helped build many of the educational and religious institutions that were set up in Saudi Arabia after the oil boom of the 1970s, when Saudi Arabia embraced political Islam as a counter against Arab nationalism and leftist ideologies. But in the early 1990s, an Islamist social movement called the Sahwa that included many leaders and sympathisers of the local branch of the Muslim Brotherhood started to criticise the ruling family for its alliance with the United States and the deployment of American troops on Saudi soil in preparation for the liberation of Kuwait.[14] It is widely believed that this episode was a turning point in the relationship between the Al Saud and the Muslim Brotherhood, and it largely explains the fears of the Al Saud and their reaction to the empowerment of Muslim Brotherhood branches across the region since 2011.[15]

Bahrain's ruling family has a long-standing alliance with the local branch of the Muslim Brotherhood. From the 1950s to the late 1970s, the main challenge to the ruling family came from leftist and Arab nationalist groups, and thereafter from Shi'a communal Islamists, and hence the Muslim Brotherhood was built up as a counter-force. Bahrain became an important centre for Islamic finance and other Muslim Brotherhood-related financial activities across the region, and some members of the Al Khalifa family were backers of the local Muslim Brotherhood branch from its inception. The political society that functions as the representative of the Bahraini Muslim Brotherhood, al-Minbar Islamic Society, has held seats in parliament since the restoration of the National Assembly in 2002.[16]

In Kuwait, the story is somewhat similar. The Kuwaiti branch of the Muslim Brotherhood broke with its mother organisation in 1990 after the latter supported the Iraqi invasion of Kuwait. The Kuwaiti branch instead became active in the Kuwaiti resistance against the Iraqis, thereby gaining considerable local goodwill. The Kuwaiti branch has also participated in parliamentary elections for a long time and has at times allied itself with different factions of the ruling family.[17] But supporters of the Muslim Brotherhood have also been involved in the protest movement that emerged in Kuwait in 2012 and challenged the ruling family, thereby affecting relations between parts of the ruling family and the group.[18]

In the UAE, the Muslim Brotherhood was founded as a charitable organisation and functioned as a cultural and social society, not as a political organisation per se. It seems to have tried to represent itself as a force that champions feelings of alienation among some Emirati citizens against the perceived 'Westernisation' of their society and the overwhelming presence of foreigners in the UAE.[19] Oman has also experienced political mobilisation by groups sympathetic to the Muslim Brotherhood, even though the Brotherhood is confined to Sunni Muslims, who make up slightly less than half of the Omani population.[20] The protest movement that emerged in Oman in 2011 and that was quickly suppressed did have some sectarian undertones in that most protests were held in areas inhabited by Sunnis.[21]

This brief overview illustrates that the Muslim Brotherhood has a presence in all six GCC states, and in most of them it also has a long history of cooperation with the regimes and the ruling families. In some, such as Qatar, Bahrain, and, to a certain extent, Kuwait, regimes continue to cooperate with the Muslim Brotherhood in public. In others, such as Saudi Arabia, there was close cooperation with the Muslim Brotherhood until the regime became aware of the political mobilisation efforts of the movement in the country, and the possible dangers this could pose to the regime's survival. This history of Muslim Brotherhood activities in the Gulf to a large extent informed the GCC's response towards the transformations in North Africa and shaped the divisions within the GCC over this issue. It is thus a classic example of how domestic political issues, and fears of domestic unrest and instability, shape foreign policy decision-making.

Qatar had a history of providing a safe haven to Muslim Brotherhood exiles and continued to welcome them and give them airtime on Al-Jazeera. At the same time, Saudi Arabia and the UAE, given their past experience with the Muslim Brotherhood and their realisation that it could pose a serious threat (as opposed to the overblown threat of Shi'a radicalism in the Saudi Eastern Province, which was used to rally the Sunnis around the flag but which did not pose an existential challenge to the Saudi state), became the leaders of the regional anti-Muslim Brotherhood alliance. Bahrain's historical experience, and its stoking of anti-Shiism as a survival mechanism, should have made for a more nuanced policy towards the Muslim Brotherhood. But because Bahrain witnessed the intervention of GCC troops in March 2011 in support of government attempts to restore order after the Pearl uprising, and because of massive diplomatic and financial cover especially from Saudi Arabia and the UAE, it also found itself in the anti-Muslim Brotherhood camp. As a result, Bahrain joined Saudi Arabia and the UAE in withdrawing its ambassador from Qatar in early 2014 in a row that was partly the result of Qatar's backing of the Muslim Brotherhood.[22]

It is fair to assume that the anti-Muslim Brotherhood Gulf states did play an important role in the Egyptian coup of 2013. Saudi Arabia maintained channels of communication with the Morsi government and the Muslim Brotherhood, in particular with Khairat al-Shater.[23] At the same time, however, Prince Bandar bin Sultan, the Director General of the Saudi General Intelligence Directorate from July 2012 to April 2014, met with Egyptian military figures and urged Western countries to support a military takeover if it was going to take place. The Egyptian Salafi Nour Party, which is said to have close ties to Saudi Arabia, endorsed the coup.[24] The leadership transition in Qatar just eight days before the coup in Egypt also deprived the Morsi government of a significant part of its regional support.

The international political economy of Khaleeji capital

But the economic dimension that was highlighted by Egypt's March 2015 conference should not be overlooked. The new interventionism of the GCC states has an economic rationale to it and the Egyptian case shows most clearly how political support and strategic investments are intertwined. While none of the GCC's regional investment strategies are profitable from a purely economic perspective, they make more sense when political, military, diplomatic, symbolic, and economic influences are combined and seen as complementing each other. In such a worldview, it is logical that the UAE should announce the building of Egypt's new capital, and that Emirati (and Saudi) companies should be among Egypt's biggest foreign investors since 2013. To some extent, this mirrors Qatar's approach in 2012 and the first half of 2013 (although many Qatari companies have suffered since the coup of 2013). The increasing importance of Khaleeji (Gulf) capital across the region, and its investment in key sectors of the most important regional states even before 2011, formed another reason for the GCC states to become so involved in the transitions in North Africa. In part, then, GCC interventionism has gone hand in hand with a major expansion of investments by Khaleeji companies, private investors, and GCC sovereign wealth funds in North Africa and the wider Arab world. The capital accumulation in the Gulf over the past decades, as part of high oil prices, has led Gulf investors to seek out investment opportunities abroad, in particular in other Arab countries.[25]

On the other hand, these investments only make sense as long as Egypt does not default on its debt or is not engulfed in a serious civil-war-type situation. Moreover, Egypt is currently only able to sustain itself fiscally because of financial help from the GCC. In a worst-case scenario, Egypt and, increasingly, the other Arab states that heavily depend on Gulf help, such as Jordan (and even GCC member states such as Bahrain and Oman), risk becoming 'black holes'—countries that need financial help indefinitely and whose deficit may also increase over time because of corruption, mismanagement, and huge expenditures for the military and the security sectors. Therefore, the GCC investments are only profitable if they are underwritten in the long term through massive direct loans to the debtor states themselves, as well as through security guarantees. Owing in part to the increase of investable funds in the GCC over the past decade or so, these states remain a preferred outlet for investors, precisely because they seem to grant influence and symbolic capital. But as oil prices decline, these economic adventures might not be as sustainable as they seemed to be in the period from 2011 to 2014, as the regional uprisings, which provided opportunities for interventionism, were coupled with historically very high oil prices (around or over $100/barrel).

Overthrowing Gaddafi: Qatar, the UAE and NATO

The leaders of virtually all GCC states had personal issues with the Libyan dictator Muammar Gaddafi. Gaddafi had alienated them and in 2009 directly attacked King 'Abdullah of Saudi Arabia during an infamous Arab League meeting in Doha. This in part explains the GCC's quick endorsement of the plans to attack Libya and remove Gaddafi from power with the direct participation of several GCC states in the NATO-led intervention between March and October 2011.[26] A meeting between US Secretary of State Hillary Clinton and UAE leaders on 14 March 2011 in Paris was crucial because it conveyed the UAE position that an intervention would have significant Arab support. In return for Arab support for the Libyan intervention, the US response to the simultaneous GCC military intervention in Bahrain was extremely muted.[27]

The Libyan intervention initially was thus more an opportunity for some Gulf states to show that they were valuable NATO allies than an attempt to strengthen Gulf security or prevent the emergence of a strong ideological force that would run counter to GCC strategies. Moreover, the UAE and Qatar's direct participation in the air strikes on Libya gave NATO the cover of having 'regional participation', something that had become increasingly important after the failure of the American-led intervention in Iraq. The UAE had participated in NATO missions before, including in Afghanistan, Bosnia, and elsewhere, and saw this as an opportunity to strengthen ties and possibly even become a full member of the alliance.[28] Since 2004, the UAE, Qatar, Bahrain, and Kuwait had been participants in NATO's partnership programmes through the Istanbul Cooperation Initiative.[29] In the Libyan intervention, participating partners were given the same access as full members to discussions and decision-making in the North Atlantic Council (NAC), the principal political decision-making body of NATO.[30]

Qatar and the UAE put six and twelve fighter jets, respectively, at NATO's disposal and they engaged in combat and surveillance missions. In addition, Qatar trained hundreds of Libyan rebels in Qatar and, from April 2011 onwards, supplied the rebels with French Milan antitank missiles and Belgian FN rifles. In total, Qatar supplied more than eighteen shipments amounting to 20,000 tons of weapons to the Libyan rebels. Many of these shipments went directly to rebel forces, including to Abdul-Hakim Belhaj of the Tripoli Military Council, and therefore-bypassed the internationally-backed National Transitional Council.[31]

Qatari and Emirati Special Forces also became involved on the ground in Libya. UAE Special Forces deployed at least one team to the Nafusa Mountains in western Libya, from where they provided equipment, support, and training to the rebels.[32] Qatari Special Forces were important in the final assault on Tripoli in August 2011. They thereby gained valuable battlefield experience, which the Gulf states had largely lacked previously. According to some accounts, by conducting these ground operations, 'Qatar almost certainly made the most important military contribution by a NATO partner, despite the fact that this clandestine operation was run independently of NATO'.[33]

Pouring oil into the fire: the Gulf states and the Libyan civil war

After the initial phase of cooperation between GCC states under the leadership of NATO in the anti-Gaddafi alliance, frictions soon emerged reflecting the abovementioned differences between Qatar and the UAE over the vision for the future of the Middle East in general, and over the role of the Muslim Brotherhood and Islamist forces in particular.

Qatar used some of the Libyan exiles in Doha as conduits for support, such as 'Ali al-Sallabi, a cleric and dissident. Qatar also supported Fawzi Abu Katif's 17 February Brigade in Benghazi and became the primary patron of Abdul-Hakim Belhaj's Tripoli Military Council. Belhaj is a veteran Libyan Islamist opposition activist and former head of the jihadist Libyan Islamic Fighting Group.[34]

The UAE had long-standing business interests in Libya, such as in Libya's largest oil refinery (in Ras Lanuf) as well as in First Gulf Libyan Bank and power plants in Tripoli. But it appears that UAE involvement was also a function of Qatari involvement, and vice versa. The UAE channelled support through Mahmoud Jibril, a key Libyan nationalist politician, who, even though he was based in Doha during the uprising, had business ties to the UAE and later relocated to the UAE. In addition, 'Aref 'Ali Nayed, who later became Libyan ambassador to the UAE, was a key interlocutor. In some ways, then, the UAE came to support the internationally recognised National Transitional Council, while Qatar started to back directly more Islamist forces and leaders from the peripheries.[35] But Gulf support often proved to be a curse as well as a blessing. In the 2012 elections, Abdul-Hakim Belhaj, who was allegedly the main recipient of Qatari aid, and his Watan party actually performed poorly.[36] In many cases, too open an association with a Gulf backer has also undermined the local support of North African clients.

The aftermath of the Libyan revolution is highly complex, and the characterisation of the conflict as one between 'secular forces' and 'Islamists' is a broad generalisation. But for an analysis of the international relations of the Libyan civil war, the characterisation of Islamists versus secularists makes sense because this is likely how their backers in the Gulf perceived the conflict.

In the non-Muslim Brotherhood Islamist scene, there are a plethora of groups, many of whom have ties to groups in Saudi Arabia. Some of them subscribe to the official interpretation of Islam in Saudi Arabia, while others are close to Saudi clerics who have emerged as critics of Saudi Arabia's political system and have hence fallen out of favour with the Al Saud. These different forces include Libyan Salafis who were educated in Saudi Arabia and were students of or were influenced by figures such as Sheikh Ibn Baz, Sheikh al-Albani, and Sheikh Ibn al-Uthaymin. These would be classified as mainstream Salafis or clerics from the official Wahhabi tradition. In addition, there are others who are followers of Sheikh Rabi' al-Madkhali, a Saudi cleric and professor at the Islamic University in Medina, who is a staunch supporter of the Saudi government. And a third strand could be classified as Salafis who take inspiration from people like Salman al-Awda or the Kuwaiti-based Umma party (the Libyan Asala party sees itself as inspired by the Umma party).[37] They have emerged as critics of the authoritarian monarchical systems in the Gulf and have adopted democracy as the solution for Arab and Muslim countries. Many of these Libyan Salafi forces have since joined Libya Dawn, a coalition of Islamist forces.

Qatar has supported Libya Dawn, which is to a large extent a Muslim Brotherhood-led coalition of Islamist forces and militias from Misrata. Apart from Qatar, Turkey has become the strongest international backer of the Libya Dawn coalition.[38] The UAE, on the other hand, has emerged as the main backer, together with neighbouring Egypt (under Sisi), of the coalition led by General Khalifa Haftar. Haftar, who proclaims himself to be a nationalist and secularist, has vowed to counter the influence of the Islamists. The UAE continues to host Mahmoud Jibril.[39] In 2014, the UAE again conducted air strikes in Libya, but this time without NATO consent. This was seen as a way to strengthen the military and political relationship with the Sisi regime in Cairo and prepare for future cooperation.[40] In 2015, it seemed as though the UAE-backed forces were gaining the upper hand in Libya while the Qatari-backed forces were in decline.

Tunisia: too small to fail

The GCC states had close relations with Ben 'Ali's regime in Tunisia, and when he had to flee the country in the wake of mass protests in late 2010 and early 2011, he left to live in exile in Saudi Arabia. The Tunisian Revolution started the Arab uprisings, and was hence a threat to the Gulf ruling families. In the aftermath, the GCC states sought to influence the political development of post-Ben 'Ali Tunisia. However, this involvement was less pronounced, less visible, and arguably less divisive there than in Egypt and Libya (or Syria for that matter). In the words of one Gulf analyst, 'Tunisia is simply too unimportant and too small to warrant much investment of political capital by the GCC, and that is a major factor why it has developed in a relatively stable and democratic manner.'[41] Having said that, the relative success of Tunisia is also largely a product of the local political context and the relative moderation of the rival political factions, in particular the Muslim Brotherhood, represented in Tunisia by the Nahda movement and its founder, Rashid al-Ghannouchi. However, similar divisions to those in other North African states have been playing out in Tunisia, albeit on a less violent and destructive scale. Qatar backed the

Nahda party and the Qatari National Bank gave Tunis $500 million to bolster its foreign currency reserves as pressure by the IMF increased. In addition, Qatar invested heavily in the country. Qatar bought a 75 per cent stake in the telephone operator Tunisiana for $1.2 billion and it also owns the Tunisian Qatari Bank in addition to many other investments.[42]

Saudi Arabia and the UAE, on the other hand, have supported forces opposed to Nahda, in particular Nidaa Tunis, an alliance of secularists and figures from the old regime. To many people's surprise, the founder of Nidaa Tunis, Beji Caid Essebsi, an 88-year-old veteran Tunisian politician with extensive ties to the old regime, won in the 2014 presidential elections. Nahda conceded defeat, in a rare conciliatory move in the post-Arab Spring political environment, and Tunisia drifted again more towards the UAE–Saudi orbit and away from Qatari influence.[43] Emirati business interests in Tunisia include the Tunisia Emirates Investment Bank (BTEI).[44] In 2012, the UAE said that its total investment in Tunisia was worth $2.5 billion.[45] So both the UAE and Qatar, as well as other Gulf states, have invested in Tunisia before and particularly after the Tunisian Revolution of 2011. As in the other two cases, Egypt and Libya, they coupled political support with investments. Unlike Egypt and Libya, however, the Tunisian system has so far been better able to withstand any antagonism resulting from this Gulf involvement.

Conclusion

To conclude, the Gulf states have intervened across the region since 2011 in varying yet unprecedented ways. In North Africa, this intervention took different forms from the direct Gulf interventions in Bahrain, Syria, and Yemen, while the sectarian and geopolitical rivalry with Iran was less prominent, although not absent. In the Maghreb, ideological divisions and rivalries between Sunni factions were more important than the Sunni–Shi'a split. The key aims of the Gulf States (minus Qatar) were to establish GCC hegemony over the Arab world, protect old pro-GCC regimes (while ousting others, such as Muammar Gaddafi's), and prevent the Muslim Brotherhood from maintaining power and successfully establishing an alternative Sunni Islamic political order. Given the importance of Egypt in Arab and Islamic history, the status of being the most important international allies of Egypt is seen as a source of pride and strength for the Gulf rulers, and prevents Egypt from becoming too independent and possibly a rival to the GCC.

The alliance with Sisi's Egypt also has a particularly strong military dimension, something that was highlighted at the Arab League summit in Sharm el-Sheikh on 26 March 2015. At the summit, a plan for a joint Arab military force was unveiled just days after a Saudi and GCC-led force had started air strikes on targets of the Houthi (Ansarallah) movement in Yemen. The campaign highlighted the extent of the GCC's ambition in dominating regional affairs, and underscored the military support that Egypt in particular is supposed to make to the security of the Gulf states in return for financial and political backing.[46] Egypt has also committed to contribute fighter jets, naval units, and ground personnel to the proposed Arab military force.[47] Whether this joint Arab force will ever come into being is another question. Given the long history of failed attempts at Arab military integration, this is at least questionable. While the joint force was hyped at the beginning of the Yemen military campaign in March 2015, Egypt and Pakistan later ruled out sending ground troops to Yemen, and thereafter the future of the Arab force seemed uncertain. The close relations that the Sisi regime enjoyed with Saudi Arabia under King 'Abdullah also began to show signs of tension under King Salman after he succeeded his half-brother in January 2015. King Salman has proved less hostile than King 'Abdullah towards the Muslim Brotherhood, and derogatory comments allegedly made by Sisi about Gulf rulers probably angered leaders in the Gulf.[48] In addition, Egyptian officials read out a letter from Vladimir Putin at the Arab League summit in Sharm el-Sheikh, something the Saudis disapproved of, particularly at a time of tensions with Russia over Syria and other issues.[49]

The Egyptian case highlights most strikingly the fact that the North African states, politicians, parties, and militias that are the recipients of Gulf aid are not devoid of agency in this process. Indeed, they are quite adept at 'negotiating' Gulf aid and playing off one donor against the other. Leaks from the Saudi Ministry of Foreign Affairs suggest that, when in government, the Muslim Brotherhood was negotiating with Gulf states about the release of former President Hosni Mubarak in return for a payment of $10 billion.[50] At the same time, leaked recordings attributed to Sisi suggest that the Gulf rulers had 'money like rice' and that Egypt would squeeze them and get billions out of them in return for political support.[51] Many of the financial commitments made by the Gulf states seem to be intended to make allies for a certain period, but these allies can never be 'bought' forever, and when the money dries up or when it is in the North Africans' interests, they may seek out other patrons and alliances.

The international political economy of the GCC interventions in North Africa is a crucial but understudied factor in the trajectories of the Arab uprisings and their fallouts. GCC political and diplomatic involvement has been coupled with massive financial rewards, investments, and loans, particularly for Egypt. So since 2011, the GCC states have replaced the United States, the European Union, and the IMF as the most important donors and creditors of North African states. In Egypt and Tunisia, the GCC states stepped in just as the IMF was threatening to punish the countries for their non-compliance with its requests, thereby undermining the position of the global financial institution. North African governments see the terms offered by the Gulf states, which often include adopting pro-Gulf positions in the United Nations, the Arab League, or other forms of political payback, as more favourable than the conditions offered by the IMF, the United States or the European Union.

But the new interventionism of the GCC also comes with new risks for the Gulf states, in that it has directly linked Gulf security to the security of a whole array of Arab regimes, many of whom only survive in power by relying on the repressive tools of political survival that fuelled the grievances leading to the Arab uprisings in the first place. Therefore, any future political change in Egypt, for example, will have a direct impact on the Gulf, and given the close connection of the GCC (minus Qatar) to the Sisi regime, a possible successor regime may become staunchly anti-GCC (although Egypt's budget deficit and its need for aid may limit any such anti-GCC stance). At the same time, the close alliance with Sisi, as well as with General Haftar in Libya, has led to a feeling among Islamists in the Gulf that their governments are working against the interests of what they perceive as the 'Islamic movement'. Hence, some of the GCC policies in North Africa have also undermined the legitimacy of the Gulf regimes at home.

A problem that is becoming more worrying is the fiscal aspect of Gulf support. The GCC involvement in North Africa has been costly, and particularly the Egyptian deficit is likely to continue at similar or even higher levels in the coming years, and the UAE, Saudi Arabia, and Kuwait are expected to pay for it.[52] The drop in oil prices since 2014 has led to some of the largest budget deficits the Gulf states have seen in decades. It is true that the GCC states, Saudi Arabia in particular, have huge foreign reserves that they can burn through before they will need to adjust their policies.[53] A further drop in oil prices, however, and constantly increasing expenditures and energy consumption in the GCC could force some Gulf states to reconsider their open-ended commitments to their North African clients and also begin to require increasingly stringent 'rates of return' on their support, as Saudi Arabia did in April

2016 when it demanded that Egypt transfer two islands in the Red Sea to its control.[54] Indeed, it often takes a long time for pledged investments and grants to materialise, and sometimes they do not arrive at all.[55]

The impact of this on regimes and parties in North Africa is unpredictable, and the exact trajectory of politics in North Africa is something that is quite difficult to control, even for the Gulf states that have emerged as such strong financial, military, and political backers of, at times, rival political forces in North Africa. In short, the Gulf states, like European and American imperial forces before them, can rent or occupy the casbah, but they will never own it. Nevertheless, by getting involved in the regional security dynamics of North Africa at a time of economic austerity programmes within the Gulf itself, policymakers now are exposed to new sources of external volatility and potential insecurity that they cannot easily hope to control, still less manage.

4

THE EMERGING ENERGY LANDSCAPE

ECONOMIC AND STRATEGIC IMPLICATIONS

Gawdat Bahgat

This chapter explores the rapid changes in the global energy landscape over the past decade and assesses their implications for the security and international relations of the states of the Persian Gulf. Ever since the 1973 Arab oil embargo, which marked a turning point in global energy markets, the non-interruption of supplies and stable prices have been major concerns and goals of the United States and other major energy consumers. Over the ensuing four decades, rising consumption and declining production have underscored the energy vulnerability of Washington and other major consumers. This has changed dramatically since the late 2000s with profound implications for notions of energy security more broadly and for regional and domestic security considerations with the Persian Gulf itself. The realignment of the global energy landscape adds a critical layer of external context to the difficult processes of transition within Persian Gulf economies as officials and publics respond to the prolonged fall in oil prices since mid-2014.

Energy is not just an economic commodity. It is a strategic one, with significant security implications. The US military is the world's largest energy consumer; without adequate and stable supplies the nation could not carry out its military operations and missions. Thus, the security of oil supplies from the Persian Gulf has been a major driver of American defence and foreign policies for the last several decades. The Carter Doctrine in 1980 stated clearly that the United States would use military force, if necessary, to defend its national interests in the Persian Gulf. Since the 1970s, US strategic relations with the Gulf Cooperation Council (GCC) states (Bahrain, Kuwait, Qatar, Oman, Saudi Arabia, and the United Arab Emirates) have steadily grown, and Washington has been the region's major security guarantor. To be sure, oil has not been the sole goal of American policy in the Persian Gulf region. One can argue that other objectives, such as promoting democracy, the security of Israel, counter-terrorism, and the non-proliferation of weapons of mass destruction, also have been pursued.

The United States has never accepted this energy vulnerability and deep dependence on foreign supplies, particularly from the Middle East. Since the Nixon administration, all American presidents have sought to reduce the nation's dependence on imported oil and achieve a state of 'energy independence'. President George W. Bush bluntly warned that the nation was 'addicted to oil'. In pursuing these goals, the United States has implemented a multidimensional strategy, mainly diversifying both the energy mix and energy sources. In other words, efforts have been made to increase domestic production; reduce the share of oil in the energy mix and increase those of natural gas, nuclear, and renewable resources; import less oil from the Middle East; and improve energy efficiency.

These investments have paid off. Since the early 2000s, US energy consumption has declined despite a growing economy and population. Equally significant, oil and natural gas production has been on the rise, largely because of technological innovations known as hydraulic fracturing (fracking) and horizontal drilling. The combination of reducing consumption and rising production has significantly improved the United States' energy outlook. These emerging trends are likely to persist for a long time. Efficiency is projected to improve further, and oil and gas production is projected to increase.

This improved energy outlook has started paying dividends. Instead of importing gas and oil, the United States is itself becoming a net exporter. The millions of dollars the nation would have spent on imports will now be spent or invested domestically. This is helping to lower the trade deficit, restrain the inflation rate, and create jobs. At the same time, Washington has earned more leverage in pursuing its foreign policy. The United States is increasingly becoming less dependent on imported oil supplies and less vulnerable to the fluctuation in oil prices. This gives the nation more freedom in pursuing its national interests.

Probably it is too early to fully comprehend the strategic implications of the emerging energy landscape. Still, the fundamental changes in the US outlook raise several important questions. Will the United States reduce its military and strategic engagement in the Middle East? Will Asian powers and the European Union member states, who are becoming more dependent on Middle Eastern oil supplies, shoulder more security responsibilities? And how might oil and gas producers in the Middle East respond to these new dynamics?

This chapter seeks to provide preliminary answers to these questions. I argue that the improved US energy outlook has substantially strengthened the nation's economy and foreign policy leverage. These less-restrained American foreign and defence policies do not, however, mean less engagement in the Middle East. On the other hand, Middle Eastern oil and gas producers are not net losers. Facing less favourable global markets, they have pursued different economic and strategic options to counter the emerging dynamics. In order to fully appreciate the shale revolution, I discuss briefly the main trends that characterise the global energy market. This will be followed by an analysis of the shale revolution and its security and strategic implications. I discuss the declining US dependence on imported oil from the Persian Gulf and China's move in the opposite direction. The following section will focus on the energy and strategic relations between the GCC states and the other major energy consumer—the European Union (EU). The final section will address how oil and gas producers are reacting to this evolving environment. The analysis is based on the assumption that the GCC states rely heavily on foreign powers to contain threats to their national security. In pursuing such strategies, the GCC states utilise energy interdependence to cement security and strategic relations with these foreign powers.

The global energy outlook

In the second half of 2014, oil prices dropped by more than 50 per cent and continued their fall throughout most of 2015. This sharp decline has particular significance, given the political instability in a number of oil-producing countries such as Libya and Iraq and the sanctions on the Iranian oil sector.

Several years ago these geopolitical factors would have pushed prices higher. In 2014 they had little, if any, impact because of the steady improvement in energy efficiency, which leads to lower consumption and rising production, particularly on the part of the United States.

Energy efficiency can be defined as the delivery of more services for the same energy input or the same services for less energy input. For a long time, the contribution of energy efficiency to energy security was not fully appreciated and was identified as 'the hidden fuel'. In recent years, efficiency has attracted more attention and has been labelled by International Energy Agency (IEA) analysts as 'the first fuel'.[1] A recent report by the IEA stated that total final consumption in the IEA countries was estimated to be 60 per cent lower in 2014 because of energy efficiency improvements over the last four decades. Stated differently, efficiency helped to avoid over 1,700 million tonnes of oil-equivalent from being consumed.[2] Thus, in addition to improving energy security, efficiency is a good business that offers high returns on investments, increases the sustainability of energy sources, and reduces pollution.

To further appreciate the significance of improving efficiency and reducing consumption, it is important to note that the decade between 2002 and 2012 recorded the largest-ever growth of energy consumption in volume terms over any ten-year period.[3] Both the IEA and British Petroleum (BP), among others, project a steady increase in global energy consumption. However, this rise in consumption varies across region and by fuel. Energy demand in most developed countries (mostly member states of the Organisation for Economic Cooperation and Development) has peaked and in some countries has started a steady decline. On the other hand, global demand for energy is led by Asian emerging markets (China, India, South Korea, and Japan) and the Middle East. Indeed, these two regions account for nearly all of the net global increase in consumption. According to the IEA, for each barrel of oil no longer used in OECD countries, two barrels more are used in the non-OECD countries.[4] China has already surpassed the United States as the world's largest oil importer, and the Persian Gulf region is projected to overtake the United States to become the largest per capita consumer of oil by 2033.[5]

Similarly, there is a variation in the demand for different fuels. Fossil fuels will maintain their dominance of the energy mix, with natural gas achieving the fastest rate of growth. In addition, the advanced technology and declining prices involved in setting up liquefied natural gas (LNG) facilities are slowly helping to counter the risk of supply disruptions and reducing the costs of exporting. Oil consumption will grow but its share will decline, and coal will grow faster than oil but slower than gas.

Growing concern about greenhouse gas (GHG) emissions, particularly carbon dioxide from the combustion of fossil fuels, has created renewed interest in nuclear power, which is basically carbon-free. For decades, nuclear power has been seen as a non-intermittent and readily expandable source of energy. On the other side, the industry has continued to face daunting challenges and risks that must be addressed. The list includes the high construction costs, safety, waste, and the close connection between civilian nuclear power and military applications. Thus, despite the Fukushima disaster, nuclear power capacity is projected to increase substantially. This increase, however, represents only a small growth in nuclear energy's share of global electricity generation because of the impressive rise of renewable energy.

Like nuclear power, renewable energy sources have been the topic of continued interest in both developed and developing countries. This interest is driven mainly by concern over energy security and climate change. Renewable energy is any form of energy that is replenished by natural processes at a rate that equals or exceeds its rate of use. Some renewable energy resources such as hydropower are technically mature and have been deployed at a significant scale. Other energy sources, such as wind, solar, and geothermal, are in a nascent phase of technical maturity and commercial production and deployment. The strong interest in renewable energy in many countries will raise its share in global power generation to a third by 2040.[6] Low natural gas prices (owing to the shale revolution) may reduce incentives for investing in and developing renewable energy.

This variation in the current and projected consumption of fossil fuels, nuclear power, and renewable energy has had significant impact on trading relationships. Generally, North America is emerging as a net exporter of energy, instead of a net importer, while Europe and Asia's already heavy dependence on foreign supplies is set to deepen further.

Long before the current tight oil (shale oil) boom, the United States sought to diversify its sources of foreign crude oil. Generally, the share of US imports from the Persian Gulf has declined while those from the western hemisphere have risen. Furthermore, the combination of increased production (mainly of tight oil) and reduced consumption has led to a substantial decline in imports. In 2005, the United States imported approximately 60 per cent of its demand. This rate is projected to fall to 10 per cent by 2035.[7] Even more impressive is the fact that the United States is emerging as a net natural gas exporter. These fundamental changes mean that energy supplies previously destined for the US market are being redirected to other markets in Europe and Asia.

The increase in shale gas and tight oil supplies is helping Europe to diversify its energy import sources away from Russia. European officials have been concerned about their heavy dependence on oil and gas supplies from Russia. The recent crisis over Ukraine has further deepened Europe's sense of vulnerability. The projected decrease in the transportation costs of LNG and the rise of its share in the global gas trade are likely to contribute to Europe's energy security. Meanwhile, in recent years, Asian economies, particularly China, India, South Korea, and Japan, have grown more dependent on imported energy supplies, mostly from the Persian Gulf. This trend is expected to continue in the foreseeable future.

To sum up, the global energy mix is becoming more diverse. Fossil fuels are projected to provide the majority of the world's energy needs. However, the mix will shift. Renewables and unconventional fossil fuels will take a larger share, along with gas, which is set to be the fastest-growing fossil fuel, as well as the cleanest, meeting as much of the increase in demand as coal and oil combined.[8] Meanwhile, the fall of demand in OECD countries and the rise in demand from Asia have accelerated the redirection of the oil and gas trade. Shale gas in the United States should be seen as part of this emerging global energy landscape.

Shale gas and the tight oil revolution

The use of horizontal drilling and hydraulic fracturing in the United States has greatly expanded the ability of producers to profitably recover natural gas and oil from complex geological fields. Generally, in a combination of these technologies, water, sand, and chemicals are injected into the horizontal borehole of a well at very high pressure to fracture the shale rocks and release the gas. This has allowed wider access to oil and gas in shale and tight formations in which the density of the rock has blocked the migration of hydrocarbons to conventional oil and gas reservoirs. Although experimentation in fracking dates back to the nineteenth century (and the first well was fracked in the United States in 1947),[9] efforts were intensified in the mid-1970s by means of a partnership of private companies, Department of Energy (DOE), and research institutions. This partnership helped to produce gas and oil commercially from shale rock. Since the mid-2000s, this combination of hydraulic fracturing and horizontal drilling has been widely recognised as a 'game changer' in the United States and around the world.[10]

The application of these technologies has led to a steady, impressive increase in oil and gas production, the largest in the history of the United States. In 2013, tight oil production averaged 3.22 million barrels per day (b/d), pushing the nation's overall production to an average of 7.84 million b/d, more than 10 per cent of total world production.[11] The DOE projects that crude oil production will rise from 6.5 million b/d in 2012 to 9.6 million b/d by 2020, a level not seen since 1970. Tight oil production growth accounts for 81 per cent of this increase, and its share of national crude oil production will grow from 35 per cent in 2012 to 50 per cent in 2020.[12]

The figures for shale gas are even more impressive. Whereas in 2007, shale gas production was 1,293 billion cubic feet (cf), by 2012 it had soared to 10,371 billion cf. Proven reserves rose from 23,304 billion cf (2007) to 129,396 billion cf (2012).[13] This dramatic surge in shale production has pushed national gas production to a new high of 24,398.6 billion cf in 2013.[14] BP projects that shale gas output will grow by 4.3 per cent between 2012 and 2035, enabling US gas production to rise by 45 per cent.[15]

The current and projected increase in tight oil and shale gas has significantly improved the United States' energy trade outlook. The United States has emerged as a net natural gas exporter, and the share of imported oil in its overall consumption is declining. These key changes have opened a debate about relaxing export restrictions. Current policy effectively bans crude oil exports through the Energy Policy and Conservation Act of 1975 (exports of petroleum products are generally permitted). There is more scope for exports of natural gas, although the Natural Gas Act of 1938 requires DOE authorisation to import or export natural gas to or from the United States.[16]

The large and growing body of academic literature and industry projections suggests four conclusions. First, the IEA and DOE, among others, project that the tight oil output will level off in the early 2020s and production will start to fall back. These projections, however, underestimate how far technological innovations can go. It is important to note that estimates of proven and recoverable shale gas and tight oil have continued to be revised upwards since the mid-2000s. Technology is not static. Accordingly, more reserves are becoming accessible at lower prices. Secondly, it is important neither to overestimate nor underestimate the shale revolution. The United States is moving closer to a state of 'self-sufficiency', to a greater balance between consumption and production. On the other hand, energy independence, or 'the ability to act freely without reference to the rest of the world',[17] is attractive political rhetoric but is unrealistic in today's global economy. The United States will always be affected by oil prices and policies in other countries.

Thirdly, there is significant uncertainty about the shale revolution outside the United States. On one hand, the resources are available in numerous other countries. A study issued by the DOE in 2013 surveyed 41 countries outside the United States and estimated the number of formations at 137, technically recoverable shale gas at 7,299 trillion cubic feet, and 345 billion barrels of tight oil.[18] On the other hand, a combination of individual property rights, legal systems, and government–private sector partnership has been the main driver behind the shale gas revolution in the United States. Many countries lack such a combination of factors. As a result, the United States is becoming more self-sufficient, while Europe and particularly Asia are becoming more dependent on foreign supplies.

Finally, undoubtedly significant and rising volumes of oil production from shale resources that are economically recoverable have exerted pressure on the global price of oil. Oil producers, inside and outside OPEC, are under pressure to cut production. The price of oil, like any other commodity, reflects the equilibrium between supply and demand. There has been a widespread view that, at around US$85 or $90 a barrel, the extraction of tight oil from shale would no longer be economical. However, new analysis finds that 80 per cent of new tight oil production would be economic between $50 and $69 a barrel.[19] In addition, companies will continue to improve technology and drive down costs.

Security and strategic implications

The combination of current and projected declining consumption and rising production means that the United States is growing less vulnerable to fluctuation in the global oil markets and less dependent on foreign supplies, including those from the Persian Gulf. These emerging trends give American foreign policy more leverage, flexibility, and choice. This significantly improved energy outlook has prompted some policymakers and analysts to question whether Washington can or should disengage from the Middle East. Budget austerity and a sceptical public add more incentives to this line of strategic reorientation. At the risk of simplicity, American policy in the Persian Gulf has been largely driven by the oil-for-security bargain—the United States would provide security to oil producers in the Persian Gulf against external threats in return for the non-interruption of oil supplies at reasonable prices. With the United States becoming less dependent on supplies from the Gulf, should this implicit bargain be reconsidered by both sides?

In the late 1960s and early 1970s, the British government decided to withdraw from the Persian Gulf region, opening the door for greater American involvement. This coincided with the peak of American oil production and the beginning of a steady decline that lasted till the late 2000s. The deep US (and European) reliance on oil supplies from the region was then a major driver for deploying military assets to protect the flow of oil and prevent disruption by regional or global powers.[20] The US role as a security guarantor in the Persian Gulf and a guardian of vital sea lanes 'has shaped the region's strategic landscape for most of the past half century'.[21] The rationale behind this deployment was that American and global economic prosperity depended on the steady flow of oil supplies from the Persian Gulf. Despite the improved US energy outlook, this proposition is as valid today as it was more than four decades ago. The Strait of Hormuz continues to be the world's most important oil chokepoint. In 2013, about 30 per cent of all seaborne-traded oil passed through the strait.[22]

The free flow of oil supplies from the Persian Gulf has been, and will continue to be, a major US foreign policy objective. However, American defence and foreign policies cannot be explained by only one drive. Washington has several key priorities in the region. These include counter-terrorism, the proliferation of weapons of mass destruction, and the security of Israel.[23] All these objectives are key US national interests. This means the United States is highly unlikely to turn its back on the region and will remain involved in ensuring security and promoting political stability. The notion that the United States can withdraw from the Middle East is 'at odds with the facts'.[24]

These broad objectives are likely to be pursued in partnership or rivalry with other global powers, particularly China (and other Asian powers). Over the last decade, economic and energy relations between Asian emerging economies and the Persian Gulf states have steadily grown. In the last two decades, China—the world's most populous country—has enjoyed one of the highest economic growth rates. This combination of a large population and rising income has made the nation the largest energy consumer in the world and the largest oil importer. The large and growing production has not kept pace with the soaring demand. The gap has been increasingly filled by imports from abroad, particularly from the Persian Gulf and Africa.[25]

Most of the Gulf oil is at present exported to Asia, not the United States. Stated differently, the United States is growing less dependent on oil supplies from the Persian Gulf while China is rapidly moving in the opposite direction. At the same time, the United States continues to take the lead as the region's major security ally. China's rise as a dominant buyer of Middle East oil presents a conundrum for both it and the United States. For Beijing, its economy is rapidly growing on oil imported from a region that is dominated by the US military. The Fifth Fleet essentially provides safety to oil tankers leaving Persian Gulf terminals for China. For Washington, reduced US dependence on Gulf oil and China's move in the opposite direction raise questions about the need for its military presence and spending in the region. Within this context, some analysts question China's willingness and capability to take responsibility in securing its oil supplies from the Persian Gulf. In other words, China is seen as a 'free rider' benefiting from the US defence of shipping lanes, without paying the price.[26]

On the other hand, China and other Asian powers are pursuing multidimensional strategies to enhance their energy security. These include establishing strong economic and political ties with Persian Gulf producers, importing oil and gas from other regions (such as Russia, Central Asia, and Africa), diversifying their own energy mix by increasing the share of renewable and nuclear energy at the expense of fossil fuels, and improving energy efficiency and reducing consumption. At one point in the future, these efforts will succeed and the soaring demand for energy will peak and start declining. In the foreseeable future, however, the increasing energy cooperation between Beijing and Persian Gulf producers is likely to grow stronger.

Unlike the United States and China, Europe has been actively involved in the Persian Gulf region for centuries. European powers have been interested in securing trade routes to South Asia and have had a heavy military presence and political influence for most of the last two centuries. The emergence of the United States as the dominant global military power significantly altered the dynamics of Europe–Gulf relations. Europe's key role in Gulf security has been largely reduced, but the EU has remained the major trade partner of the GCC states.[27]

Aside from bilateral relations between individual European countries and GCC states, the two blocs have engaged in diplomatic negotiations since the 1980s and have been involved in a long-running but as yet unsuccessful discussion of a free-trade agreement since 1989. In recent years, relations between the EU and GCC have been dominated by the following bilateral and regional issues:

• Energy security: Gulf oil and gas producers meet a large share of the EU's hydrocarbon energy demand.

- Foreign investment: Gulf sovereign wealth funds invest heavily in several European markets. These investments have helped in generating jobs and mitigating the impact of the 2008 financial crisis.
- Military sales and training: Given the colonial legacy and Europe's strategic interest in the Gulf region, Europe (particularly Britain and France) remains an important source of arms sales and training to the GCC states.
- The political and security upheavals that have swept the Arab world since early 2011 have further complicated EU–GCC relations. On one hand, the EU strongly supports the GCC states' efforts to stabilise Libya, Egypt, Syria, and Yemen. On the other hand, EU leaders have called for more political reform, accountability, and transparency in the Gulf region.
- The EU and the GCC share a similar interest in preventing the proliferation of weapons of mass destruction and fighting religious extremism.

Europe has recently been playing a major role in the Persian Gulf region. This role both complements and competes with the American and Chinese roles. Given the historical, economic, and cultural ties between Europe and the Gulf region, European powers will continue to be a major factor in Gulf security.

Oil and gas producers' response

The emerging global energy outlook seems less favourable to the Persian Gulf oil and gas producers than a few years ago. Falling demand and rising production mean lower prices and shrinking market share. Still, it is important to note that the Middle East remains the largest net regional energy exporter and is projected to maintain this status in the coming decades. Furthermore, production costs are at their lowest in the Middle East. Finally, the region has well-developed terminals and other facilities and is located next to energy-hungry markets in Europe and Asia.

These geographical and geological advantages aside, the changes in the global energy markets have been slow and gradual. In the last several years, oil and gas producers have been reassessing and readjusting their policies to meet the emerging challenges. Their goals are to maintain economic prosperity and to make sure that they have the strategic and military capabilities to overcome any external threat. Against this background, oil and gas producers have articulated and implemented multidimensional strategies.

Firstly, all Persian Gulf states have sought to diversify their energy mix by developing alternative energy, such as nuclear power and renewable

71

sources.[28] The region enjoys tremendous potential, particularly from solar power. It utilises the energy from sunlight either directly or indirectly for heating and cooling, generating electricity, water desalination, and many other residential, commercial, and industrial applications. Consuming alternative energy would reduce oil consumption and make more crude oil and petroleum products available for export. The most advanced solar-power project in the GCC states is Masdar in the UAE. The region has a long way to go to fully utilise its vast and promising renewable capability. Similarly, nuclear power is at early stage in most of the GCC states. Only the UAE appears close to adding nuclear power to its grid. In 2009, the country signed a deal with a South Korean consortium to build four reactors, and the first reactor is planned to be operational by 2017. Saudi Arabia signed agreements with different parties and plans to build up to sixteen reactors, with the first supposedly to go on line in 2022.

Secondly, many oil producers are seeking to improve energy efficiency and curb their energy consumption. The surge in consumption has negatively impacted on the Persian Gulf states both environmentally and economically. Several cities are among the most polluted in the world (largely owing to the burning of cheap oil). At the same time, rising consumption means less oil and gas available for export. In addition to these environmental and economic consequences, Persian Gulf leaders understand that oil and gas are finite resources. The high level of energy consumption cannot be divorced from the region's strong tradition of underpricing energy. In most Middle Eastern countries, subsidies for fuels and electricity constitute a significant share of government spending. Oil producers are among the largest energy subsidisers in the world. In recent years, several Middle Eastern governments have considered or started implementing strategies to address resource misallocation and reduce subsidies. These very modest attempts to curb subsidies face significant political opposition, as the social contract in the GCC states implies that the state should provide heavily subsidised goods (including fuels) and services to its citizenry.

Thirdly, several oil and gas producers have created 'oil funds' (also known as sovereign wealth funds, or SWFs) such as the Qatar Investment Authority, Kuwait Investment Authority, and Mubadala Development Company (in Abu Dhabi). The International Monetary Fund (IMF) defines SWFs as government-owned investment vehicles. They include stabilisation funds, designed to mitigate volatile international market prices on resources and commodities; saving funds, intended to share wealth across generations; and reserve investment corporations, established to reduce the opportunity cost of holding excess foreign reserves or to pursue investment policies with higher returns.[29] These funds have created additional sources of revenues (in addition to those from oil) and have helped producers to overcome financial crises during times of low oil prices.

Fourthly, for a long time, oil producers have thought to lower their heavy dependence on oil revenues and diversify their economies. True, oil revenues still provide the bulk of public expenditure and a large share of the gross national product, but it is also true that most of the Gulf economies are more diversified than they were a decade or two ago. Dubai, Manama, and Doha (among others) are emerging as important financial and business regional hubs. Certainly, more needs to be done, but they are on the right track.[30]

Fifthly, security cooperation between the GCC states and the United States is multidimensional. Most of the six GCC states have signed defence cooperation agreements with Washington, and their military officers regularly receive training and education in the United States. The two sides participate in joint military manoeuvres every few months. In recent years, the GCC states have substantially increased their spending on buying advanced US military weapons. In 2014, Saudi Arabia replaced India as the largest importer of defence equipment worldwide and took the top spot as the number one trading partner of the US. Saudi Arabia and the UAE together imported $8.6 billion in defence systems in 2014, more than the imports of Western Europe combined. The biggest beneficiary of the strong Middle Eastern market remains the United States, with $8.4 billion worth of Middle Eastern exports.[31] This close and deep military cooperation is not likely to change at any time soon.

Sixthly, the six GCC states are not putting all their eggs in the American basket. In recent years, Gulf governments have developed close military cooperation with several European countries, particularly Britain and France. British and French companies are major arms suppliers to the GCC states, and their militaries are involved in training and manoeuvres. The GCC leaders and their Russian and Chinese counterparts have also exchanged reciprocal visits and held regular consultations and negotiations, but military cooperation with these countries lags behind the level of security cooperation with Western powers.

Finally, in addition to improved national training and armament, the GCC states have different and complicated relations with regional powers (such as Pakistan, Iran, Turkey, and Egypt). Cooperation and rivalry with these powers help to maintain a level of balance of power in the region. In recent years, relations between the GCC states and each of these regional powers have witnessed fundamental changes. Generally, the Gulf states seem less challenged by external threats and more by internal pressure.

Conclusion: the post-2014 collapse in oil prices and the way forward

The security of any country depends to a great extent on the strength of its economy. The ability of any regime to meet its population's economic needs determines its survival. The decades-long talks about reducing dependence on oil revenues in the Middle East have produced very modest outcomes. Globally, Malaysia, Indonesia, and Mexico offer the best examples of countries that have been able to diversify away from oil.[32] The underlying reality is that the majority of Persian Gulf states continue to depend heavily on oil revenues. This heavy dependence has made them particularly vulnerable to the fluctuation in oil prices. The collapse of oil prices since late 2014 has dealt a heavy blow to Gulf economies, with potential implications for political stability and national security.

As discussed above, the collapse of oil prices reflects the imbalance between supply and demand. In recent years, global oil production has risen while consumption has stagnated or fallen. Both in 2014 and again in 2015, OPEC, led by Saudi Arabia and other Persian Gulf states, refused to cut production and thereby play the role of swing producer. Gulf producers have resisted demands by Iran, Algeria, Venezuela, and other OPEC members to intervene and, instead, decided to let the market correct itself. The weaker-than-expected demand growth in advanced and emerging economies and the future of shale gas and tight oil technology have all contributed to a great deal of uncertainty and unpredictability in global oil markets. In January 2015, analysts at the IMF predicted that oil prices would eventually rebound and rise to $57 per barrel in 2015 and $72 per barrel by 2019; however, oil prices actually fell to below $40 by the end of 2015 and plunged to below $30 in the opening weeks of 2016.[33] Thus, oil prices are expected recover only over the medium term in response to a decline in investment and future capacity growth, and may yet fall further.

This volatility provides both challenges and opportunities to Gulf oil producers. The breakeven prices vary considerably across the GCC states,[34] but all of them are losing billions of dollars because of lower oil prices. These losses should not be exaggerated. Over the years, Gulf states have accumulated substantial revenues and subsequently enjoy strong financial reserves. These massive reserves will help them to survive the sharp drop in oil prices with little impact in the short term, although there has been a sudden slowdown in capital spending and increasing patterns of layoffs that have predominantly affected expatriate workers rather than nationals of GCC states. Still, Persian Gulf leaders are likely to take measures to prevent any major erosion of their buffers in the longer run. These include reassessment of medium-term spending plans, particularly if oil prices fail to show signs of significant recovery. For a long time, strong GDP growth was supported by rising government spending, financed by rapidly increasing oil revenues. This model is no longer sustainable. Strong efforts should be made to reduce dependence on oil revenues and create jobs, particularly in the private sector.

The political economy of the Persian Gulf states has relied heavily upon the redistribution of oil wealth from state to society, and any weakening of these bonds will place pressure on the 'social contract' that has underpinned sociopolitical and economic stability for the past four decades. In the long term, the success of these economic readjustments would enhance the Gulf states' national security and political stability, and override any of the short-term pain that the austerity measures might cause. The precise nature of the reformulation of political and economic structures will determine whether the next phase of evolution in Persian Gulf societies—away from, rather than into, the oil era—is likely to be consensual or contested, and whether change will come from the top down, the bottom up, or a mixture of the two.

5

TOWARDS THE END OF THE OLIGARCHIC PACT?

BUSINESS AND POLITICS IN ABU DHABI, BAHRAIN, AND OMAN

Marc Valeri[1]

As the former Egyptian Prime Minister Hazem Beblawi has pointed out, in a rentier state 'citizenship is not only an affective relation between man and his homeland; it is also, or primarily, a pecuniary relation'.[2] This is especially true when the individual belongs to a social group, like the business elite, which has had a crucial role in this state's polity, even prior to the influx of rent that has taken place in the monarchies of the Persian Gulf since the 1930s. However, the evolving nature of the 'social contract' in GCC states, made more urgent by the decline in oil prices and government revenues since 2014, places new pressure on key political-economic relationships that have for decades helped to underpin regime stability and security. The changing nexus of state–business relations in the Gulf has direct implications for political stability and ruling successions in GCC states, particularly those under review in this chapter.

In the six states of the Gulf Cooperation Council (GCC), the business communities have an earlier history of political influence, alongside their related economic role—as comparative works by Crystal (on Kuwait and Qatar) in the 1990s and Moore (on Kuwait, Qatar, and Bahrain) in the early 2000s, among others, have shown.[3] Over the last decade, the nature and evolution of state–business relations in the Gulf monarchies have received greater attention, especially in the context of the Arab Spring.[4] While most of these studies have concentrated on the mutually beneficial relationship that binds together the political and business elites and on the crucial role played by the latter in supporting the established sociopolitical order and shaping political legitimacy, this chapter chooses to focus instead on the economic role and influence of the ruling families. It argues that, in all six GCC states, an increasing number of ruling family members have entered the business and private sectors over recent decades. This definitely marks a new phase in the contemporary history of state–business relations in the Gulf monarchies.

While the pre-oil period was characterised by the existence of an oligarchic pact between rulers and merchants, in which the latter's economic power allowed them to exert extended political influence, the surge in oil revenues (which took place gradually across the Arabian Peninsula between the 1930s, in Bahrain and Kuwait, and the 1970s, in Oman) disrupted this balance. Even if the ruling elite–business elite relationship has tolerated significant variations from one GCC country to another, a common tendency was that the rulers' material affluence forced the merchants to retreat from the political sphere. In return, the economic pre-eminence of the business actors was recognised and protected, and they were guaranteed a substantial part of the rentier state's subsidies.

The argument developed in this chapter is that business–ruling family relations in the Gulf monarchies have entered a third phase, in which the involvement of members of ruling families has increased dramatically, to such an extent that this has been to the detriment of the historical business elites. The ruling families' encroachment on a field that has remained for most of the twentieth century a preserve of the merchant class cannot but impinge upon the traditional strategic alliance between the two elites. Given the role of this relationship in perpetuating the post-oil sociopolitical status quo, the unprecedented intrusion of ruling family members in the private sector is likely to have major implications for the whole rentier social contract in these states and, consequently, for their domestic stability. While Qatar's ruling family has always played a greater role in commerce and members of Kuwaiti and Saudi ruling families have become much more prominent in business too, this chapter will concentrate on Abu Dhabi, Bahrain, and Oman. Beyond obvious space constraints, which prevent a full comparative study here of the six GCC countries, the choice to compare Abu Dhabi, Bahrain, and Oman is supported by the observation of the differences between the historical patterns of state–business relations in these three countries. The situation in Bahrain, where the royal family and the economic elite are historically distinct and where both have impinged on the other's preserve, contrasts with that of Abu Dhabi, where business and political elites have formed a cohesive and intermingled oligarchy, and of Oman, where the ruling family is weak and politically dependent on a bourgeoisie that has played a key role in politics. Yet, despite these historical differences, a common pattern can be observed: the long-term, sustained increase of the ruling families' involvement in local economy as well as the concomitant decline of the political and economic influence of the historical business actors. The first GCC country where this development occurred was probably Bahrain, as early as the 1970s, while it has manifested itself in Abu Dhabi and Oman much more recently.

After a first section providing a comparative overview of the main patterns governing state–business relations in the Persian Gulf monarchies, before and after oil, with a particular emphasis on Abu Dhabi, Bahrain, and Oman, this chapter will document the increasing involvement of members of the Abu Dhabi, Bahrain, and Oman ruling families in the business sector, and the concomitant growing dependence of the merchant families on the rulers. The popular protests that took place in the GCC in 2011 and 2012 revealed the business sector's resistance to change in, for example, the way national bourgeoisies remain unfailing allies of the ruling families. Even more, the protests highlighted the business sector's increasingly limited latitude of action in the political field. This chapter then argues that the nature and extent of this major shift in the quality of business politics in the GCC will have substantial implications for the wider questions of the social contract established during the rentier period in the twentieth century.

A mutually beneficial oligarchic pact

The political economy of the contemporary Gulf monarchies finds its roots in the social and political structures inherited from the pre-oil period. Prior to the influx of major oil revenues, domestic stability in the monarchies of the Arabian Peninsula was assured by an arrangement that linked rulers with a number of prominent tribal leaders and local merchant families. In particular, the merchants helped meet the rulers' financial needs and in return received political influence and protection of their economic interests. The merchants, who controlled the two main economic sectors (pearling in Kuwait, Bahrain, Qatar, and the UAE; trade in Kuwait, Bahrain, Oman, and the UAE), enjoyed not only personal proximity to the rulers (through marriage alliances) but also the protection this proximity brought them, which in turn consolidated their economic interests, usually thanks to direct intervention in the decision-making process. As explained by Albadr Abu-Baker in the case of Abu Dhabi, 'the source of merchants' political power was their economic power'.[5] In return the merchants proved indispensable to the maintenance of the political status quo; not only were they the only ones able to provide the ruler's growing need for liquid assets (through loans), but the ruler deducted from their resources taxes and customs duties, which represented the major sources of the ruler's revenue. Moreover, in the numerous instances of succession conflicts and quarrels within ruling families, the ruler and challengers to the throne were driven to forge alliances outside the family, primarily with merchants, to assert their influence within the ruling family itself. This economic power differentiated merchants from other elites, such as tribal leaders, and increased further the merchants' political influence, their involvement in the daily running of the state (through the granting of decision-making positions), and, in the end, their crucial role in the ruler's political survival.

The merchants remained key partners until the surge in oil revenues. The mutually beneficial alliance between merchants and rulers was disrupted by the unexpected material sufficiency of the rulers after oil was discovered and oil exports began. The state's monopoly on managing expenditure and development allowed the creation of a welfare state, which became the cornerstone of the ruling family's political legitimacy. Thanks to new asphalted roads, and to schools and health centres, which were built even in the smallest villages, the authority of the ruler and the burgeoning state materially and symbolically occupied the entire territory. This process was accompanied by an explosion of jobs and possibilities of income offered within the public and para-public sectors. This 'allocation state' created a public sphere that provided a huge pool of jobs open to skilled and non-skilled individuals.[6] These new civil servants, employed in the national army, the police, the intelligence service, the ministries, and governmental services, would hardly turn against the ruler since they depended on the state for their survival. Because of these jobs in the public sector, the social activities of the tribesmen, formerly restricted to the village and its vicinity, broadened into larger networks. The ruler granted key political and administrative positions to historically important tribes or families and economic monopolies to nationals, and introduced practices and laws that gave nationals rights and privileges which were not enjoyed by non-nationals. In return, the ruling families expected the non-interference of nationals and civil society in domestic politics. This bureaucratisation of society illustrates the political and social control that the ruler implemented over his territory. As Nazih Ayubi has explained, 'through the creation, expansion and maintenance of a bureaucracy, the rulers of the oil-state are paying the citizen ... Instead of the usual situation of the state taxing the citizen (in return for offering him services), here the citizen is taxing the state—by acquiring a government payment—in return for staying quiet, for not invoking tribal rivalries, and for not challenging the ruling family's position.'[7] Thus, in the Gulf, the terms of the famous formula 'no taxation without representation', raised during the United States' War of Independence by supporters of political liberalisation, have been reversed to become 'no representation without taxation'.

As for their relation with the merchants, the rulers were, at first glance, freed from their economic dependence on them. Jill Crystal explains that the development of oil production in Kuwait and Qatar forced the merchants to renounce their historical claim to participate in decision-making. This was obviously not always smooth sailing. The 1938 Reform Movements in Kuwait and Dubai, in which merchant elites played a leading role, took place while the first oil concessions were negotiated and signed by the rulers,[8] and while revenues from pearls were in steep decline. These reform movements revolved around the demand for greater accountability from the rulers regarding the use of expected revenue,[9] and more generally around the changing balance of economic power within the political–economic elite. As explained by Jill Crystal, a key determinant of the Reform Movement in Kuwait was the merchant families' motivation to protect their political and, above all, economic positions: 'these [oil] revenues, and the promise of more, sharpened cleavages both within the ruling family and between the *shaikh* and the merchants ... Merchants began asking for a say in the distribution of the new wealth.'[10]

The political failure of these movements did not signify the business families' economic marginalisation; on the contrary. With the new political order that followed the discovery and extraction of oil in Bahrain (in the 1930s and 1940s) and Abu Dhabi and Oman (in the 1950s and 1960s) came consolidation of the positions that the already prominent actors occupied. In return for the merchant families' agreement to renounce their claims to a political role, the rulers granted them a large share of oil revenues, as this chapter will now illustrate.

If the state was the major agent of economic development in the GCC states in recent decades, it has been not only through the mechanisms of 'direct' and un-individualised distribution mentioned above (such as the bureaucratisation of employment, absence of taxation, and health and education for all) but also through individualised favours, which benefited only some groups and families to whom the political authority considered itself particularly indebted. These favours have taken various forms, particularly very tough laws governing foreign investors' rights, so as to protect the national market and the pre-eminence of the well-established local merchant dynasties within it. Through the *kafil* (sponsor) system, any foreign individual or company wishing to work in a GCC country is forced to associate with a local partner, who receives regular payment. For business purposes, this favours the already well-established national companies, which enjoy political contacts in elite decision-making circles, as these leading business groups' connections are sought by foreign investors willing to take only minimum risks.

This process has become even more important with the rise in living standards; as a result there has been growing demand for consumer goods produced abroad, which has necessitated local intermediaries to allow foreign and multinational companies to enter the market. Another favour has consisted of the grant of public contracts in all sectors dealing with infrastructure and urban planning (such as roads and public buildings). The 'public works' branch has played a decisive role in the consolidation of the wealth of leading economic groups. To use Jill Crystal's phrase about Kuwait, 'in a few generations, families had made a transition from wealthy traders and pearl merchants to extremely wealthy modern contractors'.[11]

In sum, wealth distributed to political subjects by the state as salaries, social allowances, or price subsidies was regained by the old allies of the rulers (and, in particular, the merchant families) through the ownership of companies winning public contracts.[12] This compromise—abdication of political influence in return for protection of business monopolistic positions—has allowed merchants to actually strengthen their economic pre-eminence and receive a major part of the rentier state's subsidies: 'where merchants wanted to invest—trade, construction, services—the state stayed out, or offered encouragement'.[13]

This general pattern across the Gulf contains significant variations from one country to another. In Kuwait, the ruler was forced to promise to keep royal family members out of business, while in Qatar, because the merchant community was weaker and smaller, the ruler allowed his relatives into the merchants' economic territory.[14] Thus, the confusion of politics and economy observed in Qatar finds its roots in the intrusion of ruling family members into economy, but also in the exclusion of merchants from the decision-making sphere.

Bahrain: a long-lasting influential merchant community

In Bahrain, while a number of Shiite merchant families (al-Baharna, al-'Urayyid, Bin Rajab) were historical allies of the Al Khalifa ruling family, the business oligarchy has mainly been composed of Sunni families, either of Najdi background or Hawala.[15] By the beginning of the twentieth century, this business elite had a monopoly on pearling and trade while members of the ruling family acted as 'feudal lords' and owned 80 per cent of the agricultural land of the island.[16] The concomitant beginning of oil production, filling ruling family coffers, and the collapse of the pearling industry in the 1930s temporarily threatened the economic supremacy—and, as a result, the political influence—of the merchants and provided the ruling family with unprecedented financial power and autonomy.[17] However, a number of factors allowed the merchants to recover quickly and benefit immensely from the spinoffs of the oil rent in following decades. Among these factors were the explosion of purchases by the oil company to supply local fields, the greater demand for goods following the discovery of oil, and the positioning of Bahrain as an import and re-export hub for goods manufactured in the United Kingdom and United States and destined for the regional market (Qatar, Eastern Province of Saudi Arabia, and Trucial States). As explained by Mohamed G. al-Rumaihi, 'the merchants have done well for themselves by manipulating the agent system of imports and controlling the flow of goods to the retail outlets ... The granting of import licences and the setting up of agencies were rigidly controlled by the Government for the benefit of the big merchants. Any newcomer wishing to enter a particular field faced a monopoly situation which was almost impossible to break.'[18]

As a consequence of this regained influence, the first Chamber of Commerce on the southern shore of the Gulf was established in Bahrain in 1939 as the Merchants' Association in order 'to give a platform for the [larger Bahraini merchants'] complaints and to protect their interests'.[19] It continued until 1945 when it officially became the Bahrain Chamber of Commerce, before it acquired its present name, the Bahrain Chamber of Commerce and

Industry (BCCI), in 1967. Controlled since its foundation by the merchant elite,[20] the BCCI played until recently a key role in Bahraini politics, by lobbying for business interests and influencing political decisions on economic and social matters impinging upon these interests—to the extent that Fred Lawson could say in the 1980s that the head of the Chamber served 'as a de facto member of the government'.[21]

If the sovereignty ministries (*wizarat al-siyada*)[22] and most sensitive political positions have long been monopolised by the ruling family, members of the Bahraini business elite have regularly been offered cabinet positions as well, in order to maintain this mutually beneficial oligarchic pact. Until the early 1970s, the Bahraini merchants kept a firm grip over the economy while using their personal proximity to the ruler and other senior members of the Al Khalifa to act as informal advisers and make sure their interests and priorities were taken into account.

Abu Dhabi: ruling family and business elite almost intermingled

In Abu Dhabi, the situation is slightly different since oil was not exploited and exported before the early 1960s. In the pre-oil era, a few families (al-'Utaiba, al-Qubaysi, al-Suwaidi, al-Fahim, al-Muhairi) enjoyed a hegemonic position in the economy (the pearling industry and trade). While political power was firmly in the hands of the ruler, persistent disagreements (over succession issues) and lack of unity within the ruling family forced most senior Al Nahyan contenders for power to seek alliances with extra-family actors, and in particular from these merchant families. This was the case on the occasion of the accession as ruler of Abu Dhabi in 1966 of Sheikh Zayed, who had to reassert alliances with the merchants to back his power. In the 1960s, contrary to Bahrain and Kuwait, where the processes of modern state formation had already taken place, the advent of oil and the newfound affluence of Abu Dhabi's ruling family did not change drastically the state–business political balance: 'The state's financial autonomy did not provide it with political autonomy precisely because ... of the political legacy of low level of institutional development'[23] until the 1960s. Thus, the ruling family desperately needed the help and expertise of the business elite to build the new state both in the emirate of Abu Dhabi and, after the creation of the UAE in 1971, across the federation. This favoured the business elite's integration in political structures and further enhanced not only their power and influence but also their proximity to the Al Nahyan and their stake in the preservation of the authoritarian order. Abu-Baker describes this relation as an 'interdependence, and to a certain extent [a] fusion, that has evolved between the business classes and the political elites as a result of this pattern of capital accumulation ... Those who were once politically powerful became more economically powerful; and those who were economically powerful became more politically powerful.'[24] As a result, more than a pact between royal family and merchant class, as in Kuwait or Bahrain, the situation in Abu Dhabi resembled an entanglement of two dominant groups, illustrated by marriage alliances, business partnerships between members of the ruling family and the bourgeoisie, and appointments of members of the merchant families to the cabinet, the Federal National Council, and executive positions in the new state agencies and state-owned companies, in order to consolidate even more—if possible—the cohesiveness of this oligarchy and their shared interests in preserving the status quo.

Oman: the Sultan's political reliance on the business oligarchy

Unlike the other Gulf Arab monarchies, Oman is not under the rule of a tribe or a family, but a monarch who has relied on external allies for political and economic support. The former Sultan of Oman, Sa'id bin Taimur (r.1932–70), did not trust his relatives and instead relied on a few families and individuals, who were given the possibility to consolidate their political and economic positions in exchange for their support. Just like his father, Sultan Qaboos bin Sa'id (r.1970–) has chosen to impose his authority on the Al Sa'id while limiting drastically its political role as a family and drawing only a few individuals close to him. On the other hand, he has recruited heavily from some clans of the broader al-Busa'idi tribe,[25] who have been seen as neutral in internal affairs, to fill sensitive political and administrative positions such as the Diwan of the Royal Court and the Ministry of the Interior. Sultan Qaboos has allied also with Muscat and Muttrah merchant elites—a practice in keeping with the pre-1970 period. He has assured them of the protection of the political authorities, the ruling family's very limited interference in the business sphere, and privileged access to the oil windfall through public contracts. In return, the merchant families have helped the ruler to finance his nation-building endeavours. Oil has strengthened the economic and social position of the merchant and business elites inherited from the twentieth century, through the conversion of trade dynasties to rent wealth. For instance, it is widely believed that a few businessmen were awarded fixed percentages of oil revenue in 1970 in order to give them a direct stake in the new regime's stability.[26]

But this alliance with the business elite in Oman went even further. Some of the pre-eminent merchant families have been given strategic decision-making positions to secure public contracts and control over the distribution of the oil wealth. Until the late 1990s, unlike their counterparts in Kuwait or Qatar, the Omani merchants were never 'forced to choose money over formal political influence'.[27] A former chairman (1987–91) of the Chamber of Commerce, Maqbool al-Sultan, whose family acted as representatives in Oman for the British India shipping line and Lloyd's in the first half of the twentieth century, held the post of Minister for Commerce and Industry from 1991 until February 2011. The leading al-Sultan family company is W.J. Towell, which is involved in more than forty sectors and represents brands like Mars, Unilever, and Nestlé in Oman. Another obvious example of direct participation by business families in the decision-making process is the Zawawi family. Yusuf al-Zawawi, who migrated from Hijaz in modern-day Saudi Arabia to Muscat at the end of the nineteenth century to establish a trading company, became one of the unofficial advisers to Sultan Faisal (r.1888–1913). Qays al-Zawawi, Yusuf's grandson, held the position of Foreign Minister between 1973 and 1982, then became Deputy Prime Minister for Finance and Economy until his death in 1995. His brother 'Umar, possibly the richest man in Oman after the Sultan, currently holds the position of Special Adviser to the ruler for External Affairs. Economically speaking, the Omar Zawawi Establishment (OMZEST) has become one of the leading Omani holding companies. Another prominent figure, Waleed bin 'Umar, a former head of information technology services of the Sultan's Armed Forces, is vice-chairman of HBSC Oman.

But the oil rent has at the same time profoundly changed the boundaries between the political and economic sphere, as many ministers whose families were not previously active in the economy have become involved in business and built powerful conglomerates. This process has not been questioned by the ruler, as it has increased both the elite's dependency on the state and the stability of his rule. The symbolic debt owed by Sultan Qaboos at the beginning of his rule to those actors (such as merchant elites and tribal notables) who supported him after 1970 (when he relied on their funds to consolidate his authority) has thus gradually turned into a weapon in his hands, forestalling any challenges to his reign by turning the most powerful societal forces into unfailing allies. By the beginning of the twenty-first century, few members of the Council of Ministers had not personally derived material profit from the oil rent.[28] One of the most illustrative cases is the noble branch of the Khalili family—heirs to a prestigious lineage of Ibadi imams. Sa'ud al-Khalili, the nephew of a former Imam of Oman (Muhammad al-Khalili, 1920–54), became one of the four members of the very first cabinet appointed by Sultan Qaboos in August 1970. In addition, he owns the powerful Al Taher business group, founded in 1973, which is active in construction contracting (Caterpillar), food and drink (Sprite and Coke), and the distribution of Shell products. His nephew Salim bin Hilal, Minister for Agriculture until 2011, was formerly chairman of the Chamber of Commerce, while another of his nephews, 'Abd Al-Malik bin 'Abd Allah—who had previously held successively the positions of executive chairman of the Royal Court Pension Fund, chairman of the first Omani banking group (Bank Muscat), and Minister for Tourism (2011–12)—is currently Minister of Justice.

An altered balance

This chapter has argued that the established relation between the ruling family and the business oligarchy was well defined until recently, but has experienced very significant evolutions in recent years. These changes have taken place at a different pace in each monarchy, depending on the historical balance of power between these two dominant groups, but along a relatively similar path. In particular, this section will show that in Abu Dhabi, Bahrain, and Oman, the involvement of ruling families in the economy has grown substantially. This has gone with a concomitant reduction of the business elite's political power and, more generally, of their capacity to influence political decisions. The Arab Spring—in Bahrain and Oman—only confirmed this trend.

Bahrain: a business oligarchy in subservience to the Al Khalifa

Bahrain was the first country where the economic balance began to tilt sharply in favour of the ruling family. The rising oil revenues after 1973 and the shift towards greater authoritarianism after the suspension of the short-lived parliament in 1975 drastically transformed the pre-independence oligarchic pact. As a result, the Al Khalifa family gained extensive political room for manoeuvre vis-à-vis the merchants. Given that the Bahraini merchant elite view themselves as a minority and that their influence is not based on deep social networks, they have not been powerful enough to force the ruling family to stay out of business after the 1970s. In a confidential conversation with a British diplomat in 1977, the British head of Bahrain Special Branch, Ian Henderson, pointed out this evolution and noted that the Al Khalifa 'were moving into lucrative areas of business and squeezing out established merchants'.[29] Some senior members of the Al Khalifa in particular, such as Prime Minister Sheikh Khalifa bin Salman (in office since 1971), have become prominent post-independence business actors: 'the wealth of the state has been the Al Khalifa's to distribute as largesse to grateful citizens. In Bahrain [in the 1990s], the word "government" in common parlance still refers to the family. Most of the land on the island belongs to the Al Khalifa family and there has been no institutional accountability of the family to the public ... since' 1975.[30] In the 1990s, the Prime Minister 'allegedly became the richest person in Bahrain with extensive holdings in land, hotels, commercial property and profits on government contracts',[31] while it became a commonplace that 'you can't get permission for any project without giving a percentage to the Al Khalifas'.[32] As an illustration, 'members of prominent Sunni merchant families sympathetic to the petition movement [in 1994] had to retract their support because their families were seriously harassed'.[33]

The real estate sector has been crucial in this evolution. Much of Bahrain's prime land was locked up by the royal family until 2010, when speculators began to pay top prices to acquire properties for development. In the 2000s, twelve zones in Bahrain were designated specifically for the development of tourism, such as the mega-projects currently under construction at Durrat al-Bahrain (in the south), on the Amwaj Islands (near Muharraq), or in the Northern Town. This has led to an uncontrolled real estate boom which has served, in a large part, as a diversification policy by itself, with large real estate projects being erected on reclaimed lands, like Bahrain Bay (in which the King is a partner)[34] or Bahrain Financial Harbour (in which the Prime Minister is involved).[35] More generally, it induced a huge shift of wealth: prices of property have multiplied by ten since the late 1990s.

Furthermore, the established Bahraini business families, who control the Chamber of Commerce, could not oppose the emergence of new economic actors benefiting from diversification policies with the patronage of the Al Khalifa. The inability of the established business elite to resist the arrival of challengers has to do with their reduced economic weight compared with that of the ruling family, which does not give them sufficient bargaining capacity anymore. Moreover, most of their business interests and future opportunities depend on maintaining good relations with senior ruling family members, which means that they cannot take the risk of irritating them, for fear of being blacklisted and losing everything.

The most prominent of these 'nouveaux riches' was 'Isam Jinahi, the chairman of Gulf Finance House (GFH), Bahrain's leading Islamic bank, which has been involved in projects with an aggregate value of over US$20 billion across the Arab world. 'Isam Jinahi, who was a company clerk in the mid-1990s, was involved in several of the major real estate and infrastructure projects in Bahrain for ten years, such as Bahrain Financial Harbour, the $1.5 billion financial city on Manama corniche (in partnership with the Prime Minister).[36] Another example of these new Bahraini business actors is Khalid 'Abd al-Rahim, chairman of the leading Bahraini building and civil engineering company, Cebarco, founded in 1992. During the last ten years, Cebarco has been awarded contracts for the completion of some of the most prestigious projects, such as the Bahrain Formula One racing circuit (with the Crown Prince's support) and the King Hamad Highway.

This move into the economic sphere by members of the Al Khalifa has taken place alongside a dramatic loss in the capacity of business families to project political influence. As of May 2017, only three members of the business elite hold positions in the cabinet. Jawad al-'Urayyid, a former Minister of State for Cabinet Affairs (1973–82) and the grandson of Mansur al-'Urayyid, a leading pearl merchant in the 1930s, has held the position of Deputy Prime Minister without portfolio since December 2006. Zayed al-Zayani, the grandson of a leading pearl merchant of Najdi origin, 'Abd al-Rahman al-Zayani (whose brother was the head of Sheikh Hamad's office in the 1920s), succeeded Hassan Fakhro, another scion of a leading merchant family, as Minister of Industry and Commerce in December 2014.[37] Finally, Fa'iqa al-Salih, cousin of 'Ali al-Salih, chairman of the Majlis al-Shura and Minister of Commerce from 1995 to 2006), was appointed Minister of Social Development in December 2014.

Thus, the Bahraini business elite has lost much of its political influence and has therefore become heavily dependent both on the balance of power within the ruling family and on its good relationship with the most influential individuals among the Al Khalifa.

Abu Dhabi: the Al Nahyan at the helm of business

In Abu Dhabi, the political decision-making process has increasingly been monopolised by the sons of Sheikh Zayed and by the Bani Fatima group of full brothers in particular.[38] The composition of the key institutions of Abu Dhabi illustrates this. Among the Abu Dhabi Executive Council's sixteen members, two (its chairman, the Crown Prince of Abu Dhabi and Deputy Supreme Commander of the UAE Armed Forces, Mohammed bin Zayed; and its vice-chairman, the National Security Adviser,[39] Hazza' bin Zayed) are from the Bani Fatima, while three other members of the Executive Council (Mohammed bin Khalifa, the son of UAE President Khalifa bin Zayed; Hamad bin Zayed, chairman of Mohammed bin Zayed's court; and Sultan bin Tahnoon bin Mohammed) belong also to the ruling family. In addition, the ruling family also provides seven of the sixteen members of the Supreme Petroleum Council, which acts as the board of directors of the state-owned oil company ADNOC.[40] At the federation level, Lieutenant-General Saif bin Zayed has been concomitantly the UAE Minister of Interior since 2004 and UAE Deputy Prime Minister since 2009. Similarly, his half-brother Mansour bin Zayed has held the position of Minister of Presidential Affairs since 2004 and Deputy Prime Minister since 2009. The Minister of Foreign Affairs since 2006 has been 'Abdullah bin Zayed, who was previously Minister of Information and Culture (1997–2006). Another member of the Abu Dhabi ruling family sits in the UAE cabinet: Nahyan bin Mubarak (Minister of Culture, Youth and Social Development since 2013, and previously Minister of Higher Education and Scientific Research, from 1990 to 2013). If members of the business oligarchy retain important decision-making positions,[41] this political influence cannot match the level they held until the 1980s.

At the same time, the involvement of Al Nahyan members in business has reached an unprecedented level. Ruling family members are in control of powerful companies that dominate the economy—either personally or through sovereign wealth funds. Considered to be the second-largest wealth fund globally, with an estimated $773 billion of assets,[42] the Abu Dhabi Investment Authority (ADIA) is chaired by UAE President Khalifa bin Zayed and controlled by the ruling family of Abu Dhabi (Hamad bin Zayed is managing director and six out of nine board members are Al Nahyan). The second-largest Abu Dhabi fund, worth $110 billion,[43] is ADIC (Abu Dhabi Investment Council), which was split off from ADIA. Chaired by Crown Prince Mohammed bin Zayed since June 2015, its board is fairly similar to that of ADIA, with four (out of a total of seven) Al Nahyan members. ADIC controls 33 per cent of the shares of Abu Dhabi's largest bank, the National Bank of Abu Dhabi. Mohammed bin Zayed chairs Mubadala Development Company, which is viewed as his 'foremost investment vehicle',[44] and whose vice-chairman is his full-brother Mansour bin Zayed, since Mubadala and Abu Dhabi's third-largest wealth fund, the International Petroleum Investment Company (IPIC), merged in January 2017.[45] Mansour bin Zayed, who is married to a daughter of the ruler of Dubai, Manal bint Mohammed bin

Rashid, chairs the Emirates Investment Authority (EIA), the only wealth fund of the UAE government.[46] Mansour bin Zayed is also the head of the Abu Dhabi Judicial Department, the Abu Dhabi Fund for Development (which provides aid to developing countries in the form of concessionary loans and administers grants on behalf of the Abu Dhabi government), and the Khalifa bin Zayed Charity Foundation.[47] As Jean-François Seznec has noted, 'each of the funds is managed by a board of directors, which represent the interests of one or more clans within the royal family. Within each board, the chairman represents the royal clan who is most vested in the fund ... Nevertheless, there seems to be a major effort to include the various clans and the major Abu Dhabi merchant families in all the funds.'[48] Merchant elites retain a strong presence on the boards of directors in many, if not most, state-owned companies, which is a clear indication of the strong relationship between them and the Al Nahyan. However, there is no doubt where the final decision lies.

Other Al Nahyan members of the elite circle have been prominent businessmen. Hamdan bin Zayed, the ruler's representative in the Western Region since 2009 and former Minister of State for Foreign Affairs and Deputy Prime Minister, chairs Dolphin Energy, which is owned by Mubadala (51 per cent of the shares) and whose major project is Dolphin Gas Project, which involves the production, processing, and transportation of natural gas from Qatar to the UAE and Oman. Tahnoon bin Zayed, who is married to the sister of Nasser bin Ahmed al-Suwaidi, is chairman of First Abu Dhabi Bank, the UAE's largest bank by assets since its birth in April 2017 by the merger of FGB and NBAD banks. He also chairs Royal Group, a leading Abu Dhabi-based conglomerate.

The sons of UAE President Khalifa bin Zayed (who has no full brothers and is not a member of the Bani Fatima) have also gained prominent economic positions. Sultan bin Khalifa, Adviser to the UAE President and honorary chairman of Abu Dhabi Chamber of Commerce (1991–2005), is owner and chairman of SBK Holding, which employs 10,000 people in the UAE and has significant real estate holdings in Abu Dhabi. His brother Mohammed bin Khalifa chairs Abu Dhabi's Department of Finance and has headed the emirate's Retirement Pensions and Benefits Fund. A number of more distant Al Nahyan members control business assets, including 'Issa bin Zayed, a prominent real estate developer through its holding, Pearl Properties; Zayed's cousin's grandson, Nahyan bin Mubarak, owner and chairman of Abu Dhabi Group, which has considerable investments in Pakistan (where it owns two leading banks, United Bank and Bank Alfalah), and chairman of UAE's public joint stock Union National Bank (owned 50 per cent by ADIC); his brother

Hamdan, chairman and main shareholder of the National Company for Tourism and Hotels, which is responsible for Saadiyat Island and the Grand Millennium hotel, among others; Zayed's cousin's son, Tahnoon bin Mohammed, Khalifa's representative in the Eastern Region (al-'Ayn) since 1971, who together with his son Sa'id reportedly held 'a monopoly on all al-'Ayn projects' in 2003, to the point that 'only Shaykh Zayid and Khalifa [could] veto their business activities in the Eastern Region'.[49]

Oman: growing presence of the Al Sa'id in business

In Oman, only a handful of Qaboos's relatives occupied a visible role in the private sector until recently. The ruler's paternal uncle, Shabib bin Taimur, who has held the position of Special Adviser to the Sultan for Environmental Affairs since 1991, created Tawoos Group in 1982. Tawoos has become one of the leading Omani business groups, involved in various sectors from agriculture, telecommunications, and services (through its main division, Renaissance Services) to leisure and oil, and has concluded contracts with Petroleum Development Oman (PDO), the Diwan of the Royal Court, and the Ministries of Defence and Oil. If Shabib and his son Tariq, Tawoos's vice-chairman, were the first Al Sa'id members directly active in the economic sector, the involvement in business of royal family members has become much more visible in the 2000s. This is true of three of the sons of Qaboos's paternal uncle and former Prime Minister (1970–1), Tariq bin Taimur, who are also the more likely candidates for the eventual succession to Sultan Qaboos in the absence of any named heir.

Former Brigadier-General As'ad bin Tariq has been the Personal Representative of the Sultan since 2002 and the Deputy Prime Minister for International Cooperation since March 2017. He was chairman of Oman Merchant Bank, which was established in 2007 and in which he was one of the main shareholders, together with the Gulf Merchant Bank, partially owned by Saudi Arabia's al-Rajhi family. However, this project did not get off the ground. As'ad has also been chairman of the board of trustees of the University of Nizwa, the largest private university in Oman. He runs several companies, including Asad Investment Company, which operates as his personal investment vehicle and which is said to control more than $1 billion in worldwide assets. As'ad's son Taimur, who is married to Salma bint Mustahil al-Ma'ashani, the daughter of Qaboos's maternal uncle, is considered to be the leading candidate in his generation for succession to the throne. Taimur served until 2011 on the board of directors of Bank Dhofar, the second-largest Omani bank in term of assets, and since 2012 has been chairman of Alizz Bank, Oman's second Islamic bank.

As'ad's half-brother, Haitham, has held the position of Minister of National Heritage and Culture since 2002. Haitham set himself up as a businessman in 1991 when he became one of the main shareholders, in partnership with the Special Adviser to the Sultan, 'Umar al-Zawawi, and the former Minister of National Economy, Ahmed Makki, of the newly privatised Sun Farms agricultural company, one of the biggest owners of lands in Batina and the largest producer of vegetables in Oman.[50] Haitham has substantially increased his involvement in business ventures since the early 2000s, especially through a holding company for investment and project development, National Trading Company, which he owns and chairs. The holding has been involved in the construction of two major power plants (Manah and Suhar) and is agent in Oman for several multinational companies (Alstom, ThyssenKrupp). Haitham also shared with another Omani investor a 30 per cent stake in the Blue City project, a massive tourism-devoted new city supposedly worth $20 billion south of Suhar. However, mismanagement and legal battles between the project's owners, combined with the 2008 regional real estate crisis, resulted in Oman's most spectacular bankruptcy ever and the controversial intervention of the state's sovereign wealth fund OIF in 2011 and 2012 to buy Blue City bonds. Since December 2013, Haitham has chaired the main committee responsible for developing and drafting the new long-term national strategy, 'Oman Vision 2040.'

Shihab, a full brother of Haitham, former Rear-Admiral and Commander of the Royal Navy of Oman, has served as Adviser to the Sultan since 2004. Shihab chairs the Seven Seas group of companies, which has invested worldwide in petroleum, mutual funds, properties, and medical supplies. In particular, his company AMNAS was granted by royal decree in 2003 the exclusive rights to navigational aids in Oman's territorial waters. Another prominent business figure is Turki bin Mahmood, the brother of the Deputy Prime Minister for the Council of Ministers, Fahd bin Mahmood. Turki, who is State Adviser for Penal Affairs, is the president and founder of Al Turki Enterprises, one of the leading Omani companies in the construction sector and a contractor for the construction of several government buildings, Sultan Qaboos University, and the Great Mosque in Bawshar.

A final example of ruling family involvement in economic affairs is the maternal uncle of Sultan Qaboos, Sheikh Mustahil al-Ma'ashani, a former

Minister of Labour and Social Affairs in the late 1980s. He has chaired Muscat Overseas, which is probably the most active business group in Dhofar, especially in the agriculture, banking, and real estate sectors. Mustahil's elder son, Salim, a former chairman of the Nawras telecommunications private company (the second Omani mobile telecommunication operator), now holds the post of Adviser to the Diwan of the Royal Court with ministerial rank. Another of Mustahil's sons, Khalid, is chairman of the first Omani banking group, Bank Muscat.[51] Khalid is also chairman and majority shareholder of Dhofar International Development and Investment Company, which is the main shareholder (27.5 per cent) of Bank Dhofar.[52]

This massive intrusion in the economy of ruling family members and relatives of the Sultan may be the first sign of a crucial qualitative shift in the relationship between business and politics in Oman, where the ruler hitherto has relied politically and economically on the merchant elite more than on his own family since the 1970s. In the light of the growing unrest in Oman over deep-seated flaws in the state and the perceived lack of a long-term economic and political vision for the country,[53] what will be the impact of this evolution on the post-Qaboos polity, as each of the possible successors has already built up a considerable business empire even before acceding to the throne? Is there a risk that the candidates that are not selected can use their economic assets to build patronage networks and undermine the new ruler's legitimacy? This probably cannot be anticipated, but, amid mounting popular frustration, criticism of Sultan Qaboos has emerged since 2011, including his management of the oil rent and the country, which some young protesters likened to that of a private firm. The eventual successor to Sultan Qaboos will confront tremendous social and economic challenges and is likely to face these grievances again, only on a far more prominent scale given the increasing visibility of the crossover between money and power.

The business elite and the Arab Spring

If anything, the popular movements that have occurred in the Gulf since 2011 have revealed the business elites' strong inclination to privilege the political status quo over any kind of reform debate. Even more so, the protests also illustrated the extent to which the interests of the main business actors are intrinsically linked to—and increasingly dependent on—those of the ruling families in GCC states. Since the vast majority of business elites in the GCC states have vested interests in keeping the political and economic systems as they are, their absence of support to peaceful protesters, and usually their active backing of their repression by the regimes, have been made out of a rational choice. In the UAE, it was not surprising that no member of the business elite signed a petition by more than a hundred intellectuals in March 2011 for more legislative power to be given to the elected Federal National Council. The business oligarchy sided with the government and, if anything, showed greater support for the leadership than ever before.

In Oman, the business elite, accused of corruption, unwarranted privileges, and political and economic opposition to change, was one of the main targets of the protesters. From this perspective, it is not insignificant that early attempts by Sultan Qaboos to show his supposed benevolence towards people in the street led to an extensive reshuffle of the cabinet in March 2011, with the removal of long-serving ministers widely perceived as embodying the conflict of interest between business and politics (such as Ahmed Makki, the Minister for National Economy, and Maqbool al-Sultan, the Minister for Commerce and Industry).[54]

In Bahrain, except for some isolated individuals who sympathised with the protesters in 2011, business actors constantly reasserted their proximity to the regime and expressed the need to preserve the stability of the country—in an allusion to the protesters, whom they considered to be troublemakers. In a statement on 11 May 2011 referring to the Peninsula Shield Force military intervention in Bahrain, the BCCI explained that 'due to the timely measures taken by the leadership and the support of neighbouring GCC countries to ensure security and stability in the country, the [national] economy is back on track'.[55] A few days earlier, the BCCI had called on 'all business enterprises and owners in Bahrain' for a complete boycott of trade with Iran to protest against Tehran's alleged fuelling of unrest in Bahrain.[56] The massive crackdown that followed the protests in 2011 was successful in marginalising the less uncompromising component of the ruling family around the Crown Prince, in favour of the Prime Minister and his supporters, first among them the Chamber of Commerce and the business elite. The condition for business families to remain an interlocutor of the political elite in Bahrain requires adapting their strategies according to the balance of power among the Al Khalifa, on whom they remain heavily dependent, and making use of the divisions within the ruling family. This is but a pale shadow of the considerable capacity for influence that the business elite enjoyed only one generation ago.

Conclusion

The historical oligarchic pact that has linked the Gulf monarchies' ruling families and the national bourgeoisies for most of the twentieth century and that has been central to the perpetuation and consolidation of the authoritarian status quo has experienced crucial changes in recent decades. Whereas the structural patterns of the ruling elite–business elite relationship vary considerably across the GCC, as shown in this chapter, a common evolution has been taking place: the balance has recently tilted in favour of the ruling family. The business elite continues to benefit from the political status quo and shows indefectible support for the ruling family's policies—as illustrated during the Arab Spring. However, the dramatic expansion of GCC ruling families' involvement in the economy has been accompanied by a decline in the business elite's capacity to influence political decisions. In Bahrain, the business oligarchy's political influence is now secondary while their economic role is usually restricted to one of subsidiary partner in projects decided on and led by a few senior members of the Al Khalifa. In Abu Dhabi, the vast majority of the emirate's economy is controlled personally (through their own business assets) or pseudo-institutionally (through sovereign wealth funds) by the Al Nahyan (and, in particular, the Bani Fatima branch). The latter have taken care, though, to involve in all major funds and administrations members of the business oligarchy, who readily adapt to Al Nahyan's priorities and jump on the bandwagon. In Oman, while the merchants retain considerable political and economic influence, the last decade has seen an unprecedented involvement of the Al Sa'id in the local economy. It remains to be seen if these are the premises for a growing shift in business–politics relations that will occur in the post-Qaboos era. In Qatar, the ruling family has always played a greater role in commerce, and this was only accentuated under Emir Hamad (r.1995–2013); a similar evolution can be noticed in Kuwait too.

The changing dynamics in the balance between ruling families and business oligarchies in the GCC is likely to have considerable impact on the social contract, the implementation and outcomes of public policies, the balance of power within the ruling families, and, more broadly, the legitimacy of these regimes in the future.

As elsewhere in the Arab world, social and economic demands have been at the top of the agenda in demonstrations in all GCC countries since 2011, revolving in many cases around job opportunities and proactive measures to curb rising inequalities and to fight corruption among top officials. Demands of the youth in Kuwait, in Manama, or in Suhar[57] were triggered by resentment and anger at an elite seen as busily safeguarding its privileges, together with a growing disparity between the happy few who have access to the economic spinoffs and the vast majority who do not. These popular protests have given a first but tangible indication of the sensitivity of this question among the broader population. The increasing personal involvement of many ruling family members in business is likely to fuel this popular frustration. While un-individualised distribution of rent (free health care, free education, public sector jobs for nationals) was a key pillar of the system's legitimacy, the young, educated, and informed generations have become aware that this rentier bargain is, in many respects, out of date and that they will not benefit from the same rentier spinoffs as their parents and grandparents did. Under uncertain political conditions, loyalty to the system still seems to be the most rational choice for the business oligarchy, even if its political and economic privileges tend to be squeezed. More open to debate is the broader population's loyalty to a system which was, despite all its imperfections, at least capable of providing a minimum level of economic security to almost everybody but which lately has moved towards an increasingly predatory model (the epitome of which is Bahrain).

The growing involvement of ruling family members in business may be considered as a ruler's answer to the increasing difficulty of controlling his own expanding family. More and more individuals and branches of the family know that their chances of acceding to the throne or even getting senior political positions are close to zero. This is probably true now of Kuwait, where the Jaber branch has effectively sidelined the Salem branch, and even of Saudi Arabia, after the crowning of Salman bin 'Abdul 'Aziz in 2015 and the concentration of succession in one branch of the Al Sa'ud. Furthermore, it has become increasingly difficult for the ruler to buy off other members of the ruling family by granting them managing positions in the civil sector or in the security sector. As a safety valve, he may then encourage them to enter business and to choose money over political power, in a bargain comparable to the one concluded between rulers and merchants after oil was discovered. However, it remains to be seen whether this significant long-term evolution of power dynamics within ruling families will have implications for the regime's stability. This strategy may well raise the same issues that it was initially intended to address, reviving internal tensions within the ruling families themselves, since the economic weight of an individual or a branch of the family is likely to increase their political weight. Economic assets are political resources which royals involved in business will not hesitate to use in their struggle for power and influence within the family.

Another fundamental question regarding this evolution relates to the political-economic conflict of interest at the top levels in these countries. Each ruling family will face a growing conflict of priorities between the nation's general interests, which it is supposed to promote (such as the fight against local youth unemployment and the nationalisation of jobs in the private sector), and the particular stakes that some of its members defend as businessmen. This conflict of interest will have an impact on the direction taken by the state's economic policies, since labour market reforms favouring nationals are usually at odds with neoliberal policies enhancing incentives for businesses and favouring foreign direct investment, deregulation, and privatisation. But it may also raise divisions between the royals invested in power politics and those motivated by more entrepreneurial interests.

6

INDIA

A RISING POWER IN THE PERSIAN GULF?

Dionysis Markakis

India has a long-standing, rich, and intimate relationship with the Persian Gulf region that extends from antiquity to the present day. India's emergence as a 'middle power' is underpinned by its energy security reliance upon the Persian Gulf and the further expansion of energy and trading relationships with the region. The Gulf Cooperation Council (GCC) member states collectively constitute India's most important trading partner, more so than the European Union (EU). India currently imports 80 per cent of its oil needs from the Gulf, a figure that is expected to rise to 90 per cent over the next decade.[1] Moreover, over six million Indian nationals work in the Gulf region, almost three million in Saudi Arabia alone.[2] This results in approximately US$32 billion in annual remittances, almost half of India's total remittances, and roughly equivalent to the overall annual foreign direct investment (FDI) in the country.[3]

With a rapidly ascendant economy, currently the second-fastest growing in the world and already recognised as one of the ten largest globally, and moreover with its overwhelming dependence on oil imports from the Gulf, as the world's fourth-largest consumer of energy, India's relationship with the Gulf is only going to deepen further.[4] As P.R. Kumaraswamy argues, 'With the sole exception of its immediate neighbourhood, no other region has such strong economic, political, cultural and security implications for India.'[5] Given the increasingly prominent role of India in the international system over the last decade or so, and amid the seeming decline of American unipolarity in the Gulf region, this observation appears more and more relevant today. Driven by the economics of energy, trade, and expatriate labour, India's relationship with the Gulf is undergoing a steady augmentation.[6] As India's position in the Gulf grows, so will its general presence and its role in regional politics, as reflected by the visits paid by Prime Minister Narendra Modi to the UAE in August 2015 and Saudi Arabia in April 2016.

This chapter explores India's engagement with the Persian Gulf region. The focus is limited here in the main to the Gulf Cooperation Council (GCC) member states, although reference is made to Iran, Iraq, and Yemen. Firstly, the chapter places India's role in the international system in a theoretical context, utilising middle power theory to explain India's foreign policy outlook. Secondly, it examines India's relationship with the Gulf states in terms of the dominant economic, socio-cultural, and military drivers. Finally, it explores the contemporary status of the Indian–Gulf relationship, assessing the extent to which India can be described as a rising power in the region.

India: from middle to rising power?

India's stance in the international system has long been characterised by an emphasis on multilateralism. This was exemplified during the Cold War, with India serving as a founding member of the Non-Aligned Movement (NAM), a collective of states that sought to carve a path independent of the American and Soviet superpowers—a 'third way' as such. Notably, India was the only democracy in the international system not to align itself with the West.[7] This approach defined Indian foreign policy from independence in 1947 through to the end of the 1990s; indeed, it constituted a foundational national creed. However, the collapse of the Soviet Union in 1991, which signalled the end of the bipolar international system, diminished the relevance of this guiding ideological tenet. Amid the emergence of the United States as the predominant international power, albeit one increasingly facing significant challenges to its hegemony, India has struggled somewhat to define a substantive role for itself in the international system. On the one hand, by virtue of its rapidly expanding economy, substantial population, and growing military prowess, India is widely regarded as a rising—and potentially great—power in the international system.[8] This has led to increased expectation in the West of a more assertive Indian presence internationally, not least in terms of the Gulf. In large part, this has been encouraged by the United States and other major Western powers because of India's relatively benign international profile, underscored by its domestic democratic credentials. For instance, in a 2010 visit to New Delhi, US President Barack Obama stated that 'it is my firm belief that the relationship between the United States and India—bound by our shared interests and our shared values—will be one of the defining partnerships of the 21st century'.[9] This can be seen in contrast to Western reactions towards the rise of China, which have generally been more adverse. There is far less reference to mutual interests and values in the case of Sino-Western relations, with the emphasis placed on restraining China, rather than encouraging its ascent.

India's position in the international system can be understood best in terms of the middle power paradigm. Initially developed to explain the role of countries such as Australia and Canada in the international system, as influential but not dominant actors, middle power theory has since been expanded to address a range of important contemporary powers such as Brazil, South Africa, and Iran.[10] Middle powers are described by Carsten Holbraad as 'the meeting place of once great but declining powers, tired from generations of power politics at the highest level but rich in experience, and of lesser but ascending powers, conscious of their potential and stirred by ambition'.[11] The statistical indicators of a middle power are outlined by Jonathan Ping as follows: 'population, geographic area, military expenditure, GDP, GDP real growth, value of exports, gross national income per capita, trade as a percentage of GDP and life expectancy at birth'.[12] But beyond the emphasis on material indices, middle power theory also accounts for the role of normative, behavioural, and ideational factors, which Ping himself acknowledges are necessary to consider.[13]

One of the primary characteristics attributed to middle powers is their multilateral outlook. This is explained by the fact that, as Robert Keohane argues, a 'middle-power is a state whose leaders consider that it cannot act alone effectively, but may be able to have a systemic impact in a small group or through an international institution'.[14] Middle power status therefore generally manifests itself in an interest in upholding a stable international order, based on a strong international legal system, diplomacy, and coalition-building.[15] This is particularly apposite in the case of India, given its articulation of a 'value-based' foreign policy, stressing the principles of non-alignment, neutrality, negotiation, and multilateralism—all of which carry demonstrable weight in the regions of the 'periphery', including the Gulf.[16]

Consequently, whereas power is typically defined in the realist sense in terms of military or 'hard' capabilities, middle power theory allows for a far more nuanced understanding. India is a prime example of this, given that its power abroad lies in a collective of both hard and soft tools, but more so the latter. As Joseph S. Nye claims, 'The soft power of a country rests primarily on three resources: its culture (in places where it is attractive to others), its political values (when it lives up to them at home and abroad), and its foreign policies (when they are seen as legitimate and having moral authority).'[17] In terms of India's relations with the Gulf, this can be seen in the spread of Indian culture, through the influence of its sizeable diaspora, or the popularity of Indian television shows throughout the region. The relationship is underpinned by India's long civilisational links with the region, the absence of an imperial legacy, and its contemporary articulation of a principled, non-interventionist foreign policy. Ostensibly, therefore, India's engagement with the Gulf appears to have great potential.

Yet so far, India has largely failed to live up to these expectations, as it is still attempting to carve out its niche in the broader international system. Its reluctance to engage proactively internationally, and by extension in the Gulf region, can be explained by a number of factors. First is its traditional foreign policy alignment of multilateralism. Electing to operate through a number of international institutions, including the United Nations (UN), the NAM, and, to a lesser extent, the World Trade Organisation (WTO), India has primarily adopted a consensus-based foreign policy approach.[18] Clearly there are exceptions, notably its unilateral pursuit of nuclear power, which culminated in the open testing of nuclear weapons in 1998, and also the issue of Kashmir, a territory it disputes with both Pakistan and China. But, on the whole, India has employed a restrained approach in the international system, which has limited the apparent potential of its foreign policy. As India emerges as an increasingly important international actor, this is perhaps its primary challenge: how to outline a more pro-active, rather than reactive, outlook. Sunil Khilnani refers to this when he notes:

> Historically, India has tended to position itself somewhere between the powerful and the powerless, the rich and the poor—and between contending ideological

groups. Its primary mode of exercising autonomy in the international domain has been negative: refusing to participate in alignments, treaties and markets which it viewed as skewed in favour of the more powerful. This was perhaps an extension of the Gandhian strategy of boycotts and fasts; as Nehru put it in the mid-1950s: 'Asian strength exists in the negative sense of resisting.'[19]

Secondly, the construction of a coherent foreign policy vision has been undermined by domestic institutional weaknesses. As Manjari Chatterjee Miller argues, 'New Delhi's foreign policy decisions are often highly individualistic—the province of senior officials responsible for particular policy areas, not strategic planners at the top. As a result, India rarely engages in long-term thinking about its foreign policy goals, which prevents it from spelling out the role it aims to play in global affairs.' Moreover, Chatterjee Miller notes that 'Indian foreign-policy makers are insulated from outside influences, such as think tanks, which in other countries reinforce a government's sense of its place in the world.'[20] This is compounded by the relatively small size of India's foreign service, which, with a population of over one billion, has the same number of diplomats as Singapore, whose citizens number a mere five million.[21]

Thirdly, the fact is that in essence India remains a developing country, facing multiple domestic challenges. About a third of India's population lives in poverty, while access to basic education, health care, and sanitation continues to pose significant obstacles. Oliver Stuenkel argues that 'India's rise has yet to translate into tangible benefits for the poor, most of whom live in rural areas. The Maoist Naxalite insurgency, affecting large swathes of the country, has rightly been identified by the government as '... India's most serious security concern, sapping the government's authority to take the country forward. Yet, the insurgents' continued presence can be explained precisely because growth has not been sufficiently distributive.'[22] These significant domestic weaknesses clearly undermine the projection of Indian influence abroad.

Finally, India's own internal assessments about its rise are perhaps less optimistic than those prevalent in the West. Chatterjee Miller notes that 'the Indian elite fears that the notion of the country's rise is a Western construct, which has unrealistically raised expectations for both Indian economic growth and the country's international commitments. As one senior official with experience in the prime minister's office said, the West's labelling of India as a rising power is "a rope to hang ourselves".'[23] This is reminiscent of the case of Japan, which prior to the 2000s was widely touted in the West as the next global superpower, leading the charge into the 'Asian century'. China, as one of India's ascendant contemporaries, is similarly the subject of fevered speculation about the nature of its development and its future global role. Rising assessments of international actors are often followed by increased expectations, or indeed demands, for international engagement. While India already contributes significantly, for example to UN peacekeeping operations worldwide, the concern is that, if labelled as a leading power, it may be forced to assume ever more international responsibilities.[24] Again, this is of particular relevance to the Gulf, given the multiple crises under way across the wider region, whether in Syria or Iraq, Libya, or Yemen.

Ultimately, the challenge for India lies in the transition from middle-power to great-power status which it is eventually expected to make. As Charalampos Efstathopoulos argues:

> India appears to be stuck in an intermediate position of ambivalence, struggling on the one hand to reach out for strategic partnerships with major powers but simultaneously attempting to maintain non-aligned status. This ambivalence is magnified by the heightened expectations fuelled by external factors such as notions of hegemonic decline and emergence of multipolarity which, simply put, generate collective expectations and preferences for a major power role that India is not yet in a position to deliver.[25]

As such, India's challenge is to develop a 'more positive conception, and exercise, of power'.[26] The question remains whether India has the capacity and, perhaps more importantly, the desire to become a great power. One of the more obvious contexts for the testing of this proposition is the Persian Gulf region. This is the one area where one would expect an increasingly assertive Indian presence, precisely because of India's long-standing ties with the region, and, moreover, because of its ever-growing dependence on it particularly as a source of energy and remittance flows.

India and the Gulf: the foundations of the relationship

While India's connections to the Gulf region date back some four thousand years, emerging along ancient trade routes, a more direct relationship was established in the early nineteenth century, when the British assumed control over the Gulf sheikhdoms that flanked the maritime route to India to secure the 'jewel in the crown' of the British Empire. From 1819 through to 1947, the Gulf states were administered from British India through a Political Resident based in Bushehr on the Persian coast.[27] James Onley notes that 'Britain maintained its informal empire in the Gulf in order to protect British India and its trade and communication routes. By offering a series of treaties through which Britain became responsible for the maritime protection of the Gulf sheikhdoms, Britain was able to get the local rulers to collaborate in the pacification of the Gulf and in the later exclusion of foreign influences that threatened British India.'[28] This inevitably fostered deepening interactions—primarily economic, but also socio-cultural—between India and the Gulf states. One of the legacies of this is reflected in the fact that the Indian rupee was considered legal tender in Oman, Kuwait, Bahrain, Qatar, and the Trucial States, which now form the United Arab Emirates (UAE), until the early 1960s.[29]

In the twenty-first century, India's relationship with the Gulf is primarily driven by a range of economic and sociocultural variables. These dynamic, evolving elements shape the nature of the contemporary relationship, which has been catalysed in recent years not only by India's own emerging international profile, but also by that of the Gulf states themselves. Over the last decade, the Gulf states have become increasingly important regional actors in their own right. The examples of Qatar and the UAE are of particular relevance here, alongside the traditional mainstay regional power of Saudi Arabia. Powered by their vast hydrocarbon revenues, these states have actively attempted to shape the broader regional configuration, for example during the events of the Arab Spring of 2011, whether in Libya, Egypt, or Yemen. Similarly spurred by an ascendant economy, India has so far adopted a relatively circumspect stance in the region, being far less intrusive than, say, the United States or Russia in terms of regional politics. In the main, India has focused on consolidating and, in many cases, augmenting its existing relationships with the GCC states.

As in centuries past, the bedrock of the Indian–Gulf relationship is predominantly economic in nature. Indian Prime Minister Manmohan Singh articulated this in 2005, when he described the Gulf region as 'part of our natural economic hinterland'.[30] Energy, specifically hydrocarbons, dominates this exchange. India imports approximately 80 per cent of its oil from the Gulf, when one includes Iran, Iraq, and Yemen, with three of the GCC states among its top five suppliers. Saudi Arabia alone provides around 20 per cent of India's oil, as such being its largest supplier, followed by Iraq, Venezuela, Kuwait, and the UAE.[31] Qatar, moreover, serves as the principal supplier of liquefied natural gas (LNG) to India, accounting for up to 85 per cent of total LNG imports since 2004.[32] Rahul Roy-Chaudhury notes: 'The Gulf is thus acknowledged as an "indispensable pillar of India's energy security". Consequently, any disruption of energy supplies imperils Indian economic growth and security.'[33] Over the last decade, overall trade volumes between

India and the GCC have increased rapidly. In 2014, the Economist Intelligence Unit found that 'GCC exports to India have increased by 43 percent annually over the last decade, the highest rate with any major trade partner, and imports from India have increased by 26 percent.'[34] To put this in perspective, exports to India currently account for 11 per cent of total GCC exports, whereas as recently as 2005 this figure was a mere 2 per cent.[35] Thus, if one considers the GCC as a single economic bloc, it constitutes India's largest trading partner, more so than the EU, the United States, or the Association of Southeast Asian Nations (ASEAN). While energy clearly dominates trade between India and the GCC, a gradual diversification of the economic relationship is under way. This is particularly evident in the case of the UAE, whose oil exports to India now account for less than half of its total exports to the country. Correspondingly, Indian investment has played a significant role in the UAE's economic rise, with India constituting the third-largest investor in the country.[36] A more diverse trade volume also characterises India's relationships with Oman and Bahrain, with India investing in a billion-dollar fertiliser plant in Oman.[37] And increasingly the GCC states are investing in India in areas such as power, metallurgy, and construction, although at present this investment is dominated by the UAE, which contributes around 80 per cent of total Gulf investment in India. As a whole, though, levels of Gulf investment in India, while increasing rapidly on an annual basis, still remain minimal in terms of overall FDI in the country.[38]

This economic relationship is underpinned by the substantial numbers of Indian expatriates in the Gulf, who constitute a significant sociocultural bridge. As the Gulf's largest expatriate community, the Indian diaspora there also constitutes the single largest concentration of Indians outside the country itself.[39] Interestingly, around 70 per cent of Indian expatriates in the Gulf originate from a single state, Kerala, with the state of Maharashtra also being highly represented. This concentration inevitably results in a disproportionate influence on Indian domestic politics, and issues affecting the Indian diaspora in the Gulf are prominent at the local level.[40] Saudi Arabia has the largest Indian expatriate population at 2.8 million, followed by the UAE (2.6 million), Kuwait (762,000), Oman (705,000), Qatar (500,000), and finally Bahrain (350,000).[41] In the UAE and Bahrain, Indian expatriates constitute approximately a third of the total population, and in Qatar around a quarter, thus far outnumbering the local national populations.[42] As mentioned previously, Indian expatriates in the GCC account for almost half of India's total inward flow of remittances, at around $32 billion annually.[43] The UAE alone is the source of $15 billon, considerably more than the $11 billion originating from the Indian diaspora in the United States.[44] As the largest recipient country of remittances globally, this clearly has a substantial economic impact within India itself, even more so when one considers that this amount is broadly equivalent to the total amount of annual FDI in the country.[45] And it is this expatriate population that has provided India with the greatest impetus for a more assertive regional stance. This is reflected in the mass evacuations of Indian nationals from various conflict zones across the region. An early example occurred during the first Gulf war of 1990–1, when the Indian government was forced to evacuate around 100,000 Indians from Kuwait and Iraq.[46] More recently, around 15,000 Indians were evacuated from Libya in 2011, and 4,640 from Yemen in 2015.[47] As a result of its large Gulf diaspora, the Indian state has a direct, vested interest in the stability of the GCC and the broader region.

With regard to Indian expatriates in the Gulf, Roy-Chaudhury raises an important point when he notes, 'According to resident Indian ambassadors, they are considered a "preferred community" in the Gulf, and indeed a "factor for stability" in the region, due to their expertise, law-abiding tendencies and non-involvement in local or regional politics'.[48] The last characteristic is key. The extremely high percentage of expatriate workers in the Gulf states has long been perceived as a potential domestic threat. This was evidenced during the 1990 invasion of Kuwait by Saddam Hussein's Iraq. As a result of the Palestine Liberation Organisation's (PLO) support of Hussein, Palestinian workers were expelled en masse from Kuwait and also from Saudi Arabia. While primarily a punitive measure, this reflected a broader, continuing fear on the part of the Gulf monarchies, of seditious political ideologies with the potential to challenge their legitimacy. This was true of pan-Arabism, both in its Nasserite and Ba'athist manifestations, and is now increasingly so with political Islam, particularly the variety associated with the Muslim Brotherhood.[49] As a result, Indian nationals are regarded by the Gulf states as less of a potential threat than many other expatriate nationalities, because they are not perceived as politically or ideologically subversive.

Finally, an important but often overlooked determinant of India's policy towards the Gulf, and the broader Middle East, is its own substantial Muslim minority population, the second largest in the world after Indonesia's. Perhaps more significantly, given the sectarian divisions that increasingly characterise the contemporary Middle East, India has one of the largest Shi'a Muslim populations in the world after Iran, at around 16 million.[50] Moreover, owing to high population growth, India's Muslim population as a whole is projected to become the largest in the world over the next fifteen years.[51] This has had a significant impact on India's relationship with the Gulf and the broader region over the years. Kumaraswamy argues:

> As the second largest Islamic society after Indonesia, the opinions and perceptions of Indian Muslims have contributed to the overall direction of its Middle East policy. Writing in the early 1980s, Theodore Wright drew a parallel between Indian Muslims and the American Jewish community and their influence upon the Middle East policies of both countries ... In both cases, an ethno-national community that has strong links to, and involvement with, the region wields considerable influence in the development of foreign policy. Though not as organized as the Jewish community in the US, the Indian Muslims constitute about a sixth of the national population. Key states like Uttar Pradesh, which holds 80 seats in the 543-member Lok Sabha (House of the People, or the lower house of Indian parliament), have sizeable Muslim electorates.[52]

India's Muslim population—specifically the Shi'a—was cited as a determining factor by Prime Minister Singh, amid international pressure on India to vote in favour of imposing sanctions against Iran at the International Atomic Energy Agency (IAEA) in 2005. Singh claimed, 'We have other factors [to consider] with a sizeable element of the Shi'a population in our country. We have the world's second largest Shi'a population in our country. So we have to weigh all these factors.'[53] His statement reflects the influence of this domestic constituency on Indian foreign policy formulation, which is of particular relevance with regard to the Gulf and indeed the Middle East. For instance, one of the major impediments to the development of India's now vibrant relationship with Israel in the 1990s was opposition from Indian Muslims. This was explicitly acknowledged by Jaswant Singh, then Foreign Minister, who explained in 2000 that 'India's Israel policy became a captive to domestic policy that came to be unwittingly an unstated veto.'[54]

It is therefore primarily economic factors, in the form of energy, trade, and expatriate labour, as well as important sociocultural links, that drive India's engagement with the region. This has manifested in a growing Indian military presence in the Gulf, precisely for the purpose of securing these interests, in particular the supply of energy. As the Indian Foreign Minister, Salman Khurshid, said in 2013:

> The region sits astride strategic Sea Lines of Communications (SLOCs) and any disruption to these SLOCs can have a serious impact on the Indian economy, including in terms of energy supplies. It is important to keep the region out of bounds for pirates and other nefarious non-state actors. India has the capabilities

and the will to not only safeguard India's own coastline and island territories, but also contribute to keeping our region's SLOCs open and flowing.[55]

To date, India has sought to achieve this primarily through bilateral security relationships with the individual GCC states, for example Saudi Arabia, the UAE, Qatar, and Oman, with each of which it has conducted an array of joint exercises, military training, and defence cooperation, primarily in the naval sphere.[56] One of the more comprehensive examples of these 'strategic partnerships' was India's 2011 Agreement on Security Cooperation with the UAE, which outlined joint measures to counter 'terrorism, organized crime, drug trafficking, weapons smuggling, money laundering, economic crimes and cyber crimes'.[57] This is indicative of the relative depth of India's relationship with the UAE across a range of economic and sociocultural fields. Yet, overall, India's physical presence in the region remains underdeveloped, at least relative to the size of its interests in the region.

India and the Gulf: the contemporary regional context

India's policy in the Gulf is symptomatic of its overall foreign policy. Its economy, population, and military point to its status as a rising power. In practice, however, India has yet to articulate a truly coherent, overarching vision for its role in the international system. This is particularly pronounced in the case of the Gulf, given India's long historical links with the region, its multifaceted relationships with a range of actors both in the Gulf and the broader Middle East, and its considerable strategic interests there. India has variously identified the Persian Gulf as a 'vital', 'legitimate', or 'primary' area of interest in official documents, in view of the critical economic considerations of energy, trade, and expatriates.[58] And yet, this primacy has not manifested in actual strategic or policy terms. Roy-Chaudhury has observed that 'India lacks an integrated perspective on the energy, trade, expatriate, political, defence and security dimensions of its Gulf links. Although the bilateral relationships with Saudi Arabia, Oman and Qatar have been elevated to the level of a "strategic partnership", there is no discernible impact in terms of top-level policy attention to these countries, who join a group of 25 with such a status.'[59] This can be seen in contrast to India's 'Look East' policy, introduced in the early 1990s under Prime Minister P.V. Narasimha Rao, which initiated a reorientation towards both South and South East Asia. This long-standing policy was recently reaffirmed by Prime Minister Narendra Modi, who called for a renewed 'Act East' policy.[60]

What are the reasons for this lack of engagement? First and foremost, as part of India's 'extended neighbourhood', the Gulf is denied the priority placed by India on its 'near neighbourhood', which features a host of more pressing security challenges from China, Pakistan, and Afghanistan. It is ultimately the nature of its immediate geostrategic environment that poses the biggest obstacle to India's ability to project its power in the Gulf, given that its smaller rival, Pakistan, and its larger rival, China, require its constant attention. As Efstathopoulos argues, 'The geo-strategic triangle between India, Pakistan, and China constructs an intersubjective psychology of antagonism in the interactions of the three states, obliging India to constantly engage in realist exercises of counterbalancing, military build-up, and counter-insurgency, and often transferring the realist power game to India's smaller neighbours.'[61] Pakistan's status as an Islamic country, reflected in its membership of the Organisation of Islamic Cooperation (OIC), has long complicated Indian calculations towards the Gulf. Despite its own substantial Muslim population, India has been prevented from joining the OIC because of Pakistani opposition; the latter has sought to use the OIC to internationalise the issue of Kashmir. China's recent announcement of a $46 billion development initiative linking Xinjiang in north-west China with the port city of Gwadar in south-west Pakistan, as part of a multifaceted China–Pakistan Economic Corridor (CPEC), clearly has significant implications for India in the near future, not least because of the substantial deepening of the Chinese–Pakistani relationship that this represents.[62]

Secondly, India's overtures to the West, and the United States in particular, have taken precedence in recent years. Over the last decade or so, India's relationship with the United States has become increasingly close.[63] This was evidenced by the George W. Bush administration's civil nuclear cooperation deal with India in 2005, followed by the Obama administration's designation of India as a 'rising power' and, moreover, a 'strategic partner'.[64] Crucially, the United States has sought to position India as the 'lynchpin' of its efforts to counter China, particularly in the context of South East Asia. However, India has sought to resist this designation, given that, while it perceives China as a threat, it also shares common interests with it, not least the desire to 'democratise' the international order.[65] With reference to the Gulf, the impact of India's growing relationship with the United States was reflected in its refusal to condone the Iranian nuclear programme from 2005 onwards, a reversal of previous policy, despite significant domestic opposition and also largely positive relations with Iran itself.

Thirdly, a crucial point is raised by C. Raja Mohan, who notes that 'Unlike South East Asia, where a strong mechanism for regional cooperation existed in the form of ASEAN, there was no institutional framework in the Middle East that could routinize India's engagement with the region. The political initiative, therefore, had to come from India.'[66] This feeds into the previous discussion of India's innate preference for multilateral approaches, which correspondingly blunts the impetus for unilateral initiatives. Needless to say, a more substantive Indian role in the Gulf would require a clearly defined grand strategy and also the willingness to implement it. This would inevitably alienate other regional powers. To date, India has sought, largely successfully, to maintain relations with a diverse range of actors in the Middle East, often inimically opposed, from Saudi Arabia to Iran to Israel. This was stated explicitly by Shivshankar Menon, India's National Security Adviser, in 2014: 'We have stayed out of these dichotomies, tried to insulate ourselves and our people from growing extremism and radicalism in the region, and worked with all the major actors to defend our security and economic interests. We may be one of the few powers able to do so with Iran, Saudi Arabia, Egypt, and Turkey, all at the same time. This balancing is not easy or pretty but it is necessary.'[67] A more prominent, proactive Indian role in the region would most likely undermine the viability of this stance.

Finally, India is clearly reluctant to assume a leading security role in the Gulf, given the multiple, complex crises currently under way in the broader region—Egypt, Libya, Syria, and Yemen figure most prominently. This was articulated by India's Foreign Minister, Salman Khurshid, in 2013: 'We have never played the classical role of intervening with military assistance in the same way that the US has been doing. Because of the philosophical constraints that we impose on ourselves, we don't see ourselves as a replacement for any other power. We certainly don't believe that the presence of any other power, such as China or Japan, or what have you, would necessarily contribute to the security of the region.'[68] At a time when there is a widely held perception of American disengagement from the Gulf and the Middle East, with powers such as Saudi Arabia and Iran duelling for regional hegemony, and the GCC states apparently seeking new security partners to counter Iran in the region, India would seem like an obvious candidate.[69] Yet India ultimately remains deferent to the United States' leadership of the regional security architecture.

Conclusion

The challenge for India lies in defining a more proactive, rather than strictly reactive, role in the Gulf. Beyond this, the challenge lies in assuming a more assertive presence, as compared with the subsidiary role it has largely practiced, deferring to the United States on important regional security matters, despite clearly divergent interests in some instances. One example of this is Iran, with whom India has a long-standing bilateral relationship.[70] There are many reasons to favour India as a rising power in a region long dominated by external actors, not least because it may lead to a more positive conception of regional security. Currently, the practice of regional politics is based very much on realist principles of force. In no small part, this has been perpetuated by the United States, which, as the regional security guarantor, has repeatedly used force to preserve stability and its interests in the region, for example in the Gulf wars of 1991 and 2003.

Could India's traditional stance of non-alignment and, more importantly, its contemporary emphasis on multilateralism, diplomacy, and negotiation contribute to a redefinition of the security architecture in the Gulf? A more multilateral approach to regional security could plausibly benefit the myriad conflicts and crises ongoing throughout the region. This is underscored by India's long-standing cultural links with the Gulf, spanning thousands of years, its legacy of colonial rule, and subsequently ardently anti-imperialist stance, which could potentially render India's engagement with the Gulf a new chapter in the region's history. Yet the question remains whether the Gulf states themselves truly perceive India as a viable international actor in the Gulf, one capable of counterbalancing the United States, Russia, and China, not to mention regional actors such as Saudi Arabia and Iran. Nevertheless, India is clearly a rising power in the Gulf. Ultimately, the question remains whether Indian policymakers will acknowledge this and adopt a commensurate role in regional affairs.

7

THE RISE OF ISIS

IRAQ AND PERSIAN GULF SECURITY

Nussaibah Younis

The rise of the Islamic State in Iraq and Syria (ISIS) prompted a year of soul-searching and renewed collective action for the six Gulf Cooperation Council (GCC) states, faced with a profound new challenge to regional security on their very doorstep. When the militant group made its extraordinary advances in Iraq in June 2014, the GCC was mired in internal conflict among states with different ideological responses to the Arab Spring. But the appearance of a sudden threat to collective security interests led the GCC to pull together, despite its disagreements, and to pursue its plans for a shared defence architecture with renewed vigour. An early commitment to the international anti-ISIS coalition, however, gave way to scepticism as it became increasingly clear that the United States was pursuing a limited, Iraq-first agenda that did not have the capacity to tackle the Syrian civil war. This scepticism has been compounded by the increasingly visible role that the Iranian Revolutionary Guards have played on the ground in Iraq, by the agreement reached in July 2015 at the climax of the Iranian nuclear negotiations, and by the perceived role that Iran has played in supporting the Houthi rebellion in Yemen. As a result, the threat posed by ISIS has quickly been eclipsed by the threat that many GCC states feel is presented by growing Iranian dominance in the region. Renewed GCC security cooperation is, therefore, becoming increasingly centred on countering Iranian influence, rather than on supporting the fight against ISIS.

GCC disunity before the rise of ISIS

In the months before the resurgence of ISIS in Iraq, the GCC was in disarray. Saudi, Emirati, and Bahraini frustrations with Qatar's continued support for Islamists in the Middle East and North Africa led to an unprecedented public spat among the GCC members, in a precursor to a second rift in 2017 that featured the same three countries, plus Egypt, against Qatar. The three states withdrew their ambassadors from Doha, citing Qatar's continued support of groups 'threatening the security and stability of the GCC'.[1] This split was based on fundamental differences in the threat perceptions of these Gulf states.[2] While Saudi Arabia, the UAE, and, to some extent, Bahrain have seen political Islamism as an ideological threat to their own political legitimacy, Qatar instead sees it as an opportunity to bolster its power and influence in the region. The turmoil of the Arab uprisings was largely interpreted by Saudi Arabia and its Gulf allies as a threat that needed to be actively managed and mitigated, while Qatar took the opportunity to further expand its cooperation with Islamist actors in the region. Qatar's willingness to act contrary to interests that Saudi Arabia and its allies believed to be crucial to their regime security placed enormous pressure on existing ideological cleavages within the GCC, leading to the open display of anger witnessed in the early months of 2014.

Besides these escalating ideological tensions, the GCC had for decades failed to progress significantly towards one of its key objectives, namely the development of an effective, collective security architecture.[3] GCC states' ability to lay the groundwork for an integrated ballistic missile defence system is a case in point. The lack of trust among the Gulf states means that the level of information-sharing and intelligence integration fundamental to missile defence has not been achieved.[4] Differences in threat assessments, mistrust, and poor communication and institutional structures have all hampered the ability of Gulf states to plan for their collective security.

The rise of ISIS as a threat to Gulf security

It was in a context of acrimony and stagnation among GCC member states that ISIS made its lightning advance from the Syria–Iraq border region to capture Mosul in June 2014. The ability of this group, born of al-Qaeda in Iraq, to conquer Iraq's second largest city and to advance rapidly towards Baghdad and into Diyala was a startling wake-up call for the Arab Gulf states. The ISIS advance across western Iraq was judged a critical threat by the entire GCC, and the 'level of alertness of security forces in Gulf Arab states' was raised to its highest level.[5] Like al-Qaeda before it, ISIS has reserved a distinct viciousness for its rhetoric against the Gulf monarchies, believing them to be particularly treacherous in their betrayal of Islam. In November 2014 an audio recording, believed to be released by the ISIS leader Abu Bakr al-Baghdadi, called on Saudis to launch attacks against their own government: 'O sons of al-Haramayn ... the serpent's head and the stronghold of the disease are there ... draw your swords and divorce life, because there should be no security for the Saloul.'[6] Beyond their portrayal of the Gulf monarchies as un-Islamic, ISIS depicts them also as a conduit for corrosive Western influence and dominance over the Muslim world. Abu Muhammad al-Adnani, a spokesman for ISIS, called the leaders of Saudi Arabia 'guard dogs for the Jews, and a stick in the hands of the crusaders to be used against Islam'.[7] In the face of these deliberate attempts to undermine their legitimacy as rulers and to radicalise their populations, GCC states have been extremely concerned. In November 2014, ISIS threats against the Gulf materialised as eight Shi'as were shot dead by gunmen in a mosque in Saudi Arabia's Shi'a-dominated Eastern Province. Saudi Arabia's Interior Ministry uncovered evidence that the attack was linked to ISIS,[8] and in an audio recording released by ISIS the following month Saudi citizens were explicitly called on to conduct further attacks on the Shi'a province.[9]

The spectacular advances that ISIS made in Iraq also enabled the group to radicalise and attract foreign fighters from across the Gulf, raising fears that returning jihadists could mount attacks in GCC countries, as happened after the return of al-Qaeda fighters from Afghanistan to Saudi Arabia in 2002. Though it is difficult to measure accurately the numbers of foreign fighters that have joined the conflicts in Syria and Iraq, the International Centre for the Study of Radicalisation and Political Violence estimates that up to 2,500 Saudi nationals have joined militant Islamist groups in Iraq and Syria.[10] The conflicts in Iraq and Syria have attracted the largest number of foreign fighters from Muslim countries seen in any conflict since 1945, and they are thought to surpass the estimated 20,000 who travelled to the war in Afghanistan in the 1980s.[11] Saudi Arabia's Crown Prince Salman clearly stated his concerns: 'We are concerned because we have not done enough to protect our nation from extremism, and its youths from militancy and radicalism, leading some to adopt violence and replace the doctrine of tolerance with that of takfir.'[12] The problem of local radicalisation came to the fore again in January 2015 when suspected ISIS militants attacked a location on the border between Iraq and Syria, killing three Saudi border guards. Saudi Arabia arrested three Saudi citizens for links to the attack, and sources in the Saudi Interior Ministry alleged that at least three of the four attackers were themselves Saudi nationals.[13]

Part of the difficulty of countering jihadist narratives is related to the wider identity crisis developing in the Sunni Muslim world. The popular movements that had challenged long-standing authoritarian rulers in the region raised questions about how the Gulf rulers could maintain and strengthen their legitimacy, especially at a time when political Islam was challenging the basis on which these governments rule. Paranoia in Saudi Arabia and the UAE about the Muslim Brotherhood, which was listed by both as a terrorist organisation in March 2014, played into the same fears prompted by ISIS, namely of being eclipsed or undermined by political movements with a stronger appeal to Islamic legitimacy than their own.[14] ISIS has simply been the latest in a series of challenges posed by the political crisis in the Sunni world, whose populations have sought to re-understand the basis of political legitimacy in Islam. Gregory Gause has argued that 'The Arab upheavals of 2011 were fundamentally about the basis of legitimate rule in the Arab world', and that this, combined with the electoral success of political Islamists, is what made them so 'unsettling to the Saudi leadership'.[15] The resurgence of violent Islamism, therefore, has aggravated threats already sharply felt by the Gulf states.

ISIS threat drives greater GCC security cooperation

In September 2014, Saudi Arabia's Foreign Minister, Saud al-Faisal, bluntly told the press, 'Today we face a very dangerous situation where terrorist cells have turned into armies ... that extend to all of Libya, Lebanon, Syria, Iraq, and Yemen. Faced with these dangerous facts, today we are required to take serious policy decisions to confront this vicious attack with full force. We need to move with assertive steps and fast.'[16] As part of this new 'assertive' response, the GCC regrouped and acted more strategically and in greater unison than at any time since the Gulf war of 1991. It appears that when the GCC faces significant threats to its collective security, it is able to rally together and to act in a more systematic and coherent manner than in relatively unthreatening times.[17] For one, the other members appear to have been able to rather swiftly decide to bury the hatchet with Qatar and resume normal diplomatic relations. On 25 June 2014, just fifteen days after the fall of Mosul, King 'Abdullah of Saudi Arabia congratulated the Qatari Emir on the anniversary of his accession to the throne, and a few weeks later warmly welcomed the Emir on a visit to the Saudi capital. An intense, emergency GCC meeting held in November 2014 gave the Gulf leaders another opportunity to thrash out their differences with Qatar, and they came to an agreement that resulted in Saudi Arabia, the UAE, and Bahrain returning their ambassadors to Doha later that month. As Alexey Khlebnikov notes, 'Islamic State advances in Iraq and Syria and the plummeting oil prices, which by mid-November were approximately US$70 per barrel, drove the need to be united.'[18]

The threat posed by ISIS also drove the GCC to push ahead with the establishment of common foreign and defence policies. Among the most important developments was the announcement that the Gulf would finally establish a joint military command based in Riyadh. The planned joint military command will coordinate efforts with the GCC's naval command in Bahrain and air command in Saudi Arabia.[19] GCC states are to donate capabilities to the rapid deployment force, which is designed to defend the Gulf from emerging threats in the region, and which may have the ability to target extremist cells.[20] The GCC has also decided to launch a joint police force, which will be hosted by the UAE, in an attempt to bolster information-sharing and to strengthen the region's ability to deal with cross-border threats.[21] And the Internal Security Pact between the Gulf states, which has been more than three decades in the making, has begun to be implemented, with a surge in cross-border arrests and detentions in 2015.[22]

Beyond strengthening their own military and security cooperation, GCC states have also been prepared to participate in the US-led anti-ISIS coalition, giving the United States the widest Arab public support it has received for a military operation in the region since the 1991 Gulf war. The Jeddah Communiqué, which was issued in September 2014 and which was signed by all the GCC states (among other Arab states), confirmed that participating states had agreed to join 'in the many aspects of a coordinated military campaign against ISIL'.[23] As the Qatari Emir Sheikh Tamim bin Hamad Al Thani put it in an interview with CNN's Christiane Amanpour, 'We've been asked by our American friends if we can join, and we did.'[24] The signatories of the Jeddah Communiqué even emphasised that the role played by regional states would be crucial to the success of this effort.[25] Saudi Arabia, the UAE, Qatar, and Bahrain have all participated in coalition air strikes against ISIS in Syria.[26]

After the United States, the UAE has conducted more air strikes than any other member of the anti-ISIS coalition and, according to the *Washington Post*, 'often strikes targets that are just as difficult and dangerous as those attacked by the Americans'.[27] What is more important than their contributions through direct air strikes, these countries have supported US efforts against ISIS by allowing US aircraft to deploy from bases in the Gulf, including al-Udeid Air Base in Qatar, al-Dhafra Air Base in the UAE, and ʿAli al-Salem Air Base in Kuwait.[28] The Gulf states have also been keen that their efforts against ISIS should not be dominated by military engagements, and have contributed substantially to the aid effort to provide for Iraqis displaced by the ISIS advance. Soon after the fall of Mosul, Saudi Arabia pledged to donate $500 million to the UN in order to address the humanitarian crisis in Iraq.[29] The amount was significantly more than the $312 million in emergency funds that the UN had called on the entire international community to provide. Kuwait contributed a further $10 million towards UN efforts to provide for displaced Iraqis,[30] and Qatar sent six aircraft with 300 tons of aid to the Iraqi cities hosting these refugees.[31]

Among the most significant responses of the Gulf to the rise of ISIS has been a renewed effort to crack down on the flows of funding from private Gulf citizens to jihadist organisations. This has been part of an apparent GCC effort to rehabilitate its public image in the Western world, in response to repeated accusations of moral, ideological, and financial support from the GCC for terrorist organisations, and to the reputational damage done by the GCC's support of the brutal crackdown against pro-democracy activists in Bahrain.

In a Brookings paper, Elizabeth Dickinson points out that from the start of the Syrian crisis, Kuwait 'emerged as a financing and organizational hub for charities and individuals supporting Syria's myriad rebel groups'.[32] Taking advantage of Kuwait's weak financial rules, private Kuwaiti donors have been able to use money transfers, exchange companies, and direct cargo shipments to transfer potentially hundreds of millions of dollars to various militant groups in Syria.[33] The US Undersecretary for Terrorism and Financial Intelligence, David Cohen, stated that Kuwait had become the 'epicenter of fundraising for terrorist groups in Syria', and that Kuwaiti fundraisers would 'openly advertise their ability to move funds to fighters in Syria'.[34] It has even been argued that the money flows from Salafists in Kuwait could have incentivised the growing religious conservatism of Syria's major rebel movements.[35] But since the advance of ISIS in Iraq, Kuwait's parliament has passed a strengthened financial crimes law that enhances the ability of Kuwaiti authorities to reduce terrorism financing.[36] Kuwait also arrested one of its citizens who had been listed by UN Resolution 2170 as a supporter of terrorism,[37] and vowed to pursue legal action against all Kuwaitis linked to terrorist financing.[38] On 27 October 2014, the Undersecretary of Kuwait's Ministry of Foreign Affairs further announced the creation of a special task force to combat terrorist financing.[39]

The remaining Arab Gulf states also demonstrated a renewed commitment to tackling the problem of citizens financing militant extremists. The GCC as a whole 'welcomed the Security Council Resolution of August 15, 2014,'[40] which, in terms of the binding Chapter VII of the UN Charter, declared that 'all States shall ensure that no funds, financial assets or economic resources are made available, directly or indirectly for the benefit of ISI, ANF [al-Nusra Front] or any other individuals, groups, undertakings and entities associated with Al-Qaida, by their nationals or by persons within their territory'.[41] In the Jeddah conference on terrorism, which was held in September 2014, Gulf states once again asserted that they would 'do their share in the comprehensive fight against ISIL', including by 'countering financing of ISIL and other violent extremists'.[42] In the days following this conference, Qatar passed a law to prevent charities from funnelling money to extremist groups, and the following month the UAE established a joint financial counter-terrorism force with the United States.[43] Although donations from the Gulf were only ever a small proportion of the wealth amassed by ISIS, it appears that by restricting this flow of funds, the Gulf has reduced the financial resources available to the extremist group. The Chief of Staff to the Kurdish Presidency, Fuad Hussein, said that the attempt by Gulf countries to stem the transfer of funds to ISIS was making a difference. 'I think gradually the financial resources are less than six or seven months ago', he said. 'We feel that we see it's weaker than six months ago.'[44]

Fall of Maliki heralds opportunity for stronger GCC–Iraq relations

In the early days after the fall of Mosul, the Gulf's willingness to act against ISIS was tempered by its belief that Iraq's Prime Minister, Nouri al-Maliki, was the source of the resurgent violence in Iraq and that any international military action would serve only to strengthen his grip on power. Relations between Maliki and the Gulf states, which had always been strained by Maliki's perceived sectarianism, reached rock bottom in late February 2014, just four months before the fall of Mosul, when Maliki claimed that the Gulf countries were responsible for the growing violence in Iraq. In a stunning interview with the news channel France 24, Maliki accused Qatar and Saudi Arabia of 'inciting and encouraging the terrorist movements' and of 'supporting them politically and in the media, of supporting them with money and by buying weapons for them'.[45] In the face of his plummeting legitimacy at home, it seems Maliki was trying to shore up support by blaming the Gulf states for the escalating violence in Iraq, but for them, after years of tense relations, this was the final straw. When Mosul fell to ISIS, the Gulf states were desperate to have the United States remove Maliki before it engaged in any military action in the country. Hamad bin Isa Al Khalifa, the King of Bahrain, said that his country opposed foreign intervention in Iraq,[46] while Saudi Arabia's King 'Abdullah stressed to US Secretary of State John Kerry that bringing about a new and inclusive Iraqi government was the absolute priority in addressing the rise of ISIS.[47] The Emirati Foreign Ministry stated that ISIS could not be defeated unless 'the exclusionary and sectarian policies' of the Iraqi government were addressed,[48] while Qatar's former ambassador to the United States warned that any military intervention on behalf of the Maliki government could be seen as an act of 'war' on Iraq's Sunni population.[49]

This equivocation about military action melted away when intense US diplomatic efforts, together with pressure from Iraq's clerical elite and assent from the Iranian leadership, brought about the resignation of Maliki in August 2014. With a new, and much more promising, Iraqi government in place, GCC states' rhetoric against ISIS hardened as they swung much more decisively behind US-led efforts to defeat the group. The rotating President of the GCC, Kuwait's Foreign Minister, Sabah Khaled Al Sabah, said on behalf of the group: 'We denounce vehemently the practices of those who use Islam as a pretext to kill and displace en masse Iraqis and Syrians.'[50] And in a communiqué after the GCC meeting held in August 2014, the GCC declared its assent to Security Council Resolution 2170 that condemned in the strongest terms 'gross, systematic and widespread abuse' of human rights by ISIS and the al-Nusra Front.[51] It could be argued that this shift, from opposition to any military action against ISIS towards full-throated support of it, was crucial to lending the anti-ISIS coalition legitimacy among the Arab and Muslim world. This could help to account for the fact that while 73 per cent of Arabs surveyed in the fall of 2014 believed that US foreign policy in the region was 'negative' or 'somewhat negative', 59 per cent of those surveyed nevertheless supported the coalition air strikes against ISIS.[52]

Soon after the instatement of Haider al-Abadi as the new Prime Minister of Iraq, there was somewhat more confidence and optimism among Gulf leaders that Iraq could be saved from ISIS, from sectarian governance, and from domination by Iran. In the GCC meeting held a few weeks after Abadi was designated as Iraq's new Prime Minister, a communiqué was issued which 'congratulated the Iraqi leadership, hoping the formation of the new Iraqi government will contribute to promoting national unity, and to the participation of all spectrums of the Iraqi society in the political, security and development process, thus contributing to the security, stability and sovereignty of Iraq, and to restoring it to its natural place in the Arab world'.[53] A fortnight later, in the Jeddah Communiqué, the GCC again 'hailed the formation of the new, inclusive Iraqi Government and expressed their support for the immediate steps it has pledged to take to advance the interests of all Iraq's citizens, regardless of religion, sect or ethnicity'. Furthermore, the GCC 'resolved to strengthen their support for the new Iraqi Government in its efforts to unite all Iraqis in combatting ISIL'.[54]

Beyond the positive rhetoric from the GCC states, action was taken both by Baghdad and the Gulf capitals to strengthen their long-dormant relationships. The new Iraqi President, Fuad Masum, spent two days in Saudi Arabia in November 2014 and discussed the possibility of Iraq joining the GCC as well as outlining ways in which Saudi Arabia could help to support the Iraqi government's fight against ISIS.[55] In January 2015, Saudi Arabia announced that it would reopen its embassy in Baghdad after a 25-year absence, and the Saudi Ambassador to Iraq duly took up his post in January 2016.[56] And the new King of Saudi Arabia, Salman bin 'Abdul 'Aziz Al Saud, invited Abadi to visit the kingdom, expressing 'Saudi Arabia's desire to open horizons of cooperation with Iraq'.[57] Qatar similarly 'opened new doors' to cooperation with Iraq, pledging to also reopen its embassy in Baghdad. The Qatari Emir, Sheikh Tamim bin Hamad Al Thani, received Fuad Masum in a successful visit in February 2015, after which the Iraqi President said that a 'unified Gulf vision' on strengthening relations with Iraq was 'beginning to take shape'.[58] In a similarly fruitful meeting between Abadi and the Kuwaiti Prime Minister, Sheikh Jaber Mubarak Al Sabah, in December 2014, talks led to Kuwait agreeing to suspend Iraqi payments of compensation to Kuwait (for the 1990 invasion) for one year, and to an additional 45 bilateral cooperation agreements.[59]

Fear of rising Iranian influence eclipses GCC support for anti-ISIS coalition

These promising advances in the relationship between Iraq and its Gulf neighbours were soon torpedoed by Gulf fears about the extent of Iranian involvement in Iraq's war against ISIS. Shortly after Iran assented to the removal of Maliki from power, it looked as though there might be an improvement in the hostile relations between many of the Gulf states and Iraq. In late August 2014, Iran's Deputy Foreign Minister for Arab Affairs met with Saudi Arabia's Foreign Minister, Prince Saud al-Faisal, in the highest-level meeting between the two countries since Iranian President Rouhani came to power.[60] But longstanding fears of Iranian dominance, in a region where the balance of power had been fundamentally altered by the 2003 overthrow of Saddam Hussein, reasserted themselves as Iran became increasingly visible in the training, equipping, and directing of Iraq's Shi'a militia forces in the war against ISIS. While perceptions of the threat posed by Iran differs among individual Gulf states, with countries like Qatar and Oman pursuing much more positive cooperation with Iran, the view of the majority of states in the GCC is that the spread of Iranian power is a significant threat both to the Gulf and to the wider region.

After the fall of Mosul, Iran was the first country to offer aid to the embattled Maliki government,[61] and Iran has been deeply involved in aiding the Iraqi war effort ever since. Iran, together with its Lebanese client, Hezbollah, has provided training, militant equipment, technical assistance, and strategic direction to the myriad Shi'a militias that have led the offensive against ISIS in Iraq, and Iran has even conducted its own air strikes against ISIS in the country.[62] Although Iran is thought to have only a few hundred military advisers in Iraq, they have played an extremely influential role in directing the fighting, as was symbolised by the ubiquitous presence of Qasim Soleimani, the head of Iran's Qods Force, at the front lines in Iraq.[63] One leader of the Badr militia said that Qasim Soleimani 'participates in the operation command center from the start of the battle to the end and the last thing [he] does is visit the battle's wounded in the hospital'.[64] An Iranian institute has estimated that US$16 billion in weapons transfers has been provided to Iraq since the fall of Mosul,[65] and US intelligence officers noted that Iran had deployed advanced rockets and missiles—similar to those it supplies to Hezbollah in Lebanon—to aid the Iraqi battle against ISIS in Tikrit.[66]

Both Iraqi and Kurdish politicians have acknowledged that the assistance offered by Iran has been crucial in protecting Erbil and Baghdad from ISIS. A senior Kurdish minister said that 'Iran was the first country that came to our aid' and added that in their policymaking the Kurdish cabinet needed to be 'mindful' of that fact.[67] Fuad Hussein, Chief of Staff to the Kurdish President, said similarly that Iran's influence in Iraq was 'rising', but added that 'Iran helped us, this is a fact'.[68] But while Iranian aid has been appreciated, Iraqi and Kurdish politicians have also been wary of the scope of Iran's ambitions inside the country. Iraq's Finance Minister, and former Foreign Minister, Hoshyar Zebari, pointed out that 'Iran really has influence' in Iraq and that it 'will try to expand that influence and try to control as much as it can'.[69] Referring to an interview in which an Iranian official called Baghdad the capital of an 'Iranian Empire', Zebari said that 'these comments are unacceptable' and were a 'humiliation' for Iraq and must be rejected.[70] A senior Kurdish minister also warned that the war against ISIS had 'given Iran free rein' in Iraq, and accused the Iranians of sitting 'above the [Iraqi] government'.[71] He feared that Iran was likely to 'push it too far' in its intervention in Iraq, and that this would draw in 'Gulf backers', who will 'drip-feed' support to Iraq's Sunnis.[72]

Many prominent Iraqi Sunnis have indeed implored the Gulf monarchies to step in to prevent the continued sectarianisation of the conflict in Iraq, to which they believe Iran is heavily contributing. Former Iraqi Vice-President, Tariq al-Hashemi, a Sunni, who spends much of his time in Doha after being forced to flee Iraq by the Maliki government in late 2011, complained that the Arab countries have 'left Iraqis alone' while 'Iranian power has been systematically increasing in Iraq'.[73] Hashemi admits that he has spent much time trying to convince the GCC to support Iraqi Sunnis, and says that he believes that their lack of support means that they 'bear responsibility' for Iran's takeover of Iraq.[74] Sheikh Jamaal al-Khamees, a Qatar-backed Sunni tribal leader and nephew of the notorious Sunni resistance leader Sheikh Harith al-Dhari, said that 'Qasim Soleimani and ISIS are the same' and that Iraqi Sunnis would refuse to fight ISIS if all they faced was the prospect of living under Iranian domination.[75] Al-Khamees said that 'Iran is the decision maker, not Abadi' in Iraq, and that the 'legitimate Sunni resistance have no choice except to be with ISIS, because it's either ISIS or Iran.'[76] Sheikh Nawaf Hemoud Al Maghames, another Iraqi tribal leader who has tried to win support from the Gulf states for the Iraqi Sunni cause, similarly stated that the Abadi government had failed to do anything except to 'bring Iran and Qasim Soleimani' into Iraq.[77]

These impassioned pleas from Iraqi Sunni advocates, together with reports of escalating Iranian military involvement in Iraq and perceptions of Iranian intervention in Yemen, have caused much consternation in Gulf capitals, with many seeing Iran as a more immediate threat to Gulf security than ISIS. In a joint press conference with Secretary of State John Kerry in March 2015, Saudi Foreign Minister Saud al-Faisal said, 'The situation in Tikrit is a prime example of what we are worried about. Iran is taking over the country.'[78] At a

123

GCC meeting the following week, the Gulf states rejected Iran's role in Iraq, calling for 'non-interference' in Iraq's internal affairs, and imploring Iraq to extend 'its sovereignty over all its territory'.[79] The level of Iranian influence in Iraq is deemed all the more threatening in Gulf capitals because of the wider role that Iran is playing in the region and because of the rapprochement between Iran and the United States over Iran's nuclear programme. Indeed, Saudi-led air strikes against the Houthi rebels in Yemen were launched just a week before negotiations over the Iranian nuclear programme reached their climax in Lausanne.

Iran has also supported the Assad government against Gulf-backed rebels in Syria since the start of the Syrian civil war, and has 'refused to countenance a meaningful political track on Syria'.[80] It has been argued that part of the reason the Gulf states were willing to participate in the US-led anti-ISIS effort was a hope that the military engagement would 'draw the U.S. into military action in Syria' against the Assad regime.[81] Those hopes have been dashed, as the United States has resolutely avoided any military confrontation with the Assad regime, and has inadvertently aided it by attacking its Islamist rivals. The Gulf states are extremely frustrated by the lack of a comprehensive US policy to address the civil war in Syria, and feel that the United States fails to understand that any attempt to defeat ISIS without addressing one of its root causes—the mass murder inflicted by the Assad regime—is destined to fail. The Gulf states have also been anxious that the ongoing negotiations over Iran's nuclear programme, which culminated in a framework agreement in April 2015 and a final comprehensive agreement in July, have blinded the United States to the immediate threats posed by expanding Iranian influence across the Middle East. Now that a comprehensive agreement has been reached, the Gulf states feel that they face the prospect of Iran, which is already heavily influential in Iraq, Lebanon, Syria, and Yemen, recovering its economic strength as sanctions are lifted and retaking its place as a legitimate member of the international community.[82]

Conclusion

The Gulf states must now confront an environment that they believe to be uniquely threatening, with the region's traditional security guarantor—the United States—playing a diminished leadership role during the Obama administration. Following the rise of ISIS, the GCC states patched up some of their political differences and came together to refocus on the substantial threats facing their collective security, although the areas of policy disagreement with Qatar remained unresolved and triggered renewed regional instability in the diplomatic standoff that began in June 2017. It is in this context that Saudi Arabia has been able to pull together an astounding military coalition to attack the Houthi rebels, who had been sweeping across Yemen with suspected Iranian support.[83] Although the Houthi rebellion in Yemen is a complex, domestically driven political crisis that poses little threat to most of the GCC countries involved in the military strikes, the prospect of further Iranian expansion has enabled Saudi Arabia to rally together a substantial, Arab-led military coalition to prevent the Houthis from taking over Yemen. In a joint statement, all the GCC states except Oman warned that the Houthi advances in Yemen were a 'major threat' to the region, and accused the Houthis of being 'backed by regional powers', in a naked reference to Iran.[84] Operation Decisive Storm, as the assault was labelled, pounded Yemen with air strikes for almost a month before Saudi Arabia announced a new phase, entitled Operation Restoring Hope, in which it was intended that air strikes would be limited to defensive activity and there would be a refocus on political negotiations, although the military phase of the operations continued and an attempted ceasefire in December 2015 failed to halt the fighting.[85] The extraordinary scope of the Saudi-led coalition is potential evidence of a new era in GCC politics, in which the Gulf feels that it has both the capacity and the responsibility to take a leading role in securing the region from growing Iranian power. This was also reflected in renewed efforts by Saudi Arabia—prior to the June 2017 Gulf crisis and ousting of Crown Prince Mohammed bin Nayef Al Saud—to resolve its differences with Qatar and Turkey with regard to the backing of Syrian rebels.[86] Reports indicate that Qatar is brokering talks between Turkey and Saudi Arabia about the possibility of substantially increasing support for the Syrian opposition and unifying many of the rebel groups, as Russia and Iran stepped up their support for the Assad regime during the summer and autumn of 2015.[87]

In 2015–16, the GCC showed once again that when its core interests were under threat it could pull together, resolve, or at least suppress its differences, and act in defence of its collective security. The renewal of the diplomatic crisis with Qatar in June 2017, just as ISIS was defeated in Mosul and surrounded in Raqqa, illustrated the difficulty of maintaining policy cohesion when the common threat to security was loosened. Despite the promising steps towards reconciliation with the Iraqi government, and a brief interlude in which the GCC and Iran seemed on the same side in Iraq, the continued advance of Iranian power across the region has once again emerged as the GCC's dominant security threat. In a region that felt all but abandoned by the Obama administration, the GCC has increasingly come to believe that if it is to avoid the region being pulled firmly into an Iranian orbit, it will have to mount its own defence. This has presented the incoming Trump administration with an immediate foreign policy challenge as officials attempt to rebuild damaged relationships with their Persian Gulf counterparts and ensure, at the very least, an alignment of interests with the perceptions and priorities of threats to regional security.

8

A REGIONAL GREAT GAME?

IRAN–SAUDI RELATIONS IN FLUX

Nader Entessar

As the two most salient regional powers in the Persian Gulf, Iran and Saudi Arabia have developed differing goals in their foreign policy objectives, which have presented both with serious challenges to their national security interests. The security dynamic that has arisen since the Iranian Revolution and establishment of the Islamic Republic of Iran in 1979 remains a source of regional volatility which manifests in a number of regional conflicts and flashpoints, with the war in Yemen that started in March 2015 being the latest and also the most direct instance of confrontation. Samuel Huntington has defined regional powers as countries that are 'preeminent in areas of the world without being able to extend their interests and capabilities as globally as the United States'.[1] In other words, a regional power's influence has inherent limits and is invariably subordinate to that of a great power or superpower. Furthermore, as Maxi Schoeman has noted, a regional power must be able to play a leadership role in maintaining regional security, and it should receive both regional and extra-regional acceptance of its security role. In order to exercise its leadership role effectively, Schoeman argues, a regional power must be capable of playing an active role as a peacemaker or stabiliser irrespective of the degree of amity or enmity between it and the other states in the region.[2] Similarly, Graham Fuller and John Arquilla define a regional power as a state whose policies significantly impact on the security and well-being of other states in the region.[3]

In the context of these descriptions, both Iran and Saudi Arabia can be considered regional powers that possess, to varying degrees, the ability to influence or lead countries within a specific geographic area. With a defence budget of US$80.8 billion in 2014, Saudi Arabia ranks third in the world in terms of expenditure on the military (behind the United States and China).[4] While the defence expenditure of Iran formed 2.9 per cent of the country's GDP on average during the years 1988–2014, that of Saudi Arabia formed 10.2 per cent.[5]

Of course, the efficacy of the regional roles of Iran and Saudi Arabia is determined by a variety of factors, including their national interests and motivations, the level of threat perception, the regional military balance, and the foreign and domestic political context.[6] That is, the level and degree of regional influence are not static but fluctuate with changing domestic, regional, and global political and strategic circumstances. These fluctuations have indeed characterised Iranian–Saudi relations and their regional foreign policies. This chapter examines a series of stages in the relationship between Iran and Saudi Arabia, and illustrates their implications for the volatile regional security landscape and balance of power in the Persian Gulf.

The hajj and Saudi–Iranian rivalry

The Iranian Revolution of 1978–9 was a seminal event in the history of the modern Middle East and, in the words of an American observer, the 'last great revolution' of our time.[7] The revolution's impact has certainly been felt beyond its immediate borders and has served as a catalyst for numerous challenges to the geopolitical order in the region. The Iranian Revolution was launched in the name of the oppressed (*mostazafan*) and it promised to transform not only power relations inside Iran but also to introduce a new era in world politics in which middle powers could successfully challenge the hegemony of the great powers and pursue a genuinely independent foreign policy. The revolution's mantra, 'neither East nor West', reflected the desire of the early revolutionaries to create a new Islamic regional order.

However, from the outset a myriad of security challenges confronted the newly established Islamic Republic of Iran. Some of these challenges were the result of the excessive radicalisation of the early years of the revolution, while others were the by-products of shifting alliances and changes in the constellation of power in both regional and global politics.

The Saudi reaction to the victory of the Iranian Revolution and the establishment of the Islamic Republic was characterised by a mixture of apprehension and cautious response. The pre-1979 regional security arrangement in which the Saudi monarchy played a cooperative, albeit a junior, role with Iran in maintaining a pro-Western and status quo-oriented environment in the Persian Gulf was shattered with the overthrow of the Pahlavi monarchy. The Iranian Revolution's Shi'a discourse was inevitably a source of unease for Saudi Arabia, which had long viewed itself as a bastion of Sunni conservatism with a strong anti-Shi'a orientation. Nonetheless, soon after the establishment of the Islamic Republic, Saudi Arabia dispatched a high-ranking delegation to Iran headed by the secretary general of the Jeddah-based Organisation of the Islamic Conference (now Organisation of Islamic Cooperation), congratulating Iran on its revolution. This 'goodwill' Saudi message was followed by King Khalid's statement that described the establishment of an Islamic government in Iran as a 'precursor for further proximity and understanding' between Tehran and Riyadh.[8] King Khalid's sentiments were echoed by Crown Prince Fahd as well.

This initial goodwill between Iran and Saudi Arabia soon gave way to acrimonious relations, highlighted by tense confrontations during the annual hajj pilgrimage. The divergent views of Iran and Saudi Arabia became marked when Ayatollah Khomeini, the founder of the Islamic Republic, opined that the hajj 'was not only a religious but also a political occasion' and thus the holding of demonstrations in 'disavowal of the polytheists' was an integral part of hajj ceremonies.[9] The anti-American and anti-Israeli tone of these demonstrations frightened the Saudi regime, which undertook measures to suppress them. Concomitantly, official Iranian discourse began to change by referring to Saudi Arabia as 'Hejaz' and the rulers of Saudi Arabia as the usurpers of Islam's holy places in Mecca and Medina.

In November 1979, a group of Salafi extremists seized Masjid al-Haram (the Holy Mosque) in Mecca. The siege, which lasted two weeks, was ultimately suppressed by Saudi security forces with French assistance. This violent episode was followed by a Shi'a uprising in November 1979 in the Eastern Province of Saudi Arabia. This led to an armed attack by Saudi forces on Shi'a communities, causing the death and injury of many Saudi Shi'a citizens. Ayatollah Khomeini denounced both the takeover of the Masjid al-Haram and the attack on the Shi'a as the work of 'American imperialism' and 'international Zionism', thereby further intensifying the deteriorating relations between Tehran and Riyadh. The Saudi authorities also reacted to demonstrations during the hajj pilgrimage by imposing a quota of 85,000 and 100,000 for Iranian pilgrims in 1982 and 1983, respectively. The situation improved somewhat when the Saudi authorities accepted 150,000 Iranian pilgrims during the 1984 hajj ceremonies. Concerns about the hajj continued to bedevil Iranian–Saudi relations for the next three years, but matters took a sharp turn for the worse on 31 July 1987, when 402 people were killed and several thousand pilgrims (including Khomeini's wife) were injured during a hajj demonstration. Many of the dead and the injured were Iranian pilgrims, including several women, old people, and the physically impaired. The Saudis claimed that the Iranians had instigated the riots, whereas Iran blamed the Saudi regime for unleashing heavily armed guards on defenceless Iranian pilgrims.

The 1987 hajj events had a profound impact on Iran's perception of Saudi Arabia, leading to a boycott of the hajj by Iran for two years and an escalation of the ideological war between Tehran and Riyadh. The hajj incident prompted Ayatollah Khomeini to call for the establishment of an international council of religious *ulema* to supervise Islam's holy places in Mecca and Medina. Nearly three decades after the events of 1987, the sentiments behind Ayatollah Khomeini's demands were reiterated in April 2015 by Ayatollah Seyyed Ahmad Khatami, a prominent conservative cleric and a member of the governing council of the Assembly of Experts. In Ayatollah Khatami's words, the 'al-Saud regime's indiscriminate killings of innocent Muslims in Yemen has removed any semblance of legitimacy for this regime to control Islam's most sacred places'.[10] Although the annual hajj pilgrimage no longer plays the polarising role it once did in Iranian–Saudi relations, it nevertheless remains an arena for rivalry between the two countries. In fact, during the 2015 hajj over 400 Iranian pilgrims were crushed to death in a major stampede that claimed the lives of a large number of pilgrims from many countries. Some in Iran, especially those associated with 'hardline elements', placed the blame on the Saudi government and demanded that the Iranian government respond with vigour against the Saudis. However, the pragmatists in the Iranian government, especially the Foreign Ministry, chose a diplomatic path to defuse the crisis.

Saudi Arabia's support of Saddam Hussein's invasion of Iran and its subsequent backing of Iraq during the Iran–Iraq War between 1980 and 1988 influenced strongly the development of Iran's military thinking and fighting strategy and its long-term view of the Saudi threat. The resulting decentralisation of decision-making, enabling field commanders to improvise tactics and strategies to confront the better-organised and larger Iraqi force, was arguably the most important change in Iranian military doctrine since the inception of the modern armed forces in the late 1920s. In fact, Iran's present defence doctrine 'active deterrence',[11] to use President Rouhani's term, is structured around the concept of tactical decentralisation of decision-making in military affairs. Furthermore, strengthening regular units of the Revolutionary Guards (*pasdaran*) and allowing them to function independently of, but in tandem with, the regular armed forces have introduced tactical innovations and a degree of mobility that were previously lacking in Iraq's armed forces.[12] The lessons of the Iran–Iraq War for the Iranian military would be invaluable in any future regional conflict.

In recent years, Iran has tried to narrow the defence gap created by the massive conventional military build-up of its Gulf neighbours, especially Saudi Arabia, by developing a robust indigenous military industry, particularly in missile development. However, the striking disparity between Iran's conventional weapons and those of its regional adversaries would require innovation in battlefield strategies and fighting tactics in case of a military conflict with a regional power with superpower backing.[13]

Iran's nuclear issue and the Saudi nexus

Iran's nuclear programme has long been a source of contention between Iran and Saudi Arabia. However, this issue must be contextualised within the broader connections between the nuclear and non-nuclear variables in the region. As was expected, the dialogue between Tehran and Washington that began in 2013 and the prospect of an agreement between Iran and the 5+1 countries (the five permanent members of the UN Security Council and Germany) perturbed Saudi Arabia. Some Saudi officials conveyed the impression of a US betrayal in 'caving in' to Iran, even though officially the Saudi government welcomed the nuclear deal and initially viewed it as a 'step forward'. An official Saudi 'cabinet statement' issued on 25 November 2013 read: 'If there is goodwill, then this agreement could be an initial step toward reaching a comprehensive solution for Iran's nuclear program if that leads to the removal of weapons of mass destruction, especially nuclear weapons, from the Middle East and the Arab Gulf.'[14]

However, as the details of the November 2013 interim nuclear framework and the nature of compromises on both sides became more apparent, the subsequent reaction by the Saudis turned more hostile and propelled a whole new wave of Saudi 'Iranophobia'. An example of this hostility was an opinion article by the Saudi ambassador to London, Mohammed bin Nawaf Al Saud, a member of the royal family, who expressed renewed fear of Iran's nuclear ambitions and warned that the kingdom would not 'sit idly by' if the Iranians were allowed to acquire nuclear weapons.[15]

Another official, 'Abdullah al-Askar, chairman of the Shura Council's foreign affairs committee, stated: 'I am afraid Iran will give up something on [its nuclear programme] to get something else from the big powers in terms of regional politics. And I'm worrying about giving Iran more space or a freer hand in the region. The government of Iran, month after month, has proven that it has an ugly agenda in the region, and in this regard no one in the region will sleep and assume things are going smoothly.'[16] Such comments reflect the fact that many in Saudi Arabia view the primary threat as rooted in Iran's perceived intervention in regional conflicts through support for local proxies, rather than in Tehran's nuclear programme per se.

Clearly, the perception of a Western compromise in allowing Iran's continued possession of a nuclear facility played a central role in shaping the perception of the Saudis and other conservative Arab states. Essentially, the Geneva agreement (the Joint Comprehensive Plan of Action, or JCPOA) was viewed by the Saudis as a double-edged sword, one that capped and rolled back the Iranian nuclear programme and, yet at the same time, set into motion a new dynamic in regional affairs that spurred an increase in Iran's power and status.[17] The petrochemical sector in Gulf Cooperation Council (GCC) states, for example, expressed concern about a possible resurgence of the Iranian petrochemical industry, which could once again pose a threat as a regional competitor. Nonetheless, this alone illustrated the economic pros and cons of the nuclear deal from the vantage point of the GCC states, which worried that 'in exchange for Iran's concessions regarding its nuclear project, the U.S. would give it free rein in the Arab region'.[18] As a result, a great deal of ambivalence as well as anxiety about the nuclear deal could be observed in the official and semi-official local reactions to the nuclear deal. Some Gulf Arab pundits accused the United States of 'tacitly accepting a sphere of influence for Iran—a sphere that encircles the traditional allies of the Gulf'.[19]

Reflecting a despairing Arab mood, Ghassan Charbel, writing in *Al-Hayat*, observed that the 'region has been dancing to the rhythm of Iran's tune' for a while.[20] Another writer, Tariq al-Homayed, writing in the pan-Arab daily *Asharq al-Awsat*, warned of Iran's concerted effort to expand its power 'under the banner of Shiafication' and added: 'We face a difficult period, asking ourselves how to save our region from a U.S. President whose last personal chance to make history is to reach an agreement with Iran, albeit a bad one that will be catastrophic not only for our region but for the international community.' Homayed, like many other Arab pundits, raised the alarm that 'Tehran is using the Houthis to heat up the situation in Yemen in order to place pressures on Saudi Arabia and the Arab Gulf states.'[21] (The Yemen factor will be discussed later in this chapter.) Saudi Arabia's Foreign Minister, Saud al-Faisal, expressed a similar sentiment by vehemently denouncing Iran as an 'occupation force' that was 'part of the problem' in Syria, Iraq, and Yemen.[22] Incidentally, several years earlier, in 2007, the same Saud al-Faisal had surprised many, particularly in Washington policy circles, by proposing a joint Iran–GCC consortium to enrich uranium for peaceful purposes, to which Iran's Foreign Minister, Manouchehr Mottaki, had responded favourably.[23] Unfortunately, this was a remote possibility, given the depth of Iran–GCC distrust and unresolved territorial disputes, such as that between Iran and the United Arab Emirates (UAE) over three islands in the Strait of Hormuz. The whole idea of centralising uranium enrichment in the region away from Iran's hands and subjecting it to Saudi monitoring was a non-starter as far as Iran's political elite was concerned, as was another Saudi idea of allowing the GCC to join the Iran talks.[24] The absence of any progress between Iran and the GCC states on such issues contributed a great deal to the subsequent avalanche of negative GCC publicity against Iran.

Yet, despite such a slew of negative Arab commentaries about their country, Iranians were, for the most part, oblivious to them and were, on the contrary, quite convinced that the nuclear agreement was a positive development in terms of regional affairs and had the potential to open a new chapter in Iran–GCC relations. This optimism stemmed partly from the diverse reactions to the deal by GCC member states and from the intermediary role that one GCC state, Oman, played by both facilitating the secret talks in 2013 and then hosting a bilateral US–Iran round of nuclear negotiations in October 2014. Given the signs of a policy split on Iran within the GCC, the regional organisation was confronted with a new reality that demanded serious efforts in terms of policy adjustments.[25]

One such adjustment concerned Iran, as the ongoing Iran nuclear talks and the regular US–Iran diplomatic contacts required GCC leaders to consider whether the time was ripe to foster a more cooperative relationship with their Persian neighbour, which was then advocating a 'regionalism'[26] approach and downplaying the threat of closing the Strait of Hormuz.[27] As they pondered such questions, GCC leaders also had to consider another related issue, namely the connection between the end of the Iran nuclear crisis and the ability of the United States to play a leading role in managing the Gulf's security affairs. Oman was practically the only member state that had fully resolved these concerns by concluding that this was not a 'zero-sum game' and that there was little to fear from a post-agreement Iran unrestricted by Western 'coercive diplomacy'.[28] No doubt, the growth in Iran–Oman economic and energy ties also played a key role in what the Arab media labelled Oman's 'Iran rapprochement'.[29]

In a rare visit to Tehran in May 2014, the Emir of Kuwait discussed the possibility of a gas deal with Tehran, given Kuwait's growing demand for imported natural gas.[30] With their population growth and industrial boom, Kuwait and other 'gas-hungry' GCC states may be about to enter a new period of 'economic interdependence' by receiving gas from Iran—a mutually beneficial prospect that rests, to a large extent, on the resolution of the nuclear crisis and the lifting of sanctions against Iran. According to Iran's Ministry of Foreign Affairs, the value of trade between Iran and the GCC stands at $30 billion a year, of which more than half takes place between Iran and the UAE, the latter having a relatively large Iranian expatriate community. The UAE's National Bureau of Statistics put the value of the country's exports to Iran in 2013 at roughly $11 billion.[31] In the same vein, the ruler of Dubai, Sheikh Mohammed bin Rashid Al Maktoum, told the BBC in a January 2014 interview about the need to re-engage Iran: 'everyone would benefit if Iran was given space'.[32]

But, if the interim nuclear deal and the subsequent Joint Comprehensive Plan of Action raised the prospect of a reduction of tension across the Persian Gulf, there was no comparable ambiguity expressed by the 'out-of-area' state of Israel, whose leaders adamantly opposed the deal as a 'historic mistake' and both directly and indirectly (through the pro-Israel lobby in Washington) campaigned vigorously against the Obama administration's negotiation strategy towards Iran. They constantly reminded the White House that Iran could not be trusted, was not 'a friend', and that it harboured uncompromising 'nuclear ambitions', which had led to the country's emergence as a 'nuclear threshold' state. Still, convinced that Iran would not relinquish its 'bomb-making' capability through persuasive diplomacy alone, the Israelis raised the spectre of 'going it alone' with the military option. In November 2014, as the confidential talks were taking place in Vienna, Israel made it clear that it did not feel 'bound' by any deal with Iran that fell short of 'dismantling' all of Iran's uranium enrichment capacity.[33] Israel's entrenched resistance to an Iran deal as *ipso facto* a 'bad deal' was additionally propagated by pro-Israel US lawmakers, who consistently accused Iran of supporting terrorism, citing Iran's ties with Hamas in Palestine and Hezbollah in Lebanon as irrefutable proof that Iran was a source of 'regional chaos' instead of stability.

Although such a thoroughly negative interpretation of Iran's regional intentions was not shared by the White House, to the Israelis' delight Saudi Arabia and some other Arab states echoed their sentiments, as a result of which an informal, de facto Israel–Saudi alignment of interests formed around the central and common focus on Iran's 'nuclear threat'. As was reflected in nearly identical policy assessments that the Saudis and Israelis put forth both officially (at GCC meetings) and in Washington policy circles (by pro-Israel lobby groups), these two countries precipitated a spirited and formidable resistance to a final Iran nuclear deal. After 2014, the anti-Iran political synergy between Riyadh and Tel Aviv grew into a potent force that played a significant public and behind-the-scenes role in mobilising political opinion in the United States against any 'appeasement' of Iran.[34]

Given the traditional rivalry between Iran and Saudi Arabia, on the one hand, and Iran's steadfast support for the 'Palestinian resistance', on the other hand, especially after the 2014 Gaza war,[35] neither Israel nor Saudi Arabia recognised any new era of benign Iranian foreign policy that required a reassessment of their Iran policies. Rather, in both Riyadh and Tel Aviv, the tendency was to attribute only 'cosmetic changes' and a tactical 'charm offensive' to the Rouhani 'phenomenon'. From a 'balance of threat' perspective, these two countries operated on the assumption that deterring and containing Iran formed a priority and that any new form of US–Iran cooperation was detrimental to their interests. There was not, of course, a complete correspondence of Israeli and Saudi positions towards Iran, but rather a convergence of views with respect to a nuclear deal which they both scorned.

American balancing act

At the heart of the US policy conundrum was how to bring the Iran nuclear crisis to a mutually acceptable resolution without simultaneously alienating key Middle East allies such as Israel and Saudi Arabia. Caught between conflicting priorities, the United States was forced to deal with the dilemma of how to maintain old alliances while 'bringing Iran out from the cold' by moving slowly on the Iran front and tempering its rush to reach a nuclear deal.[36] This in turn reflected an American 'paradox of preferences' inviting a negotiations 'impasse',[37] as the United States needed to assess the strategic and geopolitical implications of the end of the Iran nuclear crisis in terms of its own capacity to play a leading role in the region. Complicating the matter was the crisis of regional security instigated by the Islamic State (IS) phenomenon, plaguing Syria and Iraq like a 'growing cancer', as President Obama characterised it in July 2014.[38]

While it enlisted dozens of countries, including Saudi Arabia and other GCC states, in the anti-IS coalition, some of which contributed to the air campaign in Syria and Iraq, the United States balked at the idea of allowing Iran to participate in the coalition. Nevertheless, with both the United States and Iran backing the same forces in Iraq, namely the central government in Baghdad and the Kurds in northern Iraq, a de facto and tacit alliance between Washington and Tehran was formed, whereby US air strikes against IS fighters went hand in hand with Iran's assistance on the ground. To the surprise of US officials, Tehran acquiesced in the replacement of Iraq's Prime Minister, Nouri al-Maliki, who was accused of inciting Shi'a–Sunni sectarianism, with a new government of national unity headed by Haider al-Abadi in August 2014.[39] Nor did Iran raise any objections to the US dispatch of scores of military personnel, including advisers, to assist the Iraqi army. In fact, in an interview with US media in September 2014, President Rouhani himself implicitly called for more US ground forces as a necessary 'sacrifice' in the struggle against terrorism.[40] IS also represented a significant national security threat to Iran which, if unchecked, had the potential to spill over into Iran in addition to causing sustained regional instability. Sensing Iran's vulnerability, the United States decided to create an issue linkage between the nuclear talks and anti-terrorism, making a joint effort on anti-terrorism conditional on Iran's willingness to agree to a final deal on the United States' terms.

From the Iranians' point of view, the fact that the United States continued to resist the Iraqi government's request for new military hardware even after the change of leadership simply reinforced their suspicion of the superpower's ultimate intentions. The spokesman for the Iranian parliament's National Security and Foreign Policy Committee, Seyyed Hossein Naqavi Hosseini, went so far as to claim that 'the IS terrorist group is the joint product of the U.S., the Zionist regime [Israel] and Saudi Arabia in the region and there is no doubt about that.'[41] This was, however, in sharp contrast to the stance taken by President Rouhani, in his speech to the UN General Assembly in September 2014, which raised the prospect of cooperation between Iran and the West on terrorism once the nuclear standoff was over: 'If our interlocutors are also equally motivated and flexible, and we can overcome the problem and reach a longstanding agreement within the time remaining, then an entirely different environment will emerge for cooperation at regional and international levels, allowing for greater focus on some very important regional issues such as combating violence and extremism in the region.'[42]

While Iranians debated whether there was any connection between Sunni jihadist extremism epitomised by IS and developments within GCC states, a regional dimension came to add a new and complex aspect to the standoff over the nuclear issue. This related, in part, to the Shi'a–Sunni fault line and was highlighted by sectarian tensions in Yemen, which increased the GCC states' suspicion of Iran's regional policies.[43] In March 2014, a high-ranking Saudi official blamed the Iranian leadership for 'meddling and destabilizing efforts in the countries with Shi'a majorities, Iraq and Bahrain, as well as those countries with significant minority Shi'a communities, such as Kuwait, Lebanon, and Yemen.'[44] Such anti-Iranianism among policy elites held the potential to cause greater regional tension and was even used on occasion to raise the spectre of the Gulf states 'going nuclear' in response to Iran's nuclear threat.

Hence, the United States' conundrum was complicated by the conflicting priorities and adverse impacts of policy issues that were difficult to push forward in tandem without causing certain 'side effects', such as straining relations with traditional allies in the region.[45] For a long time, the Gulf Arabs had taken advantage of the Iran nuclear standoff for their non-nuclear national security considerations and interests to restrain Iranian power. Yet, the prospect of normalising Iran's nuclear status and lifting sanctions on the country became a cause for concern, particularly since the Gulf states had to entertain the possibility of a sub-optimal nuclear deal that would enable Iran to retain its status as a 'threshold' nuclear power, precisely at a time when Iran and its key regional ally, Lebanon's Hezbollah, were openly taking credit for turning the tide in favour of the Assad regime in the bloody conflict in Syria.[46] From the perspective of the Saudis and other GCC states, however, it appeared that the danger of Iran's proxies was 'just as much of a pressing threat as Iran's nuclear ambitions'.[47] In 2013, the Saudis turned down a seat on the United Nations Security Council ostensibly in a 'protest move' against what the monarchy saw as the ineffective and conciliatory attitude of the West towards the Syrian crisis and Iran's growing regional role.[48]

The Saudi war against Yemen: a preliminary assessment of its impact on Tehran–Riyadh relations

On 25 March 2015, Saudi Arabia, leading a coalition of nine Arab states, launched an air campaign codenamed Operation Decisive Storm against Yemen, its poor southern neighbour, ostensibly on behalf of the ousted government of Yemeni President 'Abd Rabbuh Mansur Hadi. Specifically, the Saudis claimed that the 'takeover' of the Yemeni government by the Houthis, a Zaidi group in Yemen, was aided by Iran with the aim of extending the Islamic Republic's influence in the Arabian Peninsula. The Zaidis are a Shi'a sect that emerged in the eighth century and comprise between 35 and 40 per cent of the population of Yemen. It is beyond the scope of this chapter to examine the Zaidi worldview except to note that the Zaidi belief system and theology are closer to Sunni Islam than to Twelver Shiism. For example, Zaidis do not believe in the infallibility of Shi'a imams after Hussein, the venerable third Shi'a Imam. In other words, they part company with the Twelver Shi'as on a very significant aspect of Iran's official religion. In matters of Islamic jurisprudence, the Zaidi *fiqh* is similar to the Hanafi school of jurisprudence and differs significantly from the Ja'afari school of jurisprudence followed by the Twelver Shi'as. In other words, the oft-stated but largely unexamined claim that the Iranian 'intervention' in Yemen is meant to bolster Shiism at the expense of Sunni Islam does not hold true. Until the last two decades, conflicts in Yemen were based on tribal and regional loyalties and not on religious sectarianism.[49] As Ali Scotten has noted, the assertive form of Zaidism that the Houthis now follow in Yemen emerged in the early 1990s in response to the Wahhabi encroachment in Yemen and to frequent attacks on Zaidi mosques and religious shrines as well as Zaidi communities.[50]

Moreover, years of economic deprivation experienced by northern Yemenis contributed to the emergence of the Houthi movement. In the past decade alone, under the leadership of former President 'Ali 'Abdullah Saleh, Yemen government forces conducted six military campaigns against the Houthis between 2004 and 2010. These killed and displaced many thousands of Yemenis in the Zaidi heartland of northwestern Yemen. The Saudis supported these attacks on the dubious claim of preventing 'Iranian influence' in the Arabian Peninsula and launched air strikes against Houthi positions along the Saudi–Yemen boundary in 2009, which prompted Tehran to issue statements in support of the Houthis.[51] However, it is unlikely that Iran was the principal cause of the Houthis' ascendance in Yemen, as a vast pool of arms is available on the black market alone.[52] To portray the Yemeni conflict as an Iranian–instigated, sustained dispute ignores both Yemeni history and recent Saudi involvement in Yemeni politics. According to American officials familiar with intelligence regarding the Houthis' assertiveness, Iran 'discouraged Houthi rebels from taking the Yemeni capital' in September 2014, but the rebels rebuffed Iran's advice and 'walked into the city and claimed it'.[53]

Whether by accident or design, the Saudi war against Yemen has affected Tehran–Riyadh relations and exacerbated the cold war between the two regional powers. The vituperative rhetoric emanating from Tehran and Riyadh against each other has been unprecedented.[54] When Iran announced it would send aid to Yemen, Saudi Arabia and its allies tried to prevent Iranian ships from docking at Yemeni harbours, an incident that could have resulted in a direct military clash had Iran not decided to move its supplies to Djibouti for delivery to Yemen.[55] Iran's policy is now focused on preventing the expansion of the so-called coalition to fight against what the Saudis have considered as the Shi'a and Iranian 'threat' in Yemen and elsewhere in the Persian Gulf. Iran's policy in this regard experienced some success when both Pakistan and Turkey 'defected from the Saudi camp as active partners in the military campaign in Yemen—after having initially indicated they would join in'.[56] What is clear is that the Saudi war against Yemen will affect Tehran–Riyadh relations in ways that may impact on regional security and its geopolitical discourse for years to come.

Saudi–Iranian cold war redux?

With the death of King 'Abdullah in January 2015 and the accession of King Salman to the Saudi throne, there have been changes and uncertainties in Saudi Arabia's domestic and foreign policies.[57] When King Salman appointed his inexperienced 29-year-old son as the Minister of Defence and, later, the Deputy Crown Prince, Saudi Arabia, long known for its cautious foreign policy, adopted a muscular policy orientation in its immediate region and beyond. In the words of the BND, the German intelligence agency, Saudi Arabia began to pursue 'an impulsive policy of intervention'.[58] Almost from the start, Saudi–Iranian relations began to deteriorate fast. But the proverbial straw that broke the camel's back was the execution on 2 January 2016 of the dissident leader of the Saudi Shi'as, Sheikh Nimr Baqir al-Nimr. The Saudi government had long accused Nimr of being a traitor and an agent of Iran. It is beyond the scope of this chapter to analyse Nimr's politico-religious beliefs. But, as Toby Matthiesen has correctly noted, 'Nimr's relationship with Iran was always more complicated than both Iranian and Saudi leaders have claimed, and he had far more in common with the revolutionaries of the Arab Spring than with the jihadis executed alongside him or the clerics who rule in Tehran.'[59]

Analysts have offered various explanations for why the Saudi government executed Sheikh Nimr. Many analysts and scholars of Saudi politics have predicted that executing Nimr would upset Iran. As the historian Toby Jones noted, the Saudi royal court was perhaps counting on provoking Iran and stoking the flames of sectarianism.[60] In the aftermath of Sheikh Nimr's execution, protesters in Tehran sacked Saudi Arabia's embassy. In retaliation, Saudi Arabia severed its diplomatic relations with Iran. Saudi allies in the region soon followed suit and either broke their diplomatic ties with Tehran or downgraded their relationship. Shortly thereafter, the Iranian embassy in Yemen came under missile attack and was severely damaged. Tehran blamed the Saudi-led coalition for attacking its embassy and injuring several of its staff. The Iranian leadership, including President Rouhani, Foreign Minister Javad Zarif, and the head of the parliament, Ali Larijani, condemned the attack on the Saudi embassy. Tehran has arrested more than forty people whom it accused of attacking the Saudi embassy and thus damaging Iran's interests. In letters to the UN Secretary General and foreign ministers of several UN member states, Iranian Foreign Minister Zarif formally expressed regrets over the attack and declared Tehran's commitment to bring the perpetrators to justice.[61] Furthermore, Zarif reiterated Iran's desire not to escalate tension in the region. In Zarif's words, both he and Rouhani 'have indicated publicly and privately our readiness to engage in dialogue, promote stability and combat destabilizing extremism. This has fallen on deaf ears in Saudi Arabia.'[62] What is clear is that Saudi–Iranian relations have reached their nadir, with dangerous consequences for the stability of not only the Persian Gulf but the entire Middle East.

The uneasy relationship between Iran and Saudi Arabia since 1979 indicates a diplomacy deficit that has profoundly exacerbated the volatility and insecurity in the Persian Gulf and beyond. From the Saudi perspective, Iran is an expansionist state that seeks to become a regional hegemon and uses sectarianism to advance its policies. Riyadh's zero-sum view of Iranian politics has led to a skewed reading of Iran's regional policy. As Reza Marashi has noted, with the 'possible exception of Israel, no other country in the world shares Saudi Arabia's extremist reading of Iran's regional policy.'[63]

From Tehran's perspective, it is Iran that has suffered from its 'strategic loneliness', being a majority Shi'a Persian state surrounded by Sunnis and

Arabs that have threatened Iran's territorial integrity and national security. Iran may not be completely 'alone in the world' but it has no clear regional partners or allies.[64] Iran certainly sees itself as a regional power not because it has 'expansionist' tendencies, as the Saudis have claimed, but because of its size, resources, demographics, geostrategic location, and culture. Iran's perception of itself as 'first among equals' in the region is crucial to understanding the country's security mindset. Notwithstanding this, Iran has tried to repair its relations with Saudi Arabia under the Rouhani administration. Contacts between the two countries, although not frequent, have taken place. Even when the two sides use uncompromising rhetoric, they recognise the limits of what they can do. Tehran has not imposed heavy costs on Riyadh for its Yemen adventure, partly because Iranian decision-makers have come to the conclusion that 'the Saudis are already paying heavy costs for their own mistake'.[65] What is clear is that both sides will ultimately come to the realisation that the security of the Persian Gulf is not attainable in terms of a zero-sum game. As Iran's Foreign Minister Zarif recently stated, 'one cannot buy security at the expense of the insecurity of others'.[66]

9

THE POLITICS OF SUCCESSION IN SAUDI ARABIA

A STRUGGLE FOR PRIMOGENITURE

Joseph A. Kéchichian

When serious business outlets extrapolate fantasy, as occurred after King 'Abdullah bin 'Abdul 'Aziz passed away on 23 January 2015, the time was right to take cover, if for no other reason than because of a genuine fear that some of the sublime and utterly muddled prose would hit one in the face. By early 2015, dozens of journalistic and semi-academic articles were published to decipher the succession mechanism in the Kingdom of Saudi Arabia and, at least in a few cases, to draw impossible parallels with what might occur next in the Sultanate of Oman. Justin Fox, for example, wrote on the widely read *Bloomberg News* electronic site that the Al Sa'ud were comparable to a family business—a stale cliché with little resemblance to reality—arguing that for all such entities, durability did not prevent vulnerability, especially when power was transferred from one leader to another.[1] Bruce Riedel, the director of the Intelligence Project at the Brookings Institution and a veteran Central Intelligence Agency analyst, engaged in a questionable deduction from the death of King 'Abdullah in what was an eccentric speculation over Sultan

Qaboos bin Sa'id, positing that 'while the Saudi succession was transparent, Oman's is opaque'.[2] The sentence was more 'sound bite' than careful analysis as well as being somewhat tangential.

The entertaining Fox essay speculated—in the true sense of the word—whether families like the Al Sa'ud ought to 'go with the eldest son who has been groomed since birth to take over, or the younger daughter who's twice as smart? What if the kids don't get along? What if they're not interested in business? What if they can't control their anger around macadamia nuts?'—all of which was preliminary to assessing the challenges of succession in Saudi Arabia. For the brazen journalist, the Al Sa'ud was an enterprise that also happens to be a 'sovereign nation', and while Fox acknowledged that he relied on Simon Henderson and Wikipedia—the sources of 'pretty much all [of his] knowledge of Saudi succession', with the electronic encyclopedia standing as the 'best available' resource—he conceded that the matter was rather complex. Nevertheless, the *Bloomberg* author concluded that the kingdom preferred seniority over competence, even if the most recent designations of Princes Muhammad bin Nayif and Muhammad bin Salman belied such facile analyses, which, regrettably, received wide attention by experts and lay observers alike. Fox accepted the notion that the founder of the kingdom, 'Abdul 'Aziz bin 'Abdul Rahman Al Sa'ud was 'ferociously competent', though the same apparently could not be said about his successors. King Sa'ud (r.1953–64) was, according to Fox, 'a bit unreliable', and his rule was allegedly 'inept', whereas King Faisal (r.1964–75) was 'more competent'.[3] Relying on Henderson, a former journalist for the *Financial Times*, Fox repeated the latter's gossipy reportage that Faisal skipped over the next oldest son of 'Abdul 'Aziz, Muhammad, who was 'considered unsuitable due to his bad temper and frequent drunkenness', and appointed the one after, the even-tempered Khalid.[4] In turn, Fox continued, King Khalid (r.1975–82) reportedly 'passed over a couple of unimpressive brothers to choose the experienced technocrat Fahd as crown prince'. What followed, according to this legend, was 'fraught family negotiations', which resulted in naming Prince 'Abdullah bin 'Abdul 'Aziz as heir to the heir apparent.[5]

King Fahd received no particular accolades in this unabashed depiction even if his reign (1982–2005) introduced a gamut of reforms as well as significant concessions to the clergy, although his heir, 'Abdullah, assumed the burdens of power after 1995 when the monarch suffered from a debilitating stroke.[6] 'Abdullah, who accomplished far more than many realised, trod a fine line between 1995 and 2005, waiting for the moment of his accession to unleash an unprecedented set of truly epochal sociopolitical transformations. His reign, which stretched from 2005 to 2015, will long be remembered for various reforms, including extensive government scholarship programmes, the appointment of women to senior positions, a sustained effort to introduce professionalism within the judiciary, the creation of a Supreme Court, holding various national dialogues on sensitive topics, as well as convening with Spain a global interfaith dialogue between all believers.[7] Among the late ruler's most significant political transformations were the various changes associated with the country's succession mechanisms, and while observers recorded that he outlasted two heirs, Princes Sultan and Nayif, his third heir, Prince Salman, who was appointed in 2012, acceded to the throne on 23 January 2015 just as planned and without a hitch. In many ways, King Salman (r.2015–), was probably the most promising ruler on account of his five-decades-old responsibilities as the family's *consigliere*. Hardly any item of worth escaped his attention and, though he reached his eightieth birthday on 31 December 2015, he was not ill—beyond the normal wear and tear that come with age and the heavy burdens of responsibility—and did not suffer from dementia, as Henderson proclaimed ad nauseam without presenting a shred of evidence to back his assertion.[8] On the contrary, King Salman may be advanced in age, but he has no mental impairments, though those who spread such images may believe otherwise. In the event, no one made any references to King Salman's alleged health impairment after early February 2015, especially when the Saudi monarch displayed the kind of stamina that individuals half his age would struggle to muster. In fact, over the course of several weeks, Riyadh welcomed over twenty heads of states or governments, all of whom were received by the ruler and all of whom could have easily reported any lapses of attention during extensive conversations. The health rumours returned in late 2015 and early 2016, however, and were part of a carefully orchestrated narrative that presumed to provide fresh insights into 'the man in charge of the "most dangerous man in the world"'.[9] Others believed that the kingdom was 'desperate', even if the adjective was both inaccurate and frantic.[10]

Notwithstanding superficial analyses of the kingdom, succession concerns lingered in Saudi Arabia along with several conservative Arab Gulf monarchies, which deserved careful examination without the pedantic similes and irrelevant metaphors that, regrettably, filled newspapers and blanketed television programs.[11]

Like other Arab Gulf monarchies, Saudi Arabia, the country that is the focus of this chapter, entered into a transition period in 2015 that had consequences for its internal as well as regional security. In fact, succession concerns raised serious questions about security after-effects because most Gulf leaders were advanced in age. Equally important was the quest for primogeniture, which posed concrete challenges too.

Of course, age as a security factor was not unusual, nor was it exclusive to Saudi Arabia. Others confronted similar challenges though the matter gained momentum when King 'Abdullah died in January 2015. One of the most striking images of the funeral prayers ceremony was the absence of two ageing Gulf leaders—Sheikh Khalifa bin Zayed (67) of the United Arab Emirates (UAE) and Sultan Qaboos of Oman (74)—not because they did not wish to attend but because of health issues. With both men ailing, the prospects grew that their own passing would inject more instability at a time when the Arabian Peninsula confronted undeniable crises ranging from a war in Yemen to overblown but real advances by various extremist groups. To be sure, King 'Abdullah's successor, Salman bin 'Abdul 'Aziz (80), and Sheikh Sabah al-Ahmad al-Jaber Al Sabah (85), the Emir of Kuwait, were also advanced in age, which further affected the security dimension that conservative Arab Gulf monarchies confronted. Relatively young men ruled Bahrain and Qatar— King Hamad bin 'Isa (65) and Sheikh Tamim bin Hamad (36)—although the Al Khalifa and Al Thani ruling families in the two respective monarchies were not immune to developments in neighbouring states, which further compli-cated matters.

In fact, it was fair to say that succession issues received much more atten-tion than at any other time in recent memory because of the upheavals that threatened the very stability of most Arab societies. Perhaps one of the best examples of how serious succession matters had become was provided by President Barack Obama, who flew to Saudi Arabia on his way back from India at the head of an impressive American delegation after King 'Abdullah died to offer condolences, confirming Washington's apprehensions about the process. Even more problematic was the speed with which the new ruler intro-duced changes. In fact, everyone was taken aback by the 29 April 2015 appointments to office and wished to assess whether the age factor was on King Salman's mind when he selected his 55-year-old nephew, Prince Muhammad bin Nayif, as heir to the heir apparent. The designation placed Prince Muhammad second in line to the throne before the monarch elevated him to the position of nominal successor post. On his visit, Obama wished to discover the reasons behind the latest changes, and confirm or refute the speculation that the motives behind the selection from among the ruling family's younger generation were security-related. This was critical because leading powers wished to know whether such winnowing was designed to avoid a power struggle between the grandsons of the founder.

The second security outcome was the quest for primogeniture, which was now firmly established in Bahrain and Qatar as well as several of the member sheikdoms of the UAE. While it was too soon to determine if the primogeniture mechanism would be adopted again in the Sultanate with the next successor, chances were excellent that the next Sultan would restore the system, which had ensured Al Sa'id rule for centuries. Likewise, irrespective of the lateral succession mechanism in place in the Kingdom of Saudi Arabia, Riyadh toyed with the very idea, especially now that King Salman had appointed his son Muhammad as heir to the heir apparent. Of course, this was not a done deal by any stretch of the imagination even if the method gained momentum. Suffice it to say that the dramatic changes introduced in the succession line-up on 29 April 2015 upset the proverbial applecart. Indeed, this was a tectonic shift that raised many questions, including the critical quest for a primogeniture system in the Kingdom of Saudi Arabia.

Saudi Arabia was set to experience lateral shifts from existing succession lines because King Salman designated a nephew. If the pre-2011 era saw primogeniture encouraged in Egypt, Libya, and Syria (as well as in Iraq before Saddam Hussein was overthrown in 2003), what stood out was the propinquity of the mechanism in most Arab monarchies, notably in Bahrain and Qatar, though lateral succession dominated changes in Kuwait, Oman, Saudi Arabia, and the UAE. Rulers in all four pondered existing methods and were increasingly under pressure to alter them. Ironically, even if Western powers, led by the United States and the United Kingdom, attempted to mould the future of Arab leaderships, those efforts were not always successful. Many pretended to enjoy influence in the incredibly complex winnowing that occurred in strategically significant states, though what truly stood out was the mere realisation that Arab leadership succession matters remained beyond reach to most outsiders. There was, of course, an appreciation that this was probably the most sensitive political issue in the Arab Gulf monarchies and that Western officials ought to tread carefully because of internal, regional, and global security consequences. Towards that end, and aware that whatever changes occurred would only reflect family consensus and internal harmony, most foreign governments interested in flowing transitions adjusted their policies vis-à-vis emerging leaders, since no one could predict who would assume power in any state at any given time.

The Kingdom of Saudi Arabia

When King Salman bin 'Abdul 'Aziz acceded to the throne, most scholars of the kingdom concluded that he would not change the country and undo his brother's achievements, and though he moved with uncharacteristic swiftness to demonstrate his will to power, his accession was carefully orchestrated and long planned.[12] Still, many speculated that his rule would be different from that of his predecessor, and while it was only natural that a new personality would want to introduce his own ideas, the monarch was not about to abolish the Allegiance Commission, for example, or set back most of the advances recorded on socio-economic issues. Because of his consolidation of dozens of committees into two large groups, some ventured to raise concerns about direction in which the new ruler intended to take the country. A few even jumped the gun, concluding that his alleged 'overtures to the Wahhabi religious establishment and the extensive powers invested in his young son' were hazardous.[13]

For one observer of the kingdom, apparently basing herself on about two dozen interviews with 'Saudis holding a variety of political and social perspectives, many of whom declined to be identified because of the sensitivity of discussing royal politics, a recurring theme [emerged, which] was the belief that King Salman may revive the governing style of his elder brother and mentor, King Fahd bin 'Abdul 'Aziz, who reigned from 1982 to 2005'.[14] King Fahd, who was allegedly known for his autocratic style, and who 'exerted pervasive social control of the population through religion and the religious police', displayed a sharply different personality. Fahd and Salman were of course full brothers, part of the so-called Sudayri Seven because they were the sons of Hassah bint Ahmad Al Sudayri, although it was facile to conclude that political trajectories in Saudi Arabia could be traced so clearly.[15] Moreover, while some family affinities existed, policy shifts only emerged over time as individuals asserted themselves within the nascent dynastic arrangement. Consequently, the re-emergence of the powerful Sudayri branch of the family may appear to be the new nexus of power on account of King Salman's immediate appointments, but the jostling for power between this and other branches of the Al Sa'ud was neither as clear nor was it completed so soon after this latest accession. There would, most likely, be serious behind-the-scenes promotions and permutations even if that process was time-consuming. What nevertheless stood out was the tangential and largely meaningless conclusion that presumed to gauge what transpired or what would occur since leading Sudayris were left out of the changes introduced during the new ruler's first year in power. It is worth noting that Prince Bandar bin Sultan bin 'Abdul 'Aziz, a favourite son of a favourite brother, was removed from office although health reasons may have motivated that decision. Likewise, the former Minister of the Interior and a full brother of the monarch, Ahmad bin 'Abdul 'Aziz, was not entrusted with any position after he was abruptly discharged by King 'Abdullah on 5 November 2012, though rumours swirled that senior family members wanted him to replace the monarch.[16] The speculation, which mimicked intelligence reports, was taken seriously because of the way King Salman replaced his first heir apparent three months into his reign, a move that, regardless of his monarchical prerogatives, highlighted existing tensions.

Heir Apparent Muqrin bin 'Abdul 'Aziz (2014–15)

Prince Muqrin bin 'Abdul 'Aziz, a former intelligence chief, was appointed deputy heir apparent on 27 March 2014, which made the 70-year-old—the youngest son of the kingdom's founder, King 'Abdul 'Aziz Al Sa'ud—next in line to succeed after his half-brothers King 'Abdullah and the heir apparent Salman. On 23 January 2015, as expected, Muqrin, who already held the position of Second Deputy Prime Minister, a role to which he was appointed in 2013 and that traditionally but informally was the equivalent of being heir-in-waiting, was elevated to his post. There were no surprises, and as the constant companion of both the late King and his successor, only misinformed loose tongues spread rumours of his unsuitability because of his 'Yemeni' mother.[17]

What was not clear, even to Saudis themselves, was how the jump to the next generation would be managed, even if King 'Abdullah had decreed procedures to decide succession with the 2006 promulgation of the Allegiance Commission Law. The announcement that placed Prince Muqrin in the heirship reassured observers that the kingdom's long-term succession process was secure at a moment when senior members of the family sought internal stability amid conflict and political turmoil across the Middle East.[18]

It is important to note that Saudi Arabia's heir apparent normally served in one of the country's three security institutions: Ministry of Defence (MOD), Ministry of the Interior (MOI), and the Saudi Arabian National Guard (SANG). This had been the case with the past four heirs: King 'Abdullah had been commander of the SANG for nearly two decades when he was named heir in 1982. 'Abdullah's ascent to the throne in August 2005 allowed the long-time Minister of Defence, Sultan bin 'Abdul 'Aziz, to become heir. Sultan's death in October 2011 paved the way for Prince Nayif, who had led the MOI for over 35 years, to become heir in his turn. Sultan's replacement at the head of the MOD was his brother Salman, who became heir when Nayif died in June 2012. Even King Fahd bin 'Abdul 'Aziz, the man whom 'Abdullah succeeded as king in 2005, was Minister of the Interior for more than a decade before being named heir apparent in 1975. King Salman maintained this tradition intact although he introduced dramatic changes at the Ministry of Foreign Affairs.

Heir Apparent Muhammad bin Nayif (April 2015–June 2017)

Less than a hundred days after his designation as heir to the heir apparent, the Minister of the Interior, Muhammad bin Nayif, saw his fortunes change once again when King Salman replaced the heir to the Saudi throne. Muhammad bin Nayif, who was born in 1959 and who had been thought of as a contender for the throne for quite some time, assumed his new duties on 29 April 2015. In that capacity, he became the lynchpin of dramatic deviations in contemporary Al Sa'ud history, because he was the first grandson of the founder to receive the responsibility to lead the country. Although he was expected to eventually rise to the top post, the transformation shocked many Saudis, taken aback by the speed with which the ruler moved.[19]

Unlike Prince Muqrin, the new heir to the Saudi throne has a strong bloodline, as both of his parents—the late heir apparent, Nayif bin 'Abdul 'Aziz, and Jawharah bint 'Abdul 'Aziz, from the ruling family's Jiluwi branch—were full-fledged members of the Al Sa'ud. Prince Muhammad was initially known for his business dealings, first appearing in Western media in 1991 when it was reported he had been awarded a huge contract to import gas masks into Saudi Arabia.[20] He worked in the private sector until about 1990 and was appointed Assistant Minister of the Interior for Security Affairs in May 1999. It was in 2003 that he came to prominence, when the radical extremist planner 'Ali 'Abdul Rahman al-Ghamdi opted to surrender in person to the Deputy Minister.[21] In June 2004, the rapidly rising star was given the rank of minister, as he oversaw much of the Saudi terrorist rehabilitation programme since its inception. He narrowly escaped death in 2009 when a suicide bomber blew himself up within metres of him. Muhammad bin Nayif became Interior Minister in November 2012, the most senior position to be taken by a member of his generation, before King Salman appointed him heir to the heir apparent on 23 January 2015.[22] The prince, who is married to Rimah bint Sultan, the daughter of another former heir to the throne, Sultan bin 'Abdul 'Aziz, expected to eventually accede to the Saudi throne although he was not sure when that would occur. Equally important, he was not certain whether his current position would be rescinded to make room for the next rising star of the Al Sa'ud ruling family, namely Prince Muhammad bin Salman bin 'Abdul 'Aziz, who was designated heir to the heir apparent on 29 April 2015.[23]

King Salman practices 'shock and awe' in Riyadh

If the 23 January 2015 appointment of Prince Muqrin as heir apparent confirmed continuity and stability, which were classic Al Sa'ud family objectives despite disagreements that existed between the late King 'Abdullah and his heir on various issues, the new monarch added value to his predecessor's considerable innovations in succession matters when he appointed his nephew, the deputy heir apparent, Prince Muhammad bin Nayif, as his eventual successor. Doing so ensured that a new generation of leaders would come to power in what everyone concluded would be a smooth process. Yet, in what was a shocking development to all concerned, the monarch relieved Prince Muqrin of his responsibilities, reportedly upon the latter's request because that was the only way to rescind an immutable royal decree, and ordered a reshuffle that raised many questions and added to the speculation that Saudi Arabia was bound to confront serious challenges in the years ahead.

To be sure, while rumours circulated for nearly four months throughout the kingdom that Prince Muqrin would be eased out of his heirship duties and that Prince Muhammad bin Salman, the King's son, Minister of Defence, head of the Royal Court, and chairman of the Economic Committee, would assume yet another critical post, most did not expect this to occur for several more years. Instead, Saudis woke up on the morning of 29 April 2015 to hear an official royal decree read on state television that a grandson of the founder had been elevated to the heirship. Prince Muqrin was no longer heir. For his part, the affable successor was tasked to retain his thankless Ministry of Interior portfolio along with the chairmanship of the Security Committee. Simultaneously, the monarch's son, Muhammad bin Salman, added two fresh portfolios to his growing constellation, including the positions of heir to the heir apparent as well as head of a new ten-member supreme council for the state-run oil company, Saudi Aramco, even if he surrendered his Royal Court portfolio to his deputy, Hamad bin 'Abdul 'Aziz al-Suwaylim, a long-time aide to King Salman.[24]

The result of these announcements was a realisation that nearly all of the kingdom's powers were now entrusted to the two Muhammads, a situation that, under the best of circumstances, was problematic. In fact, these latest moves represented massive changes, and while some Saudis were delighted to see a grandson of the founder reach the pinnacle of power so quickly, others wondered whether the monarch was not rushing the process. From the ruler's perspective, of course, one could at least make the case that the carefully tailored procedure granted the country's youths an unparalleled degree of autonomy, energised by the type of political responsibility seldom granted them at any previous time.

Moreover, besides his monarchical prerogatives to determine the fate of the kingdom, King Salman probably decided to accelerate the pace of what he determined was an inevitable change as a new generation rose up to the challenge. Of course, time would confirm whether this calculation was the best approach, though there was no denying that Saudi leadership was now truly youthful. Still, precisely because Saudi Arabia is a monarchy that practises its succession affairs within a broad consensual framework, such serious changes were bound to have inevitable repercussions.

Indeed, one of the more troubling aspects of the King's moves concerned the state of his health, which divided observers, as some argued the ruler suffered from dementia—a state of affairs that the Royal Court vehemently denied. Naturally, while there was no evidence that the ruler suffered from dementia or any other debilitating illness, many 'experts' rushed to point to these latest developments as evidence of his desire to keep family harmony and ensure that the monarch's own son was guaranteed a spot at the top.[25] There were, of course, no such guarantees since every monarch was free to rule as he wished, even if it was amply clear that King Salman regarded primogeniture as his preferred option, given that he had entrusted his son with genuine decision-making authority. How the monarch perceived ties between the two Muhammads or what kind of guidance he provided them was anyone's guess. Suffice it to say that King Salman was confident that his directives would be carried out.

Surprisingly, the royal decree issued in April 2015 also removed Prince Sa'ud al-Faisal from the post of Minister of Foreign Affairs and replaced him with the kingdom's ambassador to Washington, 'Adil al-Jubayr. According to the statement, Prince Sa'ud 'asked to be relieved from his duties due to his health conditions', although he was sworn in by none other than the monarch on 9 March 2015 as a full-fledged member of the cabinet. The official Saudi Press Agency clarified that the veteran minister, who had held the position since 1975, was appointed an adviser and a special envoy of King Salman, as well as a supervisor for foreign affairs.[26] Given the myriad responsibilities that a Saudi Foreign Minister must assume, and because of the enviable skills of 'Adil al-Jubayr as an American specialist, what the monarch probably wished to do was entrust the post to someone who knew how to communicate with the Obama administration for the balance of Obama's term in office. Naturally, the new minister was expected to benefit from the wealth of experts working in Riyadh, though what al-Jubayr brought to the table was abundantly evident: his valuable connections in the United States at a time when that country was tilting towards Iran. The affable Foreign Minister displayed his prowess in early 2016 when leading Western news outlets embarked on a systematic anti-Saudi campaign following the execution of a convicted Saudi national, the Shi'a cleric Sheikh Nimr al-Nimr. It was a particularly effective display of determination and will that few Westerners were accustomed to witness from Saudi officials, even from the formidable Sa'ud al-Faisal whose expertise and knowledge few questioned. Backed by a far more assertive monarch, an equally confident heir apparent, and a remarkable heir to the heir apparent, al-Jubayr rose to the occasion and affirmed Saudi preferences.[27]

From an analytical perspective, therefore, the April 2015 nominations confirmed King Salman's penchant for true shock and awe. In his second cabinet reshuffle in as many months, the monarch introduced unusual appointments in terms of Al Sa'ud ruling family calculations, which may or may not sit well with the rest of the vast and influential group. For example, while the position of foreign minister was previously held by a king and his son, al-Jubayr, a non-royal, now outranked 'Abdul 'Aziz bin 'Abdullah, the son of another king serving at the Ministry of Foreign Affairs, which was unprecedented in the history of the country.[28] How senior Al Sa'ud family members absorbed this fact is too early to speculate though common sense must conclude that they might not be enthusiastic even if all were bound by the allegiance, duty, and obedience to their ruler. Equally important was the power entrusted to the two Muhammads, as older cousins and uncles—many of whom had far greater experience in domestic and international affairs—wondered what other surprises King Salman might have in store for the Al Sa'ud.[29]

Shaping the contours of power

Besides these appointments, the views imputed to King Salman about his presumed affinity with ultraconservative religious authorities were also speculative, given a near unanimous perception within the Al Sa'ud that the alliance between the ruling family and the Al al-Shaykh must remain balanced and not grant an advantage to the clerical establishment. King 'Abdullah curbed what he, as heir apparent, and the overwhelming majority of the Al Sa'ud deemed to be the excesses of the religious police, when Riyadh demoted or dismissed clerics who openly obstructed the country's sorely needed reform initiatives. It was natural that the clergy, whose members enjoyed a sort of monopoly for decades over such subjects as education, the court system, or women's opportunities, would not be enamoured of the late monarch, though it would be a total misreading to assume that King Salman would, even remotely, put clerical interests ahead of family security. Consequently, few should worry that the changes introduced after 2005 would or could be rolled back, and while King Fahd's model may appear for some to be a better balance between religion and modernisation, the natural evolutionary pattern can only be terminated at great socio-economic cost. This did not mean that some Saudis did not look askance at globalisation and, perhaps, feared that they might have to forgo their local traditions. Without a doubt, some were suspicious of the values that modernisation ushered in, and did not care for rapid changes. Still, those who held such views were certainly not in the majority.[30]

In fact, mainstream Saudis often lamented King Fahd's era as one when few social and intellectual modernisation initiatives were introduced, and though an economic boom was recorded, the price to pay was very high. In the aftermath of the 1979 takeover of the Holy Mosque in Makkah by Juhayman al-'Utaybi and his followers, Riyadh turned the clock back, allowed clerics to impose strict new rules, and otherwise distanced the country from important social reforms recorded after 1964 when King Faisal bin 'Abdul 'Aziz assumed authority.[31] By the turn of the twenty-first century, an overwhelming majority of Saudis expected genuine reforms and were far more satisfied with King 'Abdullah's rule than critics acknowledged, especially as the octogenarian launched significant educational reforms, allowed indigenous media outlets to report with relative freedom (including authorising uncovered women to present various television programmes while wearing colorful 'abayas), and otherwise encouraged women's advancement in education and the workplace.

Of course, just because the 2005–15 period was particularly encouraging for women, it did not follow that King Salman would harbour anti-women intentions or undo his brother's reforms. Simply stated, there was no evidence to suggest that Salman would not care for gender matters as much as 'Abdullah did, even if he moved fast to make several key changes, including relieving the Deputy Minister of Education for Women's Affairs, Nurah bint 'Abdullah al-Fayiz, who became the kingdom's first female minister in 2009. To be fair, the King also replaced Hamad bin Muhammad Al al-Shaykh, who was the Deputy Minister of Education for Men.

Saudi Arabia now managed by two powerful committees

During a long decade, the late King 'Abdullah bin 'Abdul 'Aziz created eleven committees and councils to run the affairs of the kingdom, which, by all accounts, found few supporters allegedly because of their bureaucratic burdens. On 29 January 2015, King Salman abolished all of them, including the powerful National Security Council (NSC), because, observers concluded, he wished to reintroduce efficiency and accountability.[32]

Two major institutions, the Council of Political and Security Affairs (CPSA), headed by the heir apparent and Minister of the Interior, Muhammad bin Nayif, and the Council of Economic and Development Affairs (CEDA), headed by the Minister of Defence, Muhammad bin Salman, replaced the eleven bodies. Both princes received open mandates to reorganise the kingdom's affairs, introduce efficient methods, and display transparency. Inasmuch as these reforms were sweeping, it is critical to assess their intrinsic capabilities, if for no other reason than to determine what patterns might emerge.[33]

The Council of Political and Security Affairs

CPSA held its first meeting on 11 February 2015 under the leadership of Muhammad bin Nayif, with Riyadh announcing in this step its renewed attention to security matters. Eight other members served on CPSA, including Prince Sa'ud al-Faisal, then the Minister of Foreign Affairs; Prince Mit'ab bin 'Abdullah, the Minister of the National Guard; Prince Muhammad bin Salman, the Minister of Defence; Sheikh Salih bin 'Abdul 'Aziz bin Muhammad bin Ibrahim Al al-Shaykh, the Minister of Islamic Affairs, Endowments, Call and Guidance; Lieutenant General Khalid bin 'Ali bin 'Abdullah al-Humaydan, the chief of General Intelligence Directorate (GID); 'Adil bin Zayd al-Turayfi, the Minister of Culture and Information; and two ministers of state, Dr Sa'ad bin Khalid al-Jabri and Dr Musa'id bin Muhammad al-Ayban.

While Princes Muhammad bin Nayif, Sa'ud al-Faisal, and Mit'ab bin 'Abdullah were well known for their service to king and country, the other five

155

CPSA members were less so, even if much was expected from them as well. Still, there was no doubt that the very existence of CPSA, which was carefully planned, highlighted the trust that the King placed in Prince Muhammad bin Nayif, whose efficiency stood out as the kingdom led a military coalition to defeat Houthi rebels in Yemen, starting in earnest on 25 March 2015. Moreover, the monarch appreciated the level of cooperation between the Minister of the Interior and various regional and international counterparts, as the kingdom fought extremists. Prince Muhammad bin Nayif's anti-terrorism policy in particular, which included a highly efficient rehabilitation component, produced favourable results in more ways than many assumed, as Riyadh coordinated with its GCC partners, various Arab states, and leading Western powers to weaken and destroy the Islamic State in Iraq and Syria (ISIS) or, as it is known by its Arabic acronym, Da'esh, and similar organisations.[34] What was unknown, however, was the level of cooperation between him and Prince Muhammad bin Salman, the newly appointed Minister of Defence, who was, by all accounts, the rising star within the ruling family.

At 30, Prince Muhammad bin Salman was probably too inexperienced to assume so many responsibilities—in addition to his Ministry of Defence portfolio, he assumed the incredibly demanding responsibilities of head of the Royal Court, although he relinquished this post on 29 April 2015, president of CEDA, and a member of CPSA. Interestingly, by virtue of his membership of both CPSA and CEDA, he became the only member of the Al Sa'ud to sit on both councils, which was an undue concentration of power in the hands of a single individual. It was possible to infer, nevertheless, that his father appointed Prince Muhammad bin Nayif as head of CPSA precisely because he wished his son to learn from a far more experienced person, and not necessarily because the Minister of the Interior occupied a higher protocol position.

Be that as it may, what was intriguing about Prince Muhammad bin Salman was what was expected of him, and while his reputation as a forthright prince who could get things done was acknowledged, it remained to be determined how he would counsel his monarch. Detractors pointed to his inability to communicate fluently in English, an essential tool for such a high-ranking leader who must carefully negotiate with leading global powers, although what was far more important was the young man's willingness to provide his sovereign with the type of advice that might not always be welcome. Over the short term, nevertheless, few observers anticipated clashes between the two Muhammads on the CPSA, with the heir apparent enjoying a slight advantage. Moreover, inasmuch as the Saudi-led coalition—which responded to calls made by President 'Abd Rabbu Mansur al-Hadi to assist Sana'a to defeat the Houthi rebellion in Yemen—was now a responsibility that fell on Prince Muhammad bin Salman's shoulders, his performance in that conflict was bound to determine his influence. Were he to record successes in the Yemen conflict, one would have to recognise that Muhammad bin Salman's influence and, consequently, his role in family affairs would grow. In the meantime, the young prince was placed under the microscope, as everyone attempted to assess his capabilities. In early 2016, Muhammad bin Salman granted *The Economist* a major interview, in which he defended his plans for the country, though detractors noted his alleged arrogance far more than any innate leadership skills.[35]

The Council of Economic and Development Affairs

CEDA met for the first time on 11 February 2015 at the Royal Court under the chairmanship of the Minister of Defence, Muhammad bin Salman. Unlike CPSA, whose entire membership consisted of nine individuals, CEDA boasted a membership of 22 and required a secretariat. Luckily, that task was entrusted to the Secretary General of the Council of Ministers, which meant that CEDA was for all practical purposes a kitchen cabinet, which concentrated on economic affairs.[36]

Inasmuch as the Council of Ministers was the chief arena of policy debates in the kingdom, and because of the burdens associated with so many tasks, it appeared that King Salman's main objective was to separate the process into two manageable groups, each entrusted with equally pertinent duties. This was certainly one interpretation that recognised how complex the day-to-day running of the government had become, requiring the type of coordination that was presumably not practised as much as the ruler hoped it would be, given that cabinet sessions were often used to reach relevant decisions. The monarch concluded that such cooperation necessitated a degree of exchange and, perhaps, cross-referrals among pertinent ministries to avoid duplication and, more important, to end waste. There was, moreover, an explicit awareness that security matters were best handled within a narrower environment, hence CPSA, whose work, he most probably reasoned, ought not to be mixed with important socio-economic decisions. In short, the goal of CEDA was to actually run the affairs of the state and be far more responsive to the needs of citizens, ranging from health care to education and myriad social and economic provisions.

Still, there was more to this story than is generally assumed, because of the identity of the CEDA president, Defence Minister Muhammad bin Salman. By virtue of his chairmanship, Prince Muhammad was on a fast track to eventual higher office, perhaps even the premiership or the deputy premiership. Like his predecessors, King Salman opted to remain his own Prime Minister, which meant that he presided over cabinet sessions. The Deputy Prime Minister and heir apparent, Muhammad bin Nayif, chaired whenever the monarch was absent. In other words, cabinet sessions were nominally the preserve of the heir, but the cabinet could now be routinely bypassed by CEDA in particular areas of responsibility. This did not mean that the cabinet was no longer a relevant institution or that its decisions were less valuable than those handled at CEDA, but that two near identical institutions could not possibly be expected to do the same work. That is why it is eminently logical to conclude that King Salman wished to streamline the institution because he intended his son would learn on the job. In short, CEDA was meant to let Prince Muhammad bin Salman be a prime minister in training, which also explained the huge amount of power concentrated in his hands.

It was worth repeating that at the age of 30, Prince Muhammad bin Salman was now expected to find the energy to handle many responsibilities, and while the King Saud University graduate remained close to his father after he earned his law degree in 2008, what was asked of him went beyond the ceremonial. Although he was a capable individual, it was still too early to determine whether the young prince had the stamina to do so many things, and do them well. The eldest son of the monarch's second wife, Princess Fahdah bint Falah al-Hithlayn, from the eastern 'Ajman tribe which backed the Al Sa'ud from the early twentieth century and whose daughters married extensively into the family, Prince Muhammad had a full brother, Turki bin Salman, who was formerly the chairman of the Saudi Research and Marketing Group, which publishes the pan-Arab daily *Asharq al-Awsat*. It was not clear what type of relations he enjoyed with several of his half-brothers, including the Deputy Minister of Petroleum, 'Abdul 'Aziz; the chairman of the Saudi Commission for Tourism and Antiquities and former astronaut, Sultan; and the governor of Madinah, Faisal, all three of whom were born to a different mother, Princess Sultanah al-Sudayri, who died in 2011. In the event, Prince Muhammad bin Salman needed all the help he could muster, given the sheer quantity of work thrown on his lap. In the aftermath of Operation Decisive Storm, the name given to the international military campaign against the Houthis in Yemen, additional burdens were placed on Defence Minister Muhammad bin Salman.[37]

The affable young man confronted another daunting hurdle, the ability to negotiate on the CEDA with veteran ministers like 'Ali al-Na'imi (Petroleum and Mineral Resources) and 'Abdul 'Aziz al-'Assaf (Finance), two men with a wealth of experience. How he handled himself with such officials was probably also part of his apprenticeship, especially when it was well known that al-Na'imi promoted his ministry's interests—in what was heretofore the most secret institution in the kingdom—in a closed circle, and had dealt directly with the monarch until then. It is critical to note that King Salman did not change this key minister despite all the shuffling within the government and might still rely on al-Na'imi in a private capacity, though it was also clear that he wished to invigorate the process by making pragmatic appointments that introduced fresh blood into the system, precisely to allow a new generation of officials to gain experience during this interim period. In time, al-Na'imi was eventually replaced in May 2016 by Khalid bin 'Abdul 'Aziz al-Falih, the former chief executive of Saudi Aramco, who had been entrusted with the Health Ministry in April 2015 and who a year later became the head of a new 'super-ministry' of Energy, Industry, and Mineral Resources.

Critics who labelled King Salman an 'old and sick man in a hurry' failed to understand how the Al Sa'ud leadership functioned, even with its periodic surprises.[38] Indeed, while the Al Sa'ud had introduced graduated changes in the past, the new monarch adopted a different method and sought advice from a variety of sources, before he made his final rulings. It was consensus decision-making par excellence, and though Saudis and others were shocked at the pace of change that occurred after King 'Abdullah passed away, with some critics lamenting that King Salman did not wait for the corpse of his late brother to be lowered into the ground before replacing top court staff members and investing one of his youngest sons with enormous powers, it did not follow that he did so out of spite. On the contrary, Salman wished to send a clear message, that the kingdom was in secure and stable hands no matter what kind of gloom and doom critics anticipated. His decision to name an heir apparent from among the ranks of the younger generation, the Minister of the Interior and counter-terrorism tsar, Muhammad bin Nayif, as heir to the heir apparent, was certainly a surprise move, more so when he quickly elevated him to the heirship.

Foreign policy challenges

Of course, there were specific reasons for these rapid transformations, including the desire to usher in a younger generation to assume the burdens of power. Yet, unlike his predecessor, Salman bin 'Abdul 'Aziz acceded to the throne amid a sea of regional and global crises, which promised to bring enduring changes to most Arab and Muslim societies. Consequently, his aim was to safeguard Saudi interests, protect the nation from numerous enemies, and allow the kingdom to prosper. While the King's goals rested on a clear ideology, which emulated those of the founder and of each monarch that ruled Saudi Arabia between 1953 and 2015, epochal changes required adaptation. Could Riyadh adjust long-held policies and, it was fair to ask, what kind of likely alterations were probable under King Salman?

It would be safe to state that the monarch inherited a great burden of problems upon his accession, and while he had been part and parcel of the collegial decision-making process for years—when every monarch reached final decisions after full consultations across the political spectrum—he was, nevertheless, now elevated to the unenviable position of final arbiter.

Today, the major foreign policy concerns from the Saudi perspective are well known, headed by an Iranian expansionist policy. Closer to Riyadh, interference in Bahrain and the prodding of local Shiʻa irredentism were all too real. In addition to these challenges, Riyadh faced the Syrian conundrum, a pro-Iran Hezbollah militia that propped up Damascus while it threatened Beirut, and a shaky Baghdad where government had become synonymous with corruption and non-governance. In both Iraq and Syria, the conservative monarchy tackled the Islamic State, even if Saudi Arabia claimed the Holy Qurʼan as its constitution and represented the ultimate Muslim state. Sunni extremist groups like the Muslim Brotherhood sought to replace the custodianship of the Two Holy Mosques by promoting rival governments in Egypt, Libya, and several other Muslim countries, though none was as bold as the Yemeni variety, which brazenly desired to revive a long-forgotten Imamate. Even Turkey, a secularised state, made a bid to contest Saudi leadership of the Muslim world ostensibly because its thoroughly Islamised leaders who appeared to be Westernised were a model worthy of emulation.[39]

Amid these overwhelming developments, shifting positions in leading Western countries, which belied long-standing accords, antagonised Riyadh as well. Starting with the George W. Bush administration, Washington embarked on a reassessment of its ties with Riyadh, which reached a peak under President Barack Obama, whose preferences for developing an opening to Iran were clear. Naturally, King ʻAbdullah bin ʻAbdul ʻAziz, Foreign Minister Prince Saʻud al-Faisal, and practically all Saudi leaders were sensitive to these developments as they worked in earnest to protect and promote their country's interests, while they preserved existing ties despite several disappointments.

Many wondered whether US foreign policymakers would eventually turn their backs on an 80-year-old partnership, though it was interesting to notice that President Obama led a large delegation to pay his condolences to the Al Sa'ud and the people of Saudi Arabia as well as to congratulate King Salman on his accession because, perhaps, some realised what was at stake. In fact, neither the short trip nor the heavyweight delegation that accompanied him was coincidental, for even Obama must have concluded that a bird in the hand was preferable to two in the bush. Washington and Tehran may yet consummate a full reconciliation and, conceivably, apply the Joint Comprehensive Plan of Action signed in Vienna on 14 July 2015 in respect of Iran's nuclear programme. Yet, American leaders knew that Riyadh could not tolerate that such an accord be at the expense of Saudi Arabia and its Gulf Cooperation Council (GCC) allies, and would react accordingly. Few could ascertain whether King Salman would tell President Obama what King 'Abdullah reportedly told US President Bill Clinton—that 'friendship has limits, Mr President'—after Clinton wanted to introduce him to Israeli officials attending King Hussein's funeral in Amman.

There were no doubts that the relationship Riyadh maintained with Washington was the most important one for the kingdom, and Saudi officials were determined to preserve it. Even after the early January 2016 break in diplomatic relations between Saudi Arabia and Iran, which followed the ransacking of the Saudi Embassy in Tehran and the Saudi consulate in Mashhad, Washington was anxious to reaffirm its security commitments to the kingdom. On 23 January 2016, coincidentally the first anniversary of King Salman's accession as ruler, US Secretary of State John Kerry declared in Riyadh that 'nothing has changed' as a result of the agreement the United States and five other world powers made with Iran. In his joint news conference with the Saudi Foreign Minister, al-Jubayr, Kerry emphasised that the relationship between Washington and the GCC, led by Saudi Arabia, was built on 'mutual interest' and 'mutual defense'. He added that there was 'no doubt' among GCC countries that the United States would 'stand with them against any external threat and defend them, if necessary'.[40] Nevertheless, few should be surprised if the approach changes, with King Salman anxious to affirm his authority in a part of the world ripped apart along sectarian lines. Even fewer should persuade themselves that the monarch would forgo that leadership role. On the contrary, a year after his accession, King Salman seemed as resolute as ever to rally his troops and forge ahead. That was why he focused on intra-Gulf relations, both to remove lingering disagreements among GCC members and to send the message that Riyadh intended to lead the Arab Gulf monarchies.

Conclusion

At the end of an official visit to the United States in early September 2015, King Salman and President Barack Obama issued a joint statement that reiterated the 'enduring relationship' between Washington and Riyadh. It acknowledged that ties had grown 'deeper and stronger over the past seven decades in the political, economic, military, security, cultural, and other spheres of mutual interest', which was telling in the light of recent tensions.[41] As expected, the two leaders stressed the importance of strategic ties, and emphasised the kingdom's leadership role in the Arab and Islamic worlds.

Importantly, while the Saudi ruler missed the 14 May Camp David summit between the leaders of the GCC and President Obama, Riyadh assented to the proposition that the US–GCC defence and security partnership would be strengthened, which was a given because of what was at stake for everyone concerned. Where divergences existed was over Iran and its attempts to destabilise the Gulf region. Interestingly, even though Riyadh was kept out of the US–Iran talks, the joint statement affirmed the need to 'counter Iran's destabilizing activities'. That sentence revealed that Washington recognised Tehran's undermining behaviour, and while King Salman expressed his support for the recent accord with Iran, what was even more telling was the monarch's emphasis that the kingdom did 'not need anything' but was 'interested in the stability of the region' because he perceived Saudi–American cooperation to be useful for the entire world. At a time when critics derided the Saudi monarch, Salman bin 'Abdul 'Aziz showed his mettle. His visit illustrated an established resolve on his part.

Notwithstanding occasional gloom and doom scenarios that question the very soundness of the monarchical system in the Kingdom of Saudi Arabia and elsewhere in the GCC states, Arab monarchies survived the post-2011 uprisings because sovereigns practised paternalism not authoritarianism, and while King Salman was an absolute ruler, he nevertheless created room for genuine freedoms to flourish. The fact that monarchies enjoyed financial cushions, introduced political systems that were fairly decentralised, and ensured that religious legitimacy existed in their realms, gave them the kind of soundness that no Arab republic managed to acquire. In Saudi Arabia, the most powerful Arab country, the Al Sa'ud drew lessons from the Arab uprisings, especially after they witnessed how quickly Western powers abandoned Hosni Mubarak of Egypt. In 2011, King 'Abdullah bin 'Abdul 'Aziz concluded that Riyadh could no longer count on the West in general and Washington in particular, and moved decisively to help Bahrain crush demonstrators who planned to change the regime in Manama. Other monarchs drew similar conclusions although their survival ought not create any ground for complacency. In fact, the primary reason for their relative success was their adaptation skills, which moved ruling families to update internal mechanisms and move towards some form of constitutionalism. Steps in that direction were taken in Kuwait, Morocco, and Jordan, and while it remains to be determined whether the Al Sa'ud and the Al Sa'id in Oman will follow suit, serious reforms were already under way in both the kingdom and the sultanate.

To be sure, this was a period of transition, with threats all around. It was thus fair to ask what would it take to destabilise Saudi Arabia, although those who anticipated the demise of the Al Sa'ud were bound to be disappointed, especially since Riyadh was amply aware of looming dangers and took decisive measures to counter various threats.[42] Despite frequent assertions that the Arab Gulf monarchies were fragile, conservative ruling families enhanced their legitimacy in the eyes of the only constituents that mattered: their populations. Indeed, barring a complete loss of religious, political, and tribal legitimacy, it is difficult to contemplate what would shake the authority of the ruling families. Naturally, one can expect foreign policy changes on account of changes in leadership, though institutional commitments gave some permanence to the way Riyadh conducts business. It was a given that King Salman and his team would adapt to circumstances even though he could not possibly destroy the framework he had helped build in the first place. Of course, challenges loomed, including succession issues that involved changes to existing mechanisms. In 2016, however, the Al Sa'ud were more secure than at any other time in contemporary history. Their rule was likely to endure precisely because of innate adaptation skills, ranging from the adoption of primogeniture mechanisms to 'will-to-power' features under the rule of a legitimate sovereign.

10

YOUTH, PROTEST, AND THE NEW ELITE

DOMESTIC SECURITY AND DIGNITY IN KUWAIT

Alanoud Alsharekh

This chapter examines the interconnections between generational change in Arabian Gulf societies and the evolving domestic security landscape in the states of the Arabian Peninsula. Over the past fifty years, the population of the six Gulf Cooperation Council (GCC) countries has grown at a phenomenal rate (from 4 million in 1950 to 46.5 million in 2010),[1] because of both a growing national population and increased inward migration. The relative youth of the GCC's native population has compounded the challenges of unemployment (which is between 5 and 15 per cent among GCC nationals),[2] and complicated the issues of resource scarcity associated with over-reliance on oil and gas exports as drivers of economic growth, which will only worsen with the post-2014 downturn in oil prices. With time on their hands to carry out acts of defiance and, increasingly, political violence, youth in Kuwait, Bahrain, Oman, and Saudi Arabia have been involved in violent anti-government protests since 2011. To ward off political unrest following the Arab Spring protests of 2011, all six GCC states raised salaries for government jobs (the main source of employment for the national population) and promised further job creation,[3] but with young people entering the market in ever-increasing numbers and pressures on national budgets to keep subsidising their lifestyles, this complicated economic issue is fast becoming a political game changer.

The educational system in GCC states has produced a generation of young people who largely fail to meet private-sector hiring standards, while the salary scale, benefits package, and lighter workload make governmental employment highly desirable to most graduates.[4] The availability of a large, skilled immigrant labour force has also stiffened private sector resistance to hiring nationals, and has resulted in overstaffing and masked unemployment in government sectors.[5] The 'youth bulge' as a demographic phenomenon (in which increasingly a national population is under the age of 25) has also led to an increase in political discontent and the questioning of societal norms. As a result, young people have been at the forefront of calls for reform since 2011, as witnessed in Oman, Bahrain, and Kuwait.

The increased integration of women into the political and economic fields and the youth bulge phenomenon have provoked resistance to established patriarchal norms that characterise the region. Both groups—women and the youth—have embraced social media tools that encourage self-expression and promote a culture of individualism, which conflict with the self-censorship and kinship-oriented ideals of their parents' generation. Young people in the GCC also lack reverence for traditions and traditional ruling structures associated with previous generations while remaining conservative in other aspects of their social life. This makes them particularly open to certain forms of politicisation that appeal to this non-traditional conservatism.

In order to accommodate demands for political and economic reforms, GCC governments have embraced some processes of Western democracy. However, the experience of Kuwait and Bahrain has shown that without legitimising political parties with clear social agendas, and without cultivating a mature political middle class to embrace and promote the egalitarian ideals inherent in electoral-based democratic systems, this political transformation will continue to be a chaotic and disruptive process. Through a close examination of the events that occurred in Kuwait leading up to and in the wake of the 'Dignity' protests in 2011–12, and the interplay with what Michael Herb calls 'the interminable political conflict' into which the country is locked,[6] this chapter will link the shifting demographic reality with the new landscape of internal challenges to security in the region.

Framing the Dignity protests

In November 2010, a Doha Debate in Qatar raised the question whether 'This House would prefer money to free elections'. There were no Arabian Gulf intellectuals on the panel but the young audience members in Doha vehemently supported the idea of an increase in political rights and government accountability despite what that could mean in lifestyle change. The choice between increased power-sharing among citizens and ruling families and the possible introduction of taxes or reduction of subsidies—both of which would dramatically change many of the benefits accruing from citizenship—has been at the heart of most political debates concerning Gulf Arabs for the past half-century.

Two years after the Doha debate, the question was no longer theoretical but a real demand of thousands of young people in Kuwait who took to the streets in what became known as the 'Dignity of a Nation' protests. The choice of the word 'dignity', though in keeping with the protest theme in other Arab Spring countries (Pope Benedict, Turkish Foreign Minister Ahmet Davutoglu, numerous journalists, and millions of Arab protesters all referred to 'renewed dignity' as an underlying theme of the Arab Spring protests), was at odds with the general perceptions of Kuwaitis held by other Arab and Arab Gulf nationals. Unlike 'police states' such as Egypt, Tunisia, Libya, Yemen, and Syria, or strictly censored neighbouring GCC countries, Kuwaitis have, by contrast, enjoyed a fair degree of free expression and democratic participation. The country's generous welfare system has ensured that citizens are sheltered from rising fuel and food costs through a subsidy system, government-assisted housing, free health care, education, and public sector jobs. So the 'indignity' of not being able to provide, or of being harassed by state security agencies, was not a burden from which many Kuwaitis suffered, unlike others in the region. From a purely benefits-oriented perspective, the 'Dignity' protests were at first criticised as a pampered child's tantrum, an accusation levelled at Kuwait's Dignity protesters and their oppositional leaders by a surprising number of Arab intellectuals and politicians such as the Lebanese socialist MP Walid Jumblat.[7] If, however, dignity is defined as the right to full political participation, a right upheld by Kuwait's constitution and by the delicate balance of loyalty and patronage that binds the agreement between rulers and ruled, a problem emerges, mostly around accusations of political interference by ruling elite members in the democratic process.

Although this political struggle dates back to the introduction of Kuwait's hybrid hereditary monarchy and unicameral legislature in 1962, it appeared

THE CHANGING SECURITY DYNAMICS OF THE PERSIAN GULF

to reach its zenith in 2012 and changed the inherently 'benevolent' relationship between monarch and citizens in a way that previous critical events, like the Iraqi occupation of 1990 for example, did not. Kuwait's national dignity was felt to have been eroded by rising corruption among the ruling and merchant elites, made more acute through the marked decrease of trickle-down benefits as the national population grew. The country had been rocked by a series of corruption scandals—including allegations of illegal transfers of hundreds of millions of dollars abroad by former Prime Minister Sheikh Nasser Mohammed al-Sabah and the deposit of millions of dollars into the accounts of pro-government MPs, to name but two.[8] As the tempo of reform demands escalated, Kuwait entered an era of instability, with levels of street violence and security crackdowns never witnessed before.[9] Many Kuwaitis tied dignity to the right to choose their political representatives within a flawed yet partially 'democratic' system. When the Emir decided to exercise his right to change the electoral system through a controversial promulgation of a 'Necessity Decree' in October 2012 at a time when the National Assembly was not in session, many of Kuwait's citizens took this direct interference as a step too far.

The Necessity (Emergency) Decree

On 7 October 2012, the Emir of Kuwait, Sheikh Sabah al-Ahmad al-Sabah, issued a bundle of 'Necessity Decrees' dealing with six different reform policies, but the one that inflamed the tribal–Islamist opposition, which had secured 35 of the 50 seats in the National Assembly the previous February, dealt with a change to the voting system for the new election to the Assembly set for December 2012. The February 2012 opposition landslide had given the tribal–Islamist opposition significant voting power and made it harder for the government to manoeuvre without their consent. It also made it easier for this bloc to propose and attempt to pass controversial legislation, including a 'blasphemy' law that carried the death sentence as punishment for those who were deemed to have transgressed against the Prophet and his kin; a 'decency' law that would enforce a conservative dress code on women; and a law that would forbid the building of new churches in Kuwait. The decree was preceded by a strange ruling by Kuwait's Constitutional Court in June 2012 which annulled the result of the February 2012 election on a technicality relating to the 'unconstitutional' dissolution of the previous parliament in December 2011. The ruling meant that the opposition-dominated National Assembly elected in February 2012 was dissolved in June 2012 and the previous parliament (elected in May 2009) was reinstated. This made the short-lived Assembly of February 2012 the first representative council in the history of Kuwait to be dissolved by a judicial ruling. However, when the former 2009 Assembly returned, it was unable to hold a single session for lack of a quorum owing to boycotts by oppositional MPs.

This controversial decree partially amended the electoral law allowing for four possible votes per person to a one person, one vote system (the single non-transferable vote), similar to the system that has for years caused contention in the Hashemite Kingdom of Jordan because of accusations that it enables the government to manipulate the outcomes of elections more easily.[10] However, Suliman al-Atiqi has argued that the four-vote system gave tribes and Islamists an unfair competitive edge which 'inflated their popularity',[11] because it allowed them to broker deals among themselves for the other three votes. According to article 71 of the constitution, the Emir is empowered to issue emergency decrees, once convened, parliament can debate the matter and vote to accept or reject the decrees. The oppositional parliamentary majority of the February 2012 Assembly—now out of office and considered role models by many of the youth protesters—refused to accept this decree, arguing that it was unconstitutional, as there was a lack of 'necessity' for amending the electoral law, and revealed the monarch's disregard of the popular will. Kuwait entered a heated political crisis that brought with it renewed marches which would change its political landscape forever, and give rise to the re-emergence of the police state in Kuwait on a scale never witnessed before.[12] The first 'Dignity of the Nation' march on 21 October 2012, organised through an anonymous Twitter account, which recycled the symbolic orange colour of the earlier 2006 protest as its emblem (the colour was thought to be a symbolic link to the Ukranian Orange Revolution), witnessed clashes between demonstrators and police forces resulting in scores of injuries on both sides, and was followed by a second march on 4 November 2012.

These marches represented a turning point in the language and tools of popular protest, and they were met with retaliation by Kuwait's security forces on a scale unprecedented in the country's history, involving tear gas, concussion grenades (sound bombs), and arrests,[13] followed by jail sentences, hefty bail amounts, and, in some cases, the revocation of citizenship. Throughout 2011, perhaps spurred by Arab Spring movements elsewhere in the region and public sympathy with their plight, Kuwait's Bedun (non-national or stateless) community also engaged in various protests to demand citizenship rights, which met with even more severe retaliation by security forces.[14] To understand how the traditionally peaceful and relatively amicable relations between government and opposition deteriorated so fast in an affluent and contented place like Kuwait, the events of the past decade have to be placed in context.

Lessons from history

The events taking place in Kuwait today cannot fully be understood without referring to three equally influential occurrences that fed into and were in turn fostered by each other. In 2003, Kuwait's late Emir, Sheikh Jaber al-Ahmad al-Sabah, who died in January 2006, broke with forty years of tradition dating back to the post-independence formation of the modern state in 1961, and split the position of Crown Prince from that of Prime Minister, to which he appointed his brother, Sheikh Sabah al-Ahmad al-Sabah, the present Emir since 2006. Most Kuwaitis accepted this change as a popular move, fuelled by a 'reformist' agenda, as both the Emir and the Crown Prince, Sheikh Sa'ad 'Abdullah al-Sabah, were in poor health at the time.[15] However, the new split in roles meant that the future ruler of Kuwait was removed from the daily task of governing, making his position a largely ceremonial and silent one. The appointment of a Prime Minister made the formerly somewhat politically-removed Emir directly accountable for the former's actions. This change also opened up the position of Prime Minister for the first time to scrutiny—a critical assessment that was not legally possible when the position was tied to the role of the Crown Prince, who, like the Emir, was constitutionally above open criticism. More importantly, the change no longer made it imperative for the Prime Minister to be a ruling family member, and as a result the inevitable next step of opposition demands was for an elected representative to fill that position.[16]

When Emir Sheikh Jaber al-Ahmad al-Sabah passed away in January 2006, the National Assembly played an important role in securing the position of ruler for his brother, Sheikh Sabah al-Ahmad al-Sabah, as the Crown Prince, Sheikh Sa'ad 'Abdullah al-Sabah was ill and thus deemed physically 'unfit to rule'. The unprecedented involvement of the National Assembly and its Speaker, the late Jassim al-Kharafi, in securing the leadership position for Sheikh Sabah during this 'crisis of transference',[17] was also due to some resistance within the ruling family council to the appointment of another sibling from the Al Jaber line within the ruling family since the position of emir usually rotated between two branches of the Al Sabah. As well as being a former Minister of Finance, Jassim al-Kharafi's family has been listed on the *Forbes* billionaire list for the past twenty years. His brother-in-law 'Ali al-Ghanim heads the Chamber of Commerce, and his position as a representative of Kuwait's merchant elite (the wealthy families that control the majority of private sector corporations) also came into play several times over the ensuing decade as an influential decision-maker in Kuwaiti politics. The marriage of Jassim al-Kharafi's granddaughter to the present Emir's grandson on 18 March 2015 could be seen as the emergence of the Kharafi–Ghanim family as more powerful than some members of the Al Sabah family itself,[18] a complaint made by Kuwaiti political commentators.

The situation among ruling family members was made more complicated by the appointment of Emir Sabah's brother as Crown Prince, thus eliminating the other branches eligible to rule from future scenarios, and by the appointment of the Emir's nephew, Sheikh Nasser al-Mohammed al-Sabah, also from the Jaber branch, as Prime Minister. For many Kuwaitis this meant that the balance between the supporters of the two branches of the ruling family was disrupted, as only those close to the Al Jaber would benefit from the new leadership.[19]

In spite of the initial wave of goodwill and optimism that supported Sheikh Sabah al-Ahmad al-Sabah as Prime Minister in 2003, three years later, while residing over his first parliament as the Emir, an 'Orange' youth movement (also referred to as 'Nabiha Khamsa' (We want five [districts])) started to protest outside the National Assembly on 14 May 2006, demanding that the number of electoral districts be reduced from 25 to 5 in order to curb gerrymandering and make it harder for government-backed MPs to win election. Although the youths behind the protests were primarily from liberal social groups, their protest was adopted and given credence by Islamist MPs at the time, especially those affiliated with the Muslim Brotherhood's political arm, the Islamic Constitutional Movement (ICM).

The Orange Movement became a convenient vehicle for some 29 MPs, who had been trying to push the redistricting agenda through parliament, to march out of the National Assembly session and converge outside its doors, usurping the spontaneous youth initiative, and turning it into an influential and more attractive platform for their political ambitions. The congregated youngsters found themselves transformed almost overnight from some two hundred friends and 'friends of friends' to an angry mob several thousand strong, with finger-wagging parliamentarians taking over their public voice.[20] Taken off guard by the outpouring of public sympathy with the Orange protests, the government announced new elections, which took place in April. The populism behind 'Nabiha Khamsa' ensured that the MPs who had promised to rally behind the district reforms made it into office in the June 2006 elections. When the new National Assembly was officially convened, the redistricting was proposed in parliament and approved by a majority. The government was forced to acquiesce in public demands and agree to the districting. This was hailed as a victory for the youth groups but it introduced a new form of political leverage for Kuwaiti MPs seeking to further their careers by jumping on the bandwagon of the youths' protests.

These developments, coupled with mounting competition within the ruling family over succession, have caused warring factions within the ruling elite to lend financial and political support to certain MPs and political movements in the hope of eliminating competitors within the family or elevating their own popularity on the 'street'. Rivalry between ruling family members, especially the heated battles between the ex-Prime Minister, Sheikh Nasser Mohammed, and his ex-Deputy Prime Minister, Sheikh Ahmad al-Fahad al-Sabah, caused additional friction within an already dysfunctional political system marked by conflict and rivalry between government and parliament. The halls of the National Assembly were rocked by score-settling and political one-upmanship, culminating in both camps losing their champion, as Sheikh Nasser Mohammed was forced to resign and Sheikh Ahmad al-Fahd shamed publicly and forced to resign to avoid hostile questioning from MPs. Cooperation between the legislative and executive branches went from being difficult to impossible, and Kuwait entered the most economically stagnant phase of its modern history, in spite of record surpluses and rocketing oil prices, with the official development plan and major government tenders stalling as consecutive governments and parliaments effectively brought the country to a halt.[21]

Escalating violence and the resurgence of tribal politics

The success of the fairly mild and non-violent Orange Movement in 2006 led to dramatic shifts in the awareness of the power of street protests in bringing about political change. Over the following seven years, what were once well-organised and law-abiding youth protests morphed into an increasingly angry series of strikes, sit-ins, and congregations, particularly among members of the Kuwaiti tribal community (those who retain, and most strongly sociopolitically identify with, the name of the tribe from which they are descended).

Increasingly, these protests were specifically tailored to promote personal and tribal positions, or as a form of political bargaining with the ruling elite to force through wage increases and other employment benefits, as over 73.2 per cent of the national population are government employees.[22]

These 'tolerated' gatherings took a turn for the worse at an infamous rally at the house of a Muslim Brotherhood-affiliated tribal MP, Jamaan al-Harbash, on 8 December 2010, where the attendees (who included politicians from both tribal and urban backgrounds, including Marzouq al-Ghanim, current House Speaker) refused to disperse when told by the authorities that they were in violation of the cap on the number of people allowed at an unlicensed gathering. Security forces were called in to force them to leave, injuring some speakers in the process.[23] It was unfortunate for the government that this show of force came just a month before the Arab Spring descended on the region, emboldening and inspiring political movements and the mobilisation of angry and frustrated youths. What followed was a year-long escalation in the tempo of reform demands and a departure from the traditionally established language of political rhetoric into calls for replacing the Prime Minister, Sheikh Nasser Mohammed al-Sabah, mimicking also Egyptian Muslim Brotherhood slogans of an 'Islamic Constitution' and an elected Prime Minister. This is partly the reason why the Muslim Brotherhood was accused of being behind these 'Dignity' protests by observers in and out of Kuwait. As a result, the Muslim Brotherhood-led government of Egypt had to issue a statement distancing itself from the turmoil.[24]

As the Emir and ruling establishment attempted to placate these demands with promises of reform, a KD1,000 (US$3,600) gift for each citizen, and increased subsidies and wage hikes, a heated political exchange developed between some tribal elements and the government. The alleged torture and murder of a young man from the Muttair tribe who was being held in police custody, and the subsequent cover-up attempts by the Ministry of the Interior soon after the violence of the Harbash incident, were taken by some as further proof of the alleged brutality of the security apparatus.[25]

Dahem al-Qahtani, a political commentator and journalist, suggests that this was a period when members of the Muttair tribe in particular felt that they were being ostracised by the government because many vocal oppositional figures in parliament belonged to it, a sentiment they expressed in media interviews and in campaign tents.[26]

The controversy around anti-tribal statements made by an urban district MP, Mohammed al-Juwaihil, tested the limits of both the tribe and government leniency, as his campaign tent was burned in the run-up to the February 2012 election.[27] In the same period, members of tribes also attacked two privately owned TV stations (both incidents were to pay back for insults), and adopted a reactionary tribal language that excluded other groups of the Kuwaiti community.[28] This included glorifying the warrior ethic of 'red-eyed free men' (a euphemism for the Muttair tribe) who put fear into communities they raided, with reports of tribes singing 'traditional war songs for its [the government's] dissolution,'[29] and revived the Bedouin ethos of favoring close kin over all others: me and my brother against my cousin, and me and my cousin against others. This insular mantra underpinned the political platforms of many tribal MPs who provided services exclusively to their tribesmen. The latter in turn ensured that the MPs made it into office by voting for them in illegal tribal primaries held before official election dates.[30] Hence, the former MP Musallam al-Barrak, who was the spearhead of the oppositional movement prior to his imprisonment in May 2015, was often referred to as 'the most popular man in Kuwait' by the foreign press for winning the highest number of votes in three consecutive elections, though he can be more accurately described as the most popular man in the al-Muttair, the tribe to which he belongs and to which he provided services.

Moreover, because of the traditional alliance with tribal elements, there was a special kinship structure and system of intermarriage between many ruling family members and tribal families, of whom great numbers were nationalised in the 1980s by the ruling elite. Many of the senior family members have intermarried with the Bedouin tribes of Kuwait. The late Emir, Sheikh Jaber al-Ahmad al-Sabah, married over ten women from the Muttair tribe,[31] including the sister of the opposition figurehead, Musallam al-Barrak. All the major Bedouin tribes, such as the Ajman, Shammar, and Otaiba, also intermarried with the late Emir and other ruling family elites. This familial relationship, the relaxed nature of Kuwait's legal prosecution in general, and their demographic numbers, which today exceed in total other non-tribal Kuwaiti ethnic groups, may have furthered a sense of being 'untouchable' among many tribal MPs and their young followers.

The opposition falters

The rise in tribal independent actions and threats of retribution added to the sense of polarisation and of the failure of Kuwait's statehood project in fostering a non-sectarian sense of citizenship based on civil responsibility and respect for the rule of law. It came at a time when developments in neighbour-ing Bahrain added to the Sunni–Shiʻa divide in the halls of the National Assembly and spilled out into the streets, lending a sense of extremist reactiv-ity to most political issues. Many of those involved in the political scene began to overemphasise ethnic and sectarian aspects of their background and affili-ation, engaging in the worst type of what Toby Matthiesen has referred to as sectarian identity entrepreneurship, forming movements 'to construct differ-ences and reinforce boundaries between their own groups and other groups'.[32]

Opposition MPs made a grave error when they overplayed their hand on 16 November 2011 and stormed the National Assembly building together with a group of youthful protesters after a failed attempt to reach the Prime Minister's home.[33] This marked a turning point in both public and govern-ment tolerance for such violent acts and made the MPs who participated subject to both social persecution, with opinions divided about the transgres-sive nature of this action, and legal persecution despite the legal immunity their positions gave them. Yet, though the Emir accepted the Prime Minister's resignation that same month, it was an incomplete victory for the tribal–Islamist opposition, as the following months would prove.

The change of tactics by the government following the Prime Minister's resignation in 2011 had especially dire consequences for youth from tribal backgrounds, many of whom had embraced the hardline rhetoric of their political idols. The figures from Kuwait's Central Statistics Bureau show a clear discrepancy between the number of youths in urban 'hadhar' (settled) areas and the much larger numbers in the mainly tribal 'bedu' districts.[34] The demo-graphic reality of Kuwait meant that much of its youth population was situ-ated in the Bedouin tribal areas, and thus likely to be exposed to two main ideologies. The first magnified the social, political, and economic importance of the tribe in guaranteeing its members' basic rights to housing, welfare, and a government job, giving increased importance to what Lambert refers to as 'new urban tribal politics'.[35] The second emphasises the narrative that belong-ing to a tribal background results in discrimination and denial of the privileges available to merchant and non-tribal Kuwaitis, which was echoed in Barrak's statement that 'there is a coalition between the government and some wealthy merchants to oppress the rest of Kuwait'.[36] This meant that, for many youths, the tribe's political leader was seen as an authority more important than the law of the land, and it made them more likely to protest, engage in altercations with law enforcement officers, and expose themselves to a greater likelihood of legal retaliation at a later stage. Whereas, historically, tribes competed with each other for the government's goodwill (for example, when a tribesman takes a high position in a ministry, he insures that his tribal brethren are well taken care of, to the detriment of other tribes), the youth protests eliminated that competition between tribes and united them against what they claimed was deliberate neglect and disrespect to all 'Bedouins'.

An exploitable and explosive generation

In spite of years of warning by non-governmental organisations (NGOs) and civil society groups of the impending youth bulge, it took the storming of the National Assembly in November 2011 for the government to realise the gravity of the situation. The 2012 statistics from the Public Authority for Civil Information showed that 57.4 per cent of Kuwait's national population was under the age of 25 and that 86.7 per cent of the population was under 40. In terms of the representation of this demographic majority in leadership positions, it became clear that both the political establishment and the government were out of touch with the youth population on whose behalf they claimed to speak. The Emir announced the establishment of a National Youth Project (NYP) at a session of the National Assembly on 15 February 2012. The aim of this project was to try to ascertain the issues that were frustrating young people in Kuwait and driving them to street protests. The hope was to provide a government-sanctioned vehicle for representative young people from different sectors of Kuwait's community to articulate their national aspirations and have direct access to MPs, ministers, and other government officials. Almost all of Kuwait's established civil society groups sent youth representatives to participate, including NGOs such as the Women's Cultural and Social Society, Injaz, the Teachers' Association, the Journalists' Society, Accountants' Association, Lawyers' Association, and Human Rights Society.[37] NGOs affiliated to the Muslim Brotherhood officially boycotted the NYP, but there were some young people present with indirect links to both the Brotherhood and to other Islamist groups. Many government officials and political figures were brought in to participate in the talks and focus on producing a comprehensive list of priorities that the government could then tackle.

The problems young people in Kuwait face today are numerous; one of the major issues being the flawed public education system, which has proved unable to provide them with a globally competitive edge in contemporary labour markets. For years, liberal academics and MPs such as Dr Aseel al-Awadhi warned the government that Islamist groups,[38] namely the Muslim

Brotherhood movement and, later, Salafist-affiliated bodies, were intervening in the educational system and watering down essential analytical curriculums in favour of overtly religious texts. This was coupled with a pro-segregation movement that culminated in turning all universities in Kuwait from coeducational facilities to single-sex institutions through a bill passed in parliament in 1996 (though it took a few years longer to be fully enforced and is still being contested in both parliament and Constitutional Court).[39] Recently, the Constitutional Court ruled that gender desegregation in education meant that opposite-sex students cannot sit next to each other in lecture halls but could otherwise mingle in the same campus.[40]

This move toward the politicisation of the educational process also involved MPs interfering in all facets of education, from teachers' recruitment to creating pressure groups for lowering the entrance requirements for colleges, and forcing governmental agencies to hire graduates with non-vocational backgrounds, to such an extent that Kuwait's Minister of Education, Bader al-Issa, complained that tribal and Islamist elements had 'kidnapped' the Public Authority for Applied Education and Training.[41] The government and, by extension, Kuwait's ruling elite turned a blind eye to these transgressions, as it was then using the Islamists to campaign against liberal MPs in parliament and co-opt the Arab nationalist movement spearheading the opposition at the time.[42]

Other issues affecting youth in Kuwait today are the lack of a spontaneous social arena in Kuwait's rigidly conservative culture, alongside a pervasive consumption-oriented culture, which means that young people spend their time in malls or various eateries, contributing to the lack of momentum in their lives. What was once a thriving communal sports scene in the 1970s and 1980s, as part of the national identity project, gradually became defunct as rivalries between ruling and merchant elites raged over leadership of these sports clubs.[43] The fracas surrounding the Public Authority for Youth and Sports has led to such an acute deterioration in sports and sporting clubs that whereas Kuwait was once the leading soccer power in the GCC (with a record nine wins in the Gulf Cup of Nations), FIFA has suspended the country three times for political interference, in 2007, 2008, and 2015. Elsewhere, excessive censorship and a lack of funding stifled the culture and arts arena in which Kuwait once led the GCC in creative output. This gaping hole in extra-curricular activities contrasted sharply with those run by organised Islamist youth groups, such as those hosted by the Muslim Brotherhood NGO Gam'iyat al-Islah or female Islamist groups such as Bayadir as-Salam, which would hold classes and sports events and run community-oriented clubs.

These political groups have succeeded in giving bored and restless young people a sense of order, identity, and belonging. The early indoctrination of Kuwaiti youth in these NGOs and social clubs meant that there was always going to be a sympathetic, engaged, and disciplined group of young people ready for mobilisation whenever Islamist groups such as the Muslim Brotherhood's political arm, ICM, entered the political arena. Islamist political groups also have established their own private schools to start the indoctrination process earlier and at a more elite level, so as to fit in with modern Kuwaiti middle-class aspirations, providing things like bilingual education and internationally accredited 'Islamic' nurseries.[44]

In other areas, young people gained a sense of belonging from the local *hussaniya* (Shiite mosque) or tribal *diwanniya* (male-only gathering house), which helped contribute to a sense of tribal, ethnic, or sectarian belonging that preceded a pan-Kuwaiti identity. A controversial planning decision in the early 1980s allowed government-allocated housing to turn into closed culs de sac where members of a single tribe or sect would live side by side, reinforcing a narrow sense of identity by eliminating the natural neighbourly interactions with other segments of Kuwait's society.[45] The result of all these factors has been a youth population that is more used to putting its faith in its elected homegrown political representative than in a wider representative government that is not focused on the immediate concerns of the local districts. Saud al-Inizi, president of Kuwait's Graduate Society, says that this national identity crisis was the inevitable result of 'a ruling elite focused on fostering loyalty for the family and ensuring the continuity of their rule, and not on state-building and presenting citizens with a set of common, law-driven values they can associate with'.[46]

Young, angry, and online

This combination of boredom, lack of direction, and social isolation made Kuwait's youth fertile ground for reactionary politics and protest movements once the Arab Spring made its way eastward from North Africa toward the Arabian Peninsula. Kuwait's fairly open political system and diverse media platforms also fuelled many aspects of this debate, and not always in ways that fostered national unity. In fact, the political dialogue in Kuwait had become so sectarian and polarised that the Emir was forced to issue a law banning hate speech (called the National Unity and Rejection of Hate Decree) within the bundle of emergency decrees of October 2012. As such, peaceful protest turned into open defiance, with alleged Molotov cocktails being thrown,[47] followed by an unprecedented government crackdown.

When the NYP finally issued its recommendations in March 2013, finding a resolution to Kuwait's housing crisis was one of its priorities.[48] While it was possible a generation ago to afford a fairly comfortable domestic lifestyle as a government employee, it has now become vastly more difficult for young adults in Kuwait to leave the parental nest, as real estate and building costs in Kuwait are among the highest in the region.[49] Housing issues are becoming increasingly contentious even in a rich country like Kuwait, where young families have to wait over seventeen years to be eligible for government-assisted housing,[50] and, even then, prices are kept at artificially inflated levels so that the landowners get to benefit. Less than 10 per cent of Kuwait's land mass is developed, as vast swathes of undeveloped land are controlled by either the Kuwait Oil Company (KOC) or the Ministry of Defence, and the government releases land for development at as slow a pace as it wishes to set.[51] In September 2013, the Netir bayt campaign (Waiting for a House) was launched as a pressure group, unsuccessful so far, that aimed to force the government to distribute 12,000 units annually.

Social media leaks, including a WhatsApp message that claimed that large tracts of prime urban land were being held by the Amiri Diwan for the benefit of ruling family newly-weds, pictures of the former Prime Minister driving a $1.6 million Bugatti in Geneva circulating on the internet,[52] and official documents from his office detailing expenditures of KD3 million (over $10 million) on incense and perfume and other gifts,[53] quickly changed the powerlessness felt by youth in Kuwait into a seething anger directed at the government and at the ruling establishment. The use of online forums and the spreading of these rumours, internal memos, and documents by both camps to try to control the dialogue are symptomatic of both the high rates of smartphone penetration in the region and the equally high rates of social media adoption by young people in Kuwait and other Arab Gulf states.[54] Similar tactics were used by both protesters and local authorities elsewhere in the GCC. In Bahrain, the use of social media to document the use of force by authorities led to many online battles between regime supporters and protesters. At one point, police in Manama would confiscate protesters' phones and use their online activities to issue arrest warrants and force them to divulge the names of others in their networks.[55] During the protests in Sohar in Oman, there were reports of circulated WhatsApp messages decrying the involvement of the UAE in Omani politics and reframing the issue as 'outside intervention' rather than a spontaneous protest movement.[56]

The limits on public debate, the lack of control on substantiated information, and the novelty of being online influencers made social media the battleground of choice for Kuwait's protest movement. Social media political activism was not a new phenomenon in Kuwait. Political blogs, such as *Sahat al-Safat*, played a pivotal role in rallying the masses to the Orange Movement in 2006. As social media tools progressed, Kuwait youth gradually moved from blogging to Twitter. Moreover, what were once creative aliases and fake photos on blogs were now replaced with full names and real photos on Twitter. The 'fear factor' among the young was gone. Various political Twitter stars with over 100,000 followers weigh in on critical issues, and for many young people their views have been taken as a more reliable and accessible source of information. Online dissent grew to such a magnitude that at one point there was a 'battery' hashtag,[57] a reference to the Emir's heart pacemaker, which was popular among young people at the beginning of the Necessity Decree debate. Criticism of the Emir or his decisions would be framed in an indirect way and the addition of the battery hashtag served as a coded reference. For the state security agency, this was a step too far. The young people involved in the hashtag were rounded up, arrested, and found guilty in spite of their veiled references and anonymous accounts, and prosecution for online offences became a real danger.[58]

The use of force by the government and security forces was directly related to three other issues that also weighed heavily on young people's minds, according to NYP findings: ensuring an independent judiciary in Kuwait, fostering national unity, and security issues, especially those to do with freedom of speech and the detention of protesters. These three concerns would gain even more urgency as the government switched gears over the next months, broke free of traditional social and cultural taboos, and struck back at Kuwait's protesters with arrests, civil and criminal suits, media campaigns, and the humiliation of the once proud opposition.

The crackdown on Dignity

One of the major impacts of the raging 'Dignity' crisis was that the electoral battle shifted from being a free competition among candidates to being a conflict between participation and boycott, with each side accusing the other of national treason. The government added to its usual pro-vote campaigns the recruitment of imams and religious authorities who equated protest and boycott with anti-Sharia disobedience, thereby embarrassing many of the protesting

Islamist MPs, who had used similar fatwas in the past to argue their case and now had to distance themselves from religious authority and ground their cause solely in secular law and the constitution. The Emir, who usually spoke to the nation on a handful of public and religious occasions, gave three speeches in one week, on 5, 7, and 11 November 2012, stressing adherence to the rule of the constitution and refusal to compromise with those who 'threaten Kuwait's stability', and followed through on his promise in a way that left many in the oppositional camp reeling from the rapid change in their fates.

On 8 December 2012, the fourth March for Dignity took place beneath the iconic symbol of Kuwait Towers, the first to occur after the National Assembly election under the contested change to the electoral law on 1 December. This was the second of these marches to be licensed by the government, and it followed five days of street protests and clashes between security forces and youths in the 'outer district' residential areas. Geographically, the 'outer districts' are commonly agreed to be those that lie beyond the sixth ring road with the exception of Al-Jahraa and Al-Fahaheel, which were once outlying villages of the old walled city of Kuwait. There are several sociopolitical stigmas attached to the outer district inhabitants, including that they are more recently settled Bedouin tribes, who were awarded citizenship on the grounds of providing feudal loyalty to the ruling family.[59] Ironically, it was this traditional government ally that by 2012 lay at the heart of the opposition protest movement, with strong support from the liberal front and from moderate Kuwaitis who saw the Emir's intervention to amend the electoral system, a key victory of the 2006 protests, as an infringement of one of the main tenets of the constitution: the 'will of the people'. This brought together unlikely political allies in the beginning, with Dr Ahmad al-Khatib, an icon of the 1960s liberal pan-Arab nationalist movement and its political arm, the National Democratic Forum, being pictured at political events with Muslim Brotherhood politicians such as ex-MP Mohammed al-Dalal. Many who did not participate in the Dignity marches boycotted the elections, whether by not running (as many inner-district urban and merchant politicians chose to do) or by not voting. In fact, Dr Khatib's op-ed about boycotting the elections, in which he explained that while Kuwaitis never wanted for food and shelter, they were nonetheless hungry for their dignity, became something of a unifying slogan for the protesters.

Estimates of the exact number of participants at the 'Dignity' marches have varied widely, with oppositional organisers claiming inflated numbers in excess of 250,000 (equivalent to almost a quarter of Kuwait's national population) and the government putting the figure at a mere 4,000, while major news agencies such as the BBC and Reuters estimated between 10,000 and 20,000 protesters at the peak. However, the size of the 8 December 2012 'Dignity' march was estimated at between only 5,000 and 10,000, as support for the boycott movement fell after the election took place. Over the next two months, two additional 'Dignity' protests saw only a few hundred protesters, as public sympathy waned and marches in residential areas became a nuisance and security hazard to many who disapproved of these protest tactics.[60]

Despite raising the ceiling of demands, the opposition and its supporters continued to stress their adherence to the current political system under the leadership of the Al Sabah family. Nevertheless, the opposition counted on the participation rate in the electoral process to be so low as to discredit the legitimacy of the Assembly, but that did not work out as hoped. Although at almost 40 per cent, participation was significantly lower than in previous elections, it was not a big enough difference to warrant a popular backlash. Also, the lack of participation by many of the stalwarts of the National Assembly meant that fresh faces, as well as the expected governmental allies, unaffiliated with any movements or political blocs, secured election, which many of the moderate Kuwaiti youth saw as a positive sign.

The disappointment with the boycott failure led to nightly protests and midnight rallies which took place in different residential areas of Kuwait, especially in the outer districts like Sabah al-Nasser, Sabahiya, and their surroundings. The arrest of stone-throwing teenagers and young tweeps for transgressing against the Emir and inciting public disorder was another blow to the youth protest movement. The consequences of their formerly tolerated activities were suddenly brought home when several were sentenced to two- and five-year jail terms and denied bail.[61] The arrest of tribal MPs and oppositional figureheads such as Musallam al-Barrak, who publicly defied the Emir in an open rally a few days after the promulgation of the Necessity Decree and introduced the slogan 'We Will Not Allow You', and their subsequent fining, release, rearrest, trial, and eventual imprisonment meant that they were reduced to a shadow of their former selves.[62] When the courts sentenced three tribal MPs to three years' imprisonment with hard labour in early February 2013, despite continuing protests, rallies and sit-ins by young people, and threats of union strikes and civil disobedience by other tribal members, the limitation of the protesters' capabilities against the might of the state was brought home. Although arrest warrants were issued for these MPs, they were not taken into custody. A week later, an appeals court suspended the sentence and the lawmakers were fined KD5,000 each and released on bail until a later retrial date. The government repeated this cycle with oppositional MPs, tweeps, and journalists in an exhausting cycle of arrests, release, and rearrest over the course of the next two years, and made a point of focusing on breaches of the law that were in the past benignly ignored.

The message to the youth and to the opposition was clear: if they chose to escalate their protest tactics, the ruling establishment would reverse its policy of tolerance and back up its threats with decisive action. Kuwait's signing of the GCC Security Agreement, after eighteen years of abstaining for 'constitutional concerns', in November 2012 was taken by the opposition to be another sign that the country was no longer a safe haven for freedom of expression and oppositional views. The agreement was signed by the Minister of the Interior, Sheikh Ahmad al-Humoud al-Sabah, but it then still needed to be officially ratified by the National Assembly.

An alternative 'youth'

In June 2013 the contested and Shi'a-heavy parliament was dissolved, and the fractured opposition saw some of its members turn their back on the coalition and run for office alongside established political players. At the same time, members of the dissolved 2012 Assembly, who had felt pressured not to participate in the December 2012 election, argued that now that a ruling of the Constitutional Court had legitimised the decree, they could once again run for office.

In the 2013 cabinet a Ministry of Youth was set up, headed by a young female member of the ruling family, the film director Sheikha al-Zain al-Sabah, as Deputy Minister. Marzouq al-Ghanim, nephew of the former Speaker and son of the head of the Chamber of Commerce, took over the role of Speaker. In what was one of the most youthful cabinets in Kuwait's recent history, four of the ministers, including a Deputy Prime Minister, Sheikh Mohammed 'Abdullah al-Mubarak, were in their early forties. Reasserting the central role of the merchant elite as the democratic core of the National Assembly meant that a new youth dialogue was opened with the government and a cooperative and results-oriented parliament installed, which had, by early 2016, weathered many developments that caused previous assemblies to disintegrate. These included the resignation of five MPs (in protest against a denial of their request to question the Prime Minister),[63] who were replaced by representatives of the merchant elite and those friendly towards the government,[64] and several protests and rallies by the remnants of the opposition.

The government produced alternative and more glamorous role models for Kuwait's youths, such as the Minister of Finance and acting Minister of Oil, Anas al-Saleh, a former member of the board of the Chamber of Commerce, thereby marking the ruling family's return to goodwill with their trusted partner, the merchant class. These three players, Sheikh Mohammed al-Mubarak, Marzouq al-Ghanim, and Anas al-Saleh, were especially adept at understanding and manipulating both traditional and social media, and the power of citizen journalism and Insta-influencers. Armed with economic incentive packages and a new parliamentary TV station that would steer the conversation away from political change and 'dignity', they were more agile and able to 'deliver' than those they replaced. Slowly, this replacement of demands for real political redistribution and voting rights with a show of selective representation from government-friendly new elites eroded the boycott movement, which fell into a cycle of infighting and internal blame.

Initially made up of Islamists (both Muslim Brotherhood and Salafist groups), merchant politicians, and tribal and liberal groups, the boycott movement was reduced by government efforts at isolation to a mostly tribal and Islamist opposition.[65] This tactic sealed the fate of what remained of the tribal–Islamist opposition further as media laws became more draconian, as it left them with a shrinking support base to draw upon. Anti-Muslim Brotherhood rhetoric reached its zenith with the fall of Mohammed Morsi's government in Egypt in July 2013,[66] and GCC states used the security agreement to chase dissidents both online and across national borders.

Mirroring the punitive actions of the Bahraini government, which revoked 31 citizenships in 2012, the Kuwaiti government crossed a hitherto-sacrosanct red line when it announced on 21 July 2014 that the citizenship of Ahmad al-Shammari, the front man of the oppositional TV station and newspaper *Al-Alam al-Yowm* (rumoured to be financed by the ousted Deputy Prime Minister, Sheikh Ahmad al-Fahad al-Sabah).[67] Four more names swiftly followed as Muslim Brotherhood figures, tribal opposition members, and others were stripped of their citizenship, as well as the citizenship of their immediate kin, as the number of revocations reached 33 by the end of 2014, according to the Human Rights Watch 2015 Kuwait Report.[68] Shi'as, Sunnis, journalists, MPs, and young people were arrested for tweeting insults, blasphemy, and even insulting neighbouring states, leading Humans Right Watch to issue a report in January 2015 that described the actions of the Kuwaiti government as targeting 'free speech throughout 2014'. The oppositional *Al-Watan* newspaper and TV station was forcibly shut down soon after for 'administrative and financial errors', despite being owned by a senior ruling family member, and many critical voices, of journalists and politicians alike, were pressured into self-censorship.[69]

The final decimation of the opposition came in the televised apology speech given by Sheikh Ahmad al-Fahad, the former Deputy Prime Minister, thought to be the instigator behind much of the protest movements and information leaks since 2011. Sheikh Ahmad apologised for supposedly misrepresenting truths and causing national disharmony on the morning of 26 March 2015,[70] and faced a KD1,000 fine and a suspended six-month jail sentence for an allegedly related issue in December 2015.[71] From September 2013 and throughout 2014, the scandal of leaked videos, supposedly showing both the former Prime Minister, Sheikh Nasser Mohammed al-Sabah, and the former Speaker, the late Jassim al-Kharafi, plotting to overthrow the current Emir and install Sheikh Nasser, as well as claims of money laundering and meeting with Hezbollah and Iranian regime representatives, was a threat that Sheikh Ahmad al-Fahad and the opposition camp used to embarrass the leadership. These videos, their validity and sources, occupied much of the oppositional rhetoric while government and high-level officials were questioned by the police. Each camp used traditional media and online channels to argue their case in spite of a gagging order issued by the Ministry of the Interior. Similarly, ex-MP Musallam al-Barrak, who had made similar allusions to bank accounts, telex transfers, and mysterious documents that, he argued, would 'prove' his accusations and topple the 'corrupt elements' in the ruling structure, including three judges, failed to provide the authorities with concrete evidence and, after evading arrests over technicalities and attempting to travel abroad for 'health reasons', he was finally jailed in May 2015 to serve a two-year sentence for insulting the Emir. The young people who had defiantly repeated his speech, tweeted, or retweeted it await similar fates and have been arrested, fined, and imprisoned themselves. Those who could do so have escaped Kuwait to seek temporary asylum elsewhere.

Having seen their heroes and their peers arrested, displaced, and humiliated, and, yet, tentatively optimistic that an economic boost may be around the corner and that their concerns will receive increased attention by the government, Kuwait's youngsters seem to be in a state of limbo. The new parliament, although labelled government-friendly by the opposition, has also fallen into a cycle of interrogations and populist demands that forced past parliaments into a 'non-cooperation' dissolution. The opposition, though no longer able to mobilise as many young people to openly challenge the ruling elite, as the cost of such behaviour has risen, is still making the most of what 'dignity' is left in being defiant and willing to protest, refusing over '50 years of constitutional violations' and a Prime Minister not elected by the people,[72] as a former Speaker of parliament, Ahmad al-Sadoun, stated at a youth power municipality congregation in February 2013. The surprising war on Yemen spearheaded by Saudi Arabia on 25 March 2015 led to a short suspension of anti-government activity by the opposition as Kuwait technically was in a 'state of war'. While these activities were fast resumed after the end of the Kuwaiti participation in the initial air strikes, the momentum and appetite for aggressive political activity were dampened by a heightened fear of sectarian resurgence, fuelled both by the ongoing crisis in Yemen and by a series of terrorist attacks on Shiite mosques by ISIS sympathisers in the Eastern Province of Saudi Arabia and Kuwait (leading to the death of 27 Kuwaitis in a mosque bombing in June 2015, a massacre unheard of since the Iraqi occupation of 1990), and the discovery of a Shiite terrorist cell in Kuwait in July 2015.[73]

Young people in Kuwait realise that the security landscape has changed dramatically in the past ten years. The introduction of mandatory DNA testing for nationals and residents alike is symptomatic of the increasingly controlled space within which Kuwaiti young men and women will have to navigate and manoeuvre in future.[74] The passing of a heavily contested electronic crimes law in January 2016, which Amnesty International warns could 'further stifle freedom of expression',[75] has restricted one of the most important avenues for young people to hold the government and influential individuals accountable. They, and the rest of Kuwait, look towards the output of this more cooperative parliament and the youthful ministers, as an era ushering in both new hope and a round of dialogue free from excessive reactivity, even as they try to weigh the necessity of an increase in security measures against the continued indignity of having their ability to protest and contest corrupt practices curtailed.

Conclusion: implications for the GCC and beyond

The struggle between the continued isolation and the successful assimilation of the national youth population into both labour markets and political systems is a double bind that the GCC states find themselves facing on a more urgent basis. What the future holds for these educated youths who seem to be unwilling to accept the political parameters of their parents, or who live in countries where the rentier bargain can no longer be upheld as in the past, will dictate many of the domestic security issues in the immediate future of the GCC. In a controversial interview with Thomas Friedman of the *New York Times*,[76] President Obama spoke about the disenfranchised, 'alienated', and unemployed youth in GCC countries, who may find the extremist ideology of the Islamic State appealing, and suggested that there was something troubling about the way GCC governments handle discontent within domestic populations, especially among their youth.

The concerns about youth unemployment in the Arab Gulf states are part of a wider economic struggle, given the current youth unemployment crisis facing the world. According to the United Nations Population Fund (UNPF), young people between the ages of 15 and 24 represent almost a quarter of the total human population (1.8 billion),[77] the highest that ratio has been in human history, and face increasingly dire employment prospects nearly everywhere. Over the past five years, these frustrated and jobless young people have fuelled international protest movements, from the Occupy movement in the United States to youth protests in Japan and across Europe, and in the Arab world and the Gulf states as well. Across the globe, youth face similar challenges in finding jobs and forging livelihoods. Most particularly, recent high school and university graduates lack the work experience that is often more important to employers than a degree. The negative effects of unemployment are also largely uniform. These include higher depression rates, decreased birth rates, rising crime, increased emigration, and increases in violent anti-establishment and protest movements.

However, youth in the Arab world face a particular set of challenges that young people in many other parts of the world do not contend with, namely a lack of freedom of expression, association, and other civil rights. In the GCC especially, there are not many public forums that focus on engaging youth and providing social and cultural outlets for young people outside the home, school, or office setting. Such outlets as do exist are usually run by politically motivated groups or NGOs that serve to entrench loyalty to the group before the country.

In his interview with the *New York Times*, President Obama referred to these issues obliquely as the lack of 'legitimate political outlet for grievances', suggesting that the political leadership in the Gulf region has nurtured governments unable or unwilling to make the necessary changes to address and resolve these and other problems, in order to give young people in the region a better future. Obama spoke of the danger within as more potentially threatening to the stability of the six GCC countries than the geographical proximity of IS in Iraq and in Syria. Nevertheless, the threat from IS to the Gulf will continue to grow and appeal to bored and disaffected young people if there is no serious political impetus to find practical solutions to the problems of masked unemployment issues and the primary concerns of this frustrated generation.

Kuwait is not unique among the Gulf states in having a mostly tribal population that can be easily manipulated to rediscover its identity within an exclusionary tribal frame of reference, which is then exploited for political power. The dwindling value of a unified national identity among many GCC youth, coupled with the resurgence of tribal values in southern Iraq after fifty years of Ba'athist rule and several attempts at demographic integration, serves as a reminder of how intractable and persistent these tribal bonds can be. The fact that these Iraqi tribes were among the early incubators of ISIS should also be a red flag for domestic security concerns within the GCC, especially after young men bombed two Shiite mosques in Saudi Arabia and one in Kuwait within the space of two months in the spring of 2015. Thus, isolating and prosecuting tribal elements will only lead to more resentment and violence, as the case of Kuwait has shown. This is not to suggest that only tribal youth is problematic; urban youth, whether Sunni or Shi'a, is equally susceptible to extremist ideologies and tend to see other nationals and residents, and even the government, as having a different, if not hostile, political agenda from their own.

So the question becomes: who sets the agenda for young people in the GCC? Though there has been some debate around the increasing independence of young people, they remain impressionable and easy to manipulate once given a 'purpose'. Shamael al-Sharikh suggests that the lack of role models for Kuwaiti millennials has made it easy for political figures to fill that gap, especially in view of their excessive materialism and the lack of success stories that youth can emulate.[78] A recent multi-stakeholder study investigating economic reforms in the kingdom found that 'beyond clear political motives, some of the reasons behind youth protests in the wealthier Arab states of the Gulf are often driven, exacerbated or compounded by idleness, boredom and the dearth of entertainment infrastructure for younger segments in society'.[79]

As tensions between Iran and GCC states continue to heighten, and play out in proxy wars in Iraq, Syria, Yemen, and elsewhere, government calls for military martyrdom in the battlefields are at odds with reforms meant to fight an insidious extremist ideology. This tension between national and fragmented identity means that young people may be attracted to more violent forms of self-expression, and may be exploited by national and personal agendas of political, religious, or other authority figures whom they admire and may seek to emulate.

In the post-digital age, identity is not bound by geography or social ties. It is systematically indoctrinated from birth to school to workplace. Since governments in the GCC have full control over the education system and many of the media outlets, it should be within their power to create an identity for their youth, about what it means to be a Kuwaiti, a Saudi, or a Bahraini, in a way that embraces all echelons of society and not just those of the ruling elite and their present allies. If the GCC countries want their youth to thrive, they need to unite them on the basis of a national identity that bridges the sectarian–tribal divide and raises them on universal citizenship ethics: abiding by the law, working hard, and giving back to their communities. Without the pursuit of this ethos, the calls to dignity will never be silenced.

There are also wider implications for the continuing tension between two competing security agendas, that of nationals within a nation-state, and that of the current power structure in these monarchies, as well as the perceptions of compatibility between the two. Young men across the Arabian Gulf states, with few notable exceptions, suffer from the same ennui, the same lack of economic and social upward mobility, and the same faltering education system, and are increasingly pushing the boundaries, online and off, of what is acceptable or tolerated. The introduction of a new and youthful ruling elite in Saudi Arabia and Qatar, and relatively young crown princes in the UAE and Bahrain, may increase expectations by the youthful populations of the GCC of being included politically as well.

What Kuwait has experienced in terms of collective bargaining by youth and the political representatives who spoke on their behalf, and the subsequent compromises made by the government since 2006, first with the redrawing of electoral districts after the Nabiha Khamsa protests and then with the resignation of the Prime Minister in 2011—a first in the GCC for a ruling family member—has two lessons for the GCC leadership. The first is that there is a real appetite for reform; and once a country commits to it, this will only fuel demands for further reform because the inherent message is that protests work. Secondly, it might be better in the long term not to compromise from the start if there is not a genuine political will to enact real, painful reforms because the corrective security measures to stem the resulting flow of protest and youth demands can be costly on a national and domestic level and hard to maintain. In spite of the current lull in protests, and the fears of exogenous intervention from Iran or IS, demand for greater democratic inclusion is likely to continue to escalate in the Gulf states, and the need for quick, cohesive, and honest re-evaluations of power-sharing between GCC rulers and those they rule can only be delayed for so long.

11

THE TRANSFORMATION
OF UAE FOREIGN POLICY SINCE 2011

Khalid Almezaini

The examination of a state's external behaviour has long been dominated by studies of superpower states using realism, the main theory in international relations studies. Over the years, this has led to the perception among scholars and policymakers of small states as weak and with a limited role to play in the international system. Yet, the end of the French and British colonialism in the 1950s and 1960s, and the collapse of the Soviet Union in 1991, led to the emergence of small states with different capabilities. Certainly, in their early stages, the newly formed small states played only a minimal role in the international system, but after almost forty to fifty years of existence, their role has changed dramatically. Several small states have emerged with considerable capabilities that allow them to influence regional or international systems. In addition, while there are great similarities between most small states that exist in the world, some can be considered an anomaly because of their peculiar external behaviour, such as Israel, Singapore, Qatar, and the United Arab Emirates (UAE).

The principal objective of this chapter is to analyse why the case of the UAE is considered an anomaly in the conduct of international relations by small states. Moreover, there are particular aspects of the UAE's behaviour that might provide better understanding of why it is a peculiar case.

Since the emergence of the UAE in 1971, the foreign policy of this small state has changed considerably. Small states, in the classical understanding, tend to avoid in engaging in any military action unless it is a reactive behaviour affecting their national security. By contrast, the UAE has moved beyond the traditional understanding of small-state behaviour. Since the Arab Spring, the foreign policy of the UAE has come to be characterized by the use of both soft and hard power through the overt resort to military diplomacy. The country's development of one of the most advanced air forces in the region has given it a confidence in engaging militarily at different levels within the Middle East and North Africa region. The case of the UAE thus necessitates a reassessment of the traditional view that small states react to regional and international political instabilities under the umbrella of strong and larger states. Instead, the UAE has opted to act individually and in alliance with regional powers, in response to security issues arising from perceived domestic and regional threats.

The case of the UAE will show that there are distinctive small states that can influence the international system through their economic and military capabilities, as well as their diplomatic skills. The chapter is structured around the following questions: Firstly, to what extent has the UAE's external behaviour changed since 2011? Secondly, what led this small state to combine the use of both soft and hard power? Thirdly, to what extent does the case of this small state reflect a return of realism and structural realism in the analysis of small-state behaviour. These questions will be answered within five sections. The first provides a conceptual definition and analysis of small states; the second consists of a brief background to UAE foreign policy before 2011; the third examines the UAE's changed behaviour since 2011; the fourth looks at the shifting combination of soft and hard power; while the fifth offers a perspective on the small state and the return of realism.

Small states in international relations

Small states have often been underestimated both because they are 'small' and because they have been seen as incapable of playing a role at the international level or even in protecting themselves from external aggression. However, with the increase in the number of small states in the international system, small states as 'small powers' have emerged as significant actors at different levels. In addition, micro-states have also received great attention. Robert Keohane points out that the literature on micro-states seems to converge around issues of sovereignty and how the capacity to formulate and conduct policy is influenced by dependence on larger polities.[1]

According to Jeanne Hey, the notion of a 'small state' is typically used to denote at least three different types of states: micro-states, small states in the developed world, and small states in the third world.[2] However, there are states in the developing world that share the characteristics of small states in the developed world, such as financial and military capabilities.

The new small states that emerged between the 1960s and the early 1990s have been defined by various criteria such as size of military power, population, economic capability, and territorial mass. In recent years, these criteria have been used extensively to examine small states and their role in the international system. However, small states can remain weak even if they acquire strong economic capability or grow demographically. What is required, therefore, is an examination of small states' foreign policy.

Robert Rothstein defines a small state as one 'which recognizes that it cannot obtain security primarily by use of its own capabilities and that it must rely fundamentally on the aid of other states, institutions, processes, or developments to do so; the Small Power's belief in its ability to rely on its own means must also be recognized by the other states involved in international politics'.[3] However, this does not mean that those types of states are weak states. According to Iver Neumann and Sieglinde Gstohl, the distinction between small and great does not coincide with the distinction between strong and weak. The former is a distinction of quantity and the latter of quality.[4] Moreover, Keohane defines a small state as 'one whose leaders consider that it can never, acting alone or in a small group, make a significant impact on the system'.[5]

The most appropriate definition that can fit the case of the UAE is that developed by Neumann and Gstohl. They define a small state as one 'with limited resources—be it natural, human or experience in conducting foreign policies—as well as limited power—as defined by the inability of the state to project its interest beyond the immediate geographical neighbourhood and the inability to pursue national interests relying solely on its own resources, thus depending on alliances or close cooperation with stronger states'.[6] Although there are states with strong economic and military capabilities such as Israel and, to some extent, the UAE, they are, by this definition, considered an anomaly.

UAE foreign policy, 1970–2011: a brief background

During the UAE's short history, the country has matured politically as state institutions developed between 1971 and 2011. This became evident in the UAE's foreign policy and in the changes that began to appear after the Arab Spring. In addition, the consolidation of the UAE as a federation was also reflected in its external behaviour and in the combination of hard and soft power tools in its conduct of foreign policy.

After its formation as a federation of seven emirates in December 1971, the UAE's foreign policy remained consistent until the death in November 2004 of Sheikh Zayed bin Sultan Al Nahyan, the nation's founding father. During this period, the UAE navigated and survived a hostile regional and international environment that encompassed the Cold War, the Islamic Revolution in Iran, the three Gulf wars between 1980 and 2003, 9/11, and the Arab–Israeli conflict.[7] While after 2004 the UAE continued the policies formulated under Sheikh Zayed, significant changes began to emerge in relation to states affected by the Arab uprisings in 2011 even as the UAE itself resisted the Arab Spring.

Two factors accounted for the consistent nature of UAE policies prior to 2004. One was the federal nature of its system, which led to the formation of a constructive foreign policy.[8] The other was the fact that the state was still in a process of formation, and most attention was paid to consolidating the fledgling federation and building up state institutions.

In the 1970s and the 1980s, the UAE's external behaviour was limited to playing a soft power role by providing foreign aid to a select group of countries in the Arab world. During this period, the formulation and conduct of foreign policy were affected by several factors, mainly related to identities and ideas. Arabism and Islamism contributed significantly to the federation's foreign policy. Although security was, and still is, a determinant factor, no imminent threats to the UAE existed during those decades. The formation of the Gulf Cooperation Council (GCC) at a summit meeting in Abu Dhabi in May 1981 contributed to the UAE's stability. In addition, there was no domestic threat.

The influence of cultural factors such as Arab nationalism varied over time. In the 1970s, Arab nationalism oriented most of the Arab states' foreign policies towards notions of 'Arab solidarity'. As a result, the UAE and most other Gulf states provided up to 10 per cent of their GDP as foreign assistance during this period to recipient countries such as Egypt, Syria, and Jordan. This aid had the political effect of supporting the existence of these small states in the Gulf. In the 1980s Islamism replaced Arab nationalism as a major ideological force, while after 1990 the UAE became more concerned about its survival and stability in view of the Iraqi invasion of Kuwait. This led the UAE to begin considering alternatives ways to ensure the survival and continuity of the state.

Although aid was an important factor in the formulation of UAE foreign and security policy, another significant dimension was the reliance on alliance policies that provided security guarantees to the UAE. Like most typical small states, the UAE sought to ways to engage at the regional and international levels to increase its visibility and create new partnerships with different countries. From the 1990s, the UAE began to take an active role in international alliances, especially in Kosovo in 1999, when the country was one of the few non-NATO members to take part in the campaign. According to Peter Hellyer, 'when in early 1999, forces from the North Atlantic Treaty Organisation (NATO) commenced a campaign of aerial bombardment to persuade the Serbian government to cease its offensive designed at expelling the Albanian population of Kosovo, the UAE was among the first non-NATO states to express support for the operation.'[9]

After the events of 9/11, the UAE joined the international campaign against terrorism assembled by the George W. Bush administration. This led to a strengthening of the UAE's security relations with various states, particularly the United States. Security concerns began to take a larger role in the UAE's foreign policy especially after the US invasion of Iraq in 2003 and the death of Sheikh Zayed in November 2004. Observers of the UAE began to notice incremental changes in the direction of a security-focused foreign policy. This has traditionally been pursued by small states owing to their lack of guarantees for survival. Recent UAE foreign policy clearly reflects the pursuit of collective security within the GCC, greater regional integration, and alliances with international influential actors.

The UAE's new security foreign policy: implications of the Arab Spring

Small states in a hostile environment like the Middle East continue to search for alternative ways to ensure survival and stability. The Arab Spring created further complications for regional stability and the security of small states. During the uprisings in 2011, the policies of Middle Eastern states focused on regime and state survival. In other word, the changing regional and political dynamics determined the foreign policies of states in the region. Although countries in the Middle East are known for having highly personalised foreign policies, according to Kenneth Waltz 'structural change affects the behaviour of states and the outcomes their interactions produce'.[10] The Arab Spring has brought many changes not only to the UAE, but also to most states in the Middle East.

The changes in the UAE's external behaviour do not only stem from regional dynamics, but also from the domestic threats that were perceived by Emirati officials to emanate from the Muslim Brotherhood. Since the start of the Arab Spring, the UAE authorities have become increasingly concerned about a number of local Islamists who, emboldened by the rise of the Muslim Brotherhood in Tunisia and Egypt, started to become more politically active within the UAE.[11] Al-Islah, the local affiliate of the Muslim Brotherhood in the UAE, sought to work with liberal pro-democracy activists, as had the parent Muslim Brotherhood organisation in Egypt.[12] However, after a number of intellectuals, academics, activists, and practitioners sent a petition in March 2011 to President Khalifa bin Zayed asking for the Federal National Council (FNC) to be given more legislative powers, the liberals seemed to lose momentum, reportedly because of a lack of grassroots support.[13] The petition was not welcomed in the UAE, and as the regional uprising had taken violent turn, the UAE government began to adopt measures to contain the Muslim Brotherhood in the UAE, particularly after al-Islah started to receive external support.[14]

Does the Muslim Brotherhood, as represented in the UAE by al-Islah, really threaten the survival of the regime or the state? According to Forstenlechner, Rutledge, and al-Nuaimi, 'Few analysts considered the Muslim Brotherhood capable of threatening the existence of the state, as too few Emiratis subscribe to the doctrine.'[15] However, there are no exact figures available for the number of followers in the UAE. The UAE government acted in response to the perceived threat from the Muslim Brotherhood, whose networks appear to have increased dramatically since 2011.

This domestic threat along with the wider political instabilities across the Middle East led the UAE to redefine its security policy. New laws were introduced, and new security agreements signed with different partners reflected the changes in the UAE's foreign policy. In an unprecedented step for a small state, the UAE cabinet approved a list of terrorist organisations and groups following the implementation of a law in 2014 on combating terrorist crimes.[16] This list included about 80 organisations, including many based in Western countries. In addition, since 2011 the UAE has signed security agreements with Algeria, Egypt, India, Afghanistan, Morocco (on security and anti-terrorism), and the United Kingdom (through a defence agreement). This list excludes military purchases from the United States.

In addition to these changes in security policy there also have been adjustments to domestic policy. The UAE leadership, particularly the President, Sheikh Khalifa bin Zayed, has followed his predecessor in acknowledging and adapting to broader shifts in the regional environment. Regime transition in Egypt, Tunisia, and Libya, the growth of movements of political Islam, and the rise of extremism and sectarianism all required significant change in the UAE's external behaviour. Leaders in the UAE, headed by the Crown Prince of Abu Dhabi, Sheikh Mohammed bin Zayed and the Foreign Minister, Sheikh 'Abdullah bin Zayed, realised that the changing dynamics in the region required a change in foreign policy. What characterised the new posture in the UAE was not only the increased use of soft power, but also the use of hard power. This, together with the increase in military spending and the strengthening of military capabilities, has made the UAE one of the most active and influential small states in the region.

Emirati political scientist Abdulkhaleq 'Abdullah has observed that it is hard not to notice that the UAE has become more visible and active in regional affairs.[17] 'Abdullah adds: 'Wherever you go, the UAE looms large on the horizon, certainly larger than it has been in the past four decades since its formation in 1971.'[18] Despite the sharp fall in oil prices since June 2014, the UAE continues to be active. 'Abdullah predicts that the UAE's political visibility, military assertiveness, economic prominence, and its growing regional role will continue into the foreseeable future.[19] One can also notice that the change in the UAE foreign policy coincided with the change in leadership and growth of instability in the region.

The UAE's foreign policy since 2011 has involved two distinct changes. Firstly, the UAE has matured politically and gained confidence in its ability as a small state both at the military and economic levels. With one of the best air forces in the region, it has played a role in Libya, Syria, and more recently in Yemen together with Saudi Arabia and other regional and international allies. Moreover, these changes have led the Emirates to develop a military collaboration with Saudi Arabia that can play a strong regional role. Secondly, the foreign ministry institutions have developed strongly in the past ten years, enabling them to play a significant role in the making of independent decisions. The UAE Foreign Minister, Sheikh 'Abdullah bin Zayed, has been very active since 2004, and has engaged the UAE in forums and relationships at various regional and international levels. It is clear that the UAE appears to be capable of taking independent decisions of its own on matters of foreign policy, unlike many other small states.[20]

Soft and hard powers: UAE's rise to hard power

The use of hard and soft power essentially involves a state's ability to influence behaviour of other states through economic and military strength. In the process, the state wields power beyond its own territory by making other states do what it wants. The concept of hard power relies heavily on the realist school of thought in international relations studies, in which power is often linked to possession of tangible resources such as military and economy strength, apart from territory, population, and natural resources. Joseph Nye argues that states that exercise hard power show command behaviour, enabling them even to set the political agendas of states that they deem weaker.[21] Hard power strategies focus on military intervention, coercive diplomacy, and economic sanctions to enforce national interests.[22] Consequently, hard power rests on a carrot and stick approach,[23] and such power is typically seen as being exercised by large states against smaller ones. The term has existed since the time of Machiavelli and Hobbes but it gained renewed attention after Nye coined the term 'soft power'.

Although soft power is coercive in nature, the way it is wielded compared with hard power varies significantly. States which exercise soft power tend to do so in a co-optive manner so as to persuade other states to do what they want. Nye defines soft power as the ability to get what one wants through persuasion or attraction rather than coercion.[24] In addition, the show of power is made apparent through the strength of intangible resources such as culture, ideology, and institutions.[25] The instruments of such a show of power could range from diplomacy to economic threats and military coercion as opposed to all-out warfare.[26] Historically, when economies were not as interdependent as they are today, it was difficult for states to exercise soft power beyond their territories. However, this has changed drastically in the present age and day. But the combination of soft and hard power wielded by small states rarely existed before the age of globalisation, with the exception of Israel and Singapore.

The combination of these two tools is normally referred to as smart power. Ernest defines smart power as 'the capacity of an actor to combine elements of hard power and soft power in ways that are mutually reinforcing such that the actor's purposes are advanced effectively and efficiently'.[27] However, the use of smart power differs from one country to another and the two components might not be used simultaneously.

Small states in the international system rarely use hard power because of their limited military capabilities. Traditionally, the use of soft power has placed small states as active players on the world map. Small states in the

Middle East such as Kuwait, Qatar, and UAE were known for their exercise of soft power from the 1970s. In particular, foreign aid was used extensively by the Gulf states for various reasons, and in the process they were able to show and exercise their power in countries that were politically and economically weak.

Foreign aid has been the most important soft power tool in UAE foreign policy since the 1970s. Over this period, the UAE has provided about 10 per cent of its GDP as foreign aid to countries around the world, but mostly to Arab and Muslim countries. This was owing to the rise of oil prices in 1974, after which the UAE became the third-largest aid donor in the region. The UAE government used this tool as a soft power to achieve many objectives, which also seem to have evolved over time.[28]

Between the 1970s and 2011, when the UAE was known for its use of foreign aid as a soft power, the country was still in process of formation, and many of its institutions were not fully developed. Thus, its limited military capability did not enable the UAE to participate in hard power projection at any level. Furthermore, the UAE's military capability was in many ways hindered by the existence of traditional armies in the Arab world which for years dominated as the military powers in the region. These countries included Iraq, Egypt, and Syria. Although the UAE relied on the United States for external defence and security, the core Arab countries provided an umbrella for small states in the Middle East during the early years of independence, and in return many received financial aid from the oil producers in the Gulf. However, with the political and economic decline in the MENA region, the security and military forces of the core Arab states also received a blow, so much so that they struggled to maintain their own state security when regime opponents began to pose a threat to the their countries' stability. At the same time, the military power of the smaller Gulf states began to be more visible particularly during and after the Arab Spring. Sultan al-Qasimi points out: 'Over the past decade the Arab world has witnessed a shifting of not only hard power—which saw the traditional armies of the Arab world in Syria, Egypt and Iraq consumed in internal turmoil— but also of what Harvard professor Joseph Nye termed "soft power", which has moved from these countries to the resource-rich Gulf states'.[29] In addition, the increase in military expenditure of the UAE in recent years has strengthened its military capability. In 2013, the UAE was the United States' second-largest arms export partner, accounting for 8 per cent of total US exports, while Saudi Arabia accounts for 41 per cent of the United

Kingdom's total arms exports, according to a SIPRI report.[30] This allowed the UAE to develop one of the most advanced air forces in the region.

One can thus trace the gradual rise of the UAE's military role in the region since 2011. The UAE began using its military power in the midst of the Arab Spring. In Libya, it contributed to the international coalition as Emirati forces provided clear support for the toppling of the Gaddafi regime. *The National*, an Abu Dhabi-based newspaper, reported that the UAE sent six Mirage and six F-16 fighter jets to join the NATO-led coalition in Libya.[31] In addition, the UAE has subsequently been a key ally in the international campaign against the Islamic State in Iraq and Syria (ISIS), although it suspended its role for a short period during the winter of 2014 before it deployed a squadron of F-16 fighters to Jordan following the ISIS capture of the Jordanian pilot Muath al-Kaseasbah. Beginning in March 2015, the UAE joined the regional coalition against the Houthis in Yemen and played a critical military role both in the air, where its 30 fighter jets formed the second-largest national contingent after Saudi Arabia, and on the ground through the dispatch of Emirati elite and regular ground forces, which played a critical role in the recapture of Aden from Houthi control in July–August 2015.

Given the increasing role of UAE military operations in the region and the rise of external security threats such as ISIS, the government instituted compulsory military service. The conscription law passed in January 2014 requires all men aged between 18 and 35 to perform nine months of military service. Additionally, and in response to the political upheaval in the Middle East in the turbulent aftermath of the Arab Spring, UAE military spending increased from US$1.9 billion in 2009 to $3.13 billion in 2015.[32]

The need for the UAE to supplement soft power with hard power arose from the challenge to meet the regional security changes coursing through much of the Arab world. The Middle East region collectively faces multiple security threats, which go beyond the borders of the Gulf countries. This is also a reflection of how transnational terrorism has become a real threat for the GCC and countries like the UAE, which are trying to avoid the overspill of instability and insecurity from neighbouring conflict zones. This explains why the UAE government opted to participate in the military operation against the Houthis in Yemen and position its military operations within a more comprehensive approach which also emphasised humanitarian aid and assistance.

The emergence of military diplomacy as the UAE's new tool has been a major factor underpinning the rising Emirati role across the region. Although at the time of writing the UAE does not face any direct security threat, defence policy has evolved to encompass threats that face other GCC and Arab states as well. In addition, while Saudi Arabia faces a more direct threat from ISIS and Bahrain confronts endemic political instability, Emirati policymakers have used both soft and hard power tools to support other GCC members and project their power and influence on the regional stage.

The UAE: small state and the return of realism

Theoretically, realism conjures up a grim image of international politics within the territorial boundaries of the formally sovereign state. It also highlights the importance of the political survival of states and regimes. In this sense, necessity, not freedom, is the appropriate or realistic starting point for understanding international relations.[33] When examining policymaking in small states, it is most often the case that realism provides the inevitable policy framework for those states. Three realist principles—state survival, state sovereignty, and self-help—underline the main rationale for the foreign policies of small states. Before the Arab Spring, constructivism provided, to a great extent, a better understanding of the UAE's external behaviour. Yet, realism has never been absent from the policy objectives of the UAE. Currently, realist politics have been revived because of the current regional conflicts that have resulted in several geopolitical outcomes, including growing Sunni extremism in Iraq, Syria, and Yemen, and increasing involvement by an assertive Iran in each of those countries.[34]

However, despite the evidence that small states tend to 'bandwagon' with stronger states, the UAE has recently begun forming smaller regional alliances. Without doubt, bandwagoning contributed to the survival of the UAE since the creation of the federation in 1971, but owing to the rise of instability in the wider region, and the changes in US foreign policy towards the Gulf, the UAE together with other states began forming regional alliances (such as UAE–Egypt military cooperation and the establishment of a combined GCC military force) even if some GCC states already had security arrangements with the United States. This diversification of security partners indicates clearly that small states continue to seek alternative assurance for survival. This is known as 'hedging', whereby small states diversify their strategies in view of unclear policies or strategies on the part of the predominant powers. However, in the case of the GCC states the formation of these alliances is meant also to confront the perceived threat from Iran. Furthermore, the Iranian nuclear deal agreed in July 2015 with international powers led by the P5+1 will push the

UAE and other GCC countries to further diversify their security partners, although they will also continue to rely on the United States.

Nonetheless, security dilemmas will remain a predominant feature for small states, and the UAE and other small states in the Gulf region will continue to search for assurance. While Iran aspires to gain greater regional influence and threats from violent non-state actors will grow, it is natural for a small state like the UAE navigating an anarchic system to acquire power and seek the assurance of regional and international coalitions. Powell points out that states functioning in the shadow of the power of larger states often engage in strategies of partnerships, coalitions, and bandwagoning.[35]

The GCC and the UAE

The UAE's position in the GCC has changed since 2011. This is owing to the fact that UAE as a small state has sought to create and support such regional organisations as the GCC to confront the rising regional threat from state and non-state actors, the perceived US retreat from the region, and the growth of new centres of global power and economic influence. Stephens has pointed out that since 2011 there has been an increasing realisation among GCC members that the United States, so long their external guarantor of security, is engaged in rethinking policy towards the Middle East as part of a reassessment of its global posture.[36]

One of the noteworthy changes in UAE foreign policy since the start of the Arab Spring has been the increasing security cooperation with other GCC states. Since 2011, they have enhanced their security arrangements and signed new agreements that boost the coordination of defence and security policies. In 2013, the GCC states established a unified military command structure, which will have a force of around 100,000 when it becomes fully operational. In addition, an internal security pact was signed in November 2012. The objective is to enhance local or regional force capability and power projection which can, over time, reduce dependence on Western power, even in the unlikely event of a US withdrawal from the Gulf.

Nonetheless, since 2011 there has been clear competition between Qatar and UAE at different levels. Both states are small, and Qatar can be considered a real micro-state with a population of about 2.1 million in 2013, while the UAE has a population of about 9 million. According to al-Buluwi, the issue in dispute between Qatar and UAE (which was resolved in November 2014) reflected the differences between leadership in the two countries. He suggested out that Doha came out in support of movements for change in the Arab world, particularly political Islamic movements, while Abu Dhabi emerged as a key player in the Middle East but in an opposing role which confronted political Islam.[37] Al-Buluwi argued further that religious space has been one of the reasons fuelling this soft conflict between Doha and Abu Dhabi because of the decline in the central role once played by Saudi Arabia in this respect.[38]

Small states in the GCC have always been supportive of the establishment of several security and military agreements, but, despite the manifest failure to protect Kuwait in 1991, all members believe that the GCC should work closely to establish an alternative means of survival to over-reliance on the external security guarantee provided by the United States. Therefore, since 2011, the Gulf states have worked closely to fully integrate their security and defence systems and, since 2015, have deployed military power in an unprecedented manner in operating as a coalition in Yemen. According to Brahim Saidy, this is to allow the GCC to become a real military alliance along the lines of NATO.[39] The aim of the GCC to pursue or establish a 'NATO-like' organisation may make significant changes in the foreign polices of these small states. If successful, it can lead to the creation of a stronger GCC at all levels and help overcome various points of tension among its members.

Conclusion

To sum up, while 'the behavior of small states on the periphery of the international system will continue to reflect structural/systematic constraints',[40] the case of the UAE shows that in some instances this argument is inapplicable in defining the behaviour of small states in the foreign policy sphere. Since 2011, the foreign policy decisions of the UAE have gone beyond traditional small-state behaviours. Especially with regard to the mixing of 'hard' and 'soft' power in the region, the UAE has performed unilaterally and independently, such as in Libya, instead of acting under the umbrella of stronger and larger states. In addition, in bilateral alliance with other regional powers such as the alliance against ISIS or with Saudi Arabia in Yemen, the UAE has shown its power above and beyond the capacity of a classical small state. The aspiration to become a strong, influential small state has helped the UAE to seek alternative security arrangements, which have had profound consequences for multiple zones of regional conflict across the Arab world.

NOTESpp. [2–6]

NOTES

1. INTRODUCTION

1. Fariborz Mokhtari, 'No One Will Scratch My Back: Iranian Security Perceptions in Historical Context', *Middle East Journal*, 59(2), 2005, p. 210.
2. Mehran Kamrava, 'Introduction', in Mehran Kamrava (ed.), *Beyond the Arab Spring: The Evolving Ruling Bargain in the Middle East* (Oxford: Oxford University Press, 2014), p. 2.
3. Christoph Reuter, 'The Terror Strategist: Secret Files Reveal the Structure of Islamic State', *Spiegel Online International*, 18 April 2015.
4. Martin Chulov, 'Isis: The Inside Story', *The Guardian*, 11 December 2014.
5. 'Oil and the Gulf States: After the Party', *The Economist*, 26 March 2016; 'Total Natural Resource Rents (% of GDP)', The World Bank, http://data.worldbank.org/indicator/NY.GDP.TOTL.RT.ZS
6. Christopher Davidson, 'Dubai and Abu Dhabi: Implosion and Opportunity', *Open Democracy*, 4 December 2009.
7. Fahad Al Mukrashi, 'Oman's Revenues from Oil Dropped by 45.5%', *Gulf News*, 30 November 2015.
8. Sarah Townsend, 'Qatar Exports Drop by over 40% in a Year', *ArabianBusiness.com*, 30 August 2015.
9. 'Kuwait Sees a Record Budget Deficit on Falling Oil Income', *Kuwait Times*, 28 January 2016.
10. 'Saudi Arabia Moves In on First Foreign Loan in 25 Years as Oil Revenues Fall', *BBC News*, 20 April 2016.
11. Martin Dokoupil, 'Gulf Arab States Should Cut State Spending Growth: IMF', *Reuters*, 29 October 2012.
12. Steffen Hertog, 'The Costs of Counter-Revolution in the Gulf', *Foreign Policy*, 31 May 2011.
13. 'Citizens Want Kuwait-Like Government Bounty', *The Peninsula*, 18 January 2011.

14. Simeon Kerr, 'Saudi Arabia Looks to Reform Energy Subsidy Program', *Financial Times*, 12 November 2015.
15. Jim Krane and Shih Yu Hung, 'Energy Subsidy Reform in the Persian Gulf: The End of the Big Oil Giveaway', Issue brief, Rice University's Baker Institute for Public Policy, 1, 2016.
16. Tim Boersma and Steve Griffiths, 'Reforming Energy Subsidies: Initial Lessons from the United Arab Emirates', Research paper, Energy, Security and Climate Initiative at Brookings, 6, 2016.
17. Shahd al-Hamdan, 'Surge of Complaints over High Tariffs', *Saudi Gazette*, 3 April 2016; Glen Carey and Zaid Sabah, 'Saudi King Fires Water Minister after Complaints over Tariffs', *Bloomberg*, 24 April 2016.
18. Marketa Hulpachova, 'Iranians Brace for Panic Hikes as Government Rolls Back on Subsidies', *The Guardian*, 28 April 2014.
19. 'Gov Says Cannot Cut Cash Subsidies to 24 Million Homes', *Tehran Times*, 19 April 2016.
20. 'Fuel Subsidy Reforms to Make Only a Modest Dent in GCC Deficits', *Gulf States News*, 40(1010), 18 February 2010.
21. 'Bahrain Planning More Subsidy Cuts, New Charges to Boost Revenues', *Khaleej Times*, 17 November 2015; Zalnab Fattah, 'Untouched for Half a Century, Kuwait Utility Bills to Rise', *Bloomberg*, 14 April 2016.
22. 'Kuwait Poll: Opposition Wins Nearly Half of Parliament', *Al-Jazeera Online*, 27 November 2016.
23. Viviam Nereim, 'Young Arabs Wedded to State Largesse Poses Test for Gulf Leaders', *Bloomberg*, 12 April 2016.
24. Ahmad Jabr, '58 Percent Unemployed Kuwaitis Unwilling to Work in Private Sector: Efforts to Kuwaitize Private Sector Largely Failed', *Kuwait Times*, 18 April 2016.
25. Nadia al-Sakkaf, 'Poor Must Be Cushioned from Fuel Subsidy Cuts', *Yemen Times*, 27 March 2014.
26. Jodi Rudoren and Ranya Kadri, 'Protests over Gas Prices in Jordan Turn Deadly', *New York Times*, 14 November 2012.
27. Charles Tripp, *The Power and the People: Paths of Resistance in the Middle East* (Cambridge: Cambridge University Press, 2013), p. 134. 'Hero of the Crossing' refers to Sadat's initial yet short-lived military achievement in crossing the Suez Canal to conduct operations in the Sinai Peninsula during the October 1973 war with Israel.
28. Barry Buzan and Lene Hansen, *The Evolution of International Security Studies* (Cambridge: Cambridge University Press, 2009), pp. 187–188.
29. Victor Cha, 'Globalization and the Study of International Security', *Journal of Peace Research*, 37(3), 2000, p. 391.
30. Mary Kaldor and Joseph Stiglitz, 'Introduction', in Joseph Stiglitz and Mary Kaldor

(eds.), *The Quest for Security: Protection without Protectionism and the Challenge of Global Governance* (New York: Columbia University Press, 2013), p. 2.

31. Christian Reus-Smit, 'Constructivism and the Structure of Ethical Reasoning', in Richard Price (ed.), *Moral Limit and Possibility in World Politics* (Cambridge: Cambridge University Press, 2008), p. 53.

32. Paul Aarts and Dennis Janssen, 'Shades of Opinion: The Oil Exporting Countries and International Climate Politics', in Gerd Nonneman (ed.), *Analyzing Middle East Foreign Policies and the Relationship with Europe* (London: Routledge, 2005), p. 225.

33. Barry Buzan, Ole Waever and Jaap de Wilde, *Security: A New Framework for Analysis* (Boulder, CO: Lynne Rienner, 1998), p. 23.

34. Barry Buzan, 'Will the "Global War on Terrorism" Be the New Cold War?', *International Affairs*, 82(6), 2006, p. 1103.

35. Keith Krause, 'Insecurity and State Formation in the Global Military Order: The Middle Eastern Case', *European Journal of International Relations*, 2(3), 1996, p. 319.

36. Fred Halliday, *The Middle East in International Relations: Power, Politics and Ideology* (Cambridge: Cambridge University Press, 2005), p. 150.

37. Edward Newman, 'Critical Human Security Studies', *Review of International Studies*, 36, 2010, p. 78.

38. Barry Buzan and Lene Hansen, *The Evolution of International Security Studies* (Cambridge: Cambridge University Press, 2009), p. 188.

39. Ibid., p. 189.

40. Mary Kaldor, *New and Old Wars: Organized Violence in a Global Era* (2nd edn, Cambridge: Polity Press, 2006), p. 4.

41. Stiglitz and Kaldor, *The Quest for Security*, pp. 4–7.

42. David Held, 'Global Challenges: Accountability and Effectiveness', *Open Democracy*, 17 January 2008.

43. 'MPs Support US Air Strikes against IS in Iraq', *BBC News*, 26 September 2014.

44. Steven Erlanger and Stephen Castle, 'British Jets Hit ISIS in Syria after Parliament Authorizes Airstrikes', *New York Times*, 2 December 2015.

45. Fred Lawson, 'From Here We Begin: A Survey of Scholarship on the International Relations of the Gulf', in Matteo Legrenzi (ed.), *Security in the Gulf: Historical Legacies and Future Prospects* (Abingdon: Routledge, 2013), p. 3.

46. Abdulkhaleq Abdulla, 'The Gulf Cooperation Council: Nature, Origin and Process', in Michael C. Hudson (ed.), *Middle East Dilemma: The Politics and Economics of Arab Integration* (New York: Columbia University Press, 1999), p. 154.

47. Henner Furtig, 'Conflict and Cooperation in the Persian Gulf: The Interregional Order and US Policy', *Middle East Journal*, 61(4), Fall 2007, p. 627.

48. Alexander Wendt, *Social Theory of International Politics* (Cambridge: Cambridge

University Press, 1999). Richard Price (ed.), *Moral Limit and Possibility in World Politics* (Cambridge: Cambridge University Press, 2008).

49. Christian Reus-Smit, 'Constructivism and the Structure of Ethical Reasoning', in Richard Price (ed.), *Moral Limit and Possibility in World Politics* (Cambridge: Cambridge University Press, 2008), p. 53.

50. Anoushiravan Ehteshami, 'Reform from Above: The Politics of Participation in the Oil Monarchies', *International Affairs*, 79(1), 2003, p. 55.

51. 'Senior Iran Official Predicts Imminent Demise of Gulf State Royals', *World Tribune*, 15 August 2008.

52. 'Saudi Arabia Tells Iran to Stop "Meddling" in the Region', *Reuters*, 20 October 2015.

53. 'UAE Calls for Iran to "Respect" Gulf Neighbours', *AFP*, 20 April 2011.

54. 'No Iranian Role Found in Bahrain Unrest', *Washington Times*, 23 November 2011.

55. Shahram Chubin, 'Iran's Power in Context', *Survival*, 51(1), 2009, p. 165.

56. Shohini Gupta, 'Oman: The Unsung Hero of the Iranian Nuclear Deal', *Foreign Policy Journal* online, 23 July 2015.

57. Mohammed Mukhashaf, 'Saudi-Backed Yemen Forces Take Aden Port from Houthis: Residents', *Reuters*, 15 July 2015.

58. 'Scores of Gulf Troops Killed in Yemen Conflict', *Al-Jazeera* online, 5 September 2015.

59. Ayesha Almazroui, 'National Identity Is Often Forged in Tough Times', *The National*, 9 September 2015; Omar Mohamed, 'First Among Equals', *Newsweek Middle East*, 2 December 2015.

60. Rami Khouri, 'The War in Yemen as a Rite of Passage', *Al-Jazeera* online, 16 September 2015.

61. David Sanger, David Kirkpatrick, and Somini Sengupta, 'Rancor between Saudi Arabia and Iran Threatens Talks on Syria', *New York Times*, 29 October 2015; 'OPEC Fails to Agree Production Ceiling after Iran Pledges Output Boost', *Reuters*, 4 December 2015.

62. Marc Lynch, *The Arab Uprising: The Unfinished Revolutions of the New Middle East* (New York: Public Affairs, 2012), pp. 10–12.

2. LINKS BETWEEN DOMESTIC AND REGIONAL SECURITY

1. Henner Furtig, 'Conflict and Cooperation in the Persian Gulf: The Interregional Order and U.S. Policy', *Middle East Journal*, 61(4), 2007, p. 639.

2. Arshin Adib-Moghaddam, *The International Politics of the Persian Gulf: A Cultural Genealogy* (London: Routledge, 2006), p. 29.

3. Abdul-Reda Assiri, *Kuwait's Foreign Policy: City-State in World Politics* (Boulder, CO: Westview Press, 1990), pp. 113–114.

4. Anthony Cordesman, *Kuwait: Recovery and Security after the Gulf War* (Boulder, CO: Westview Press, 1997), pp. 127–128.

5. Abdullah al-Shayeji, 'Dangerous Perceptions: Gulf Views of the U.S. Role in the Region', *Middle East Policy*, 5(2), 1997, pp. 1–13.

6. Ibid.

7. Mary Ann Weaver, 'Qatar: Revolution from the Top Down', *National Geographic*, March 2003.

8. 'Jihad against Jews and Crusaders', World Islamic Front Statement, 23 February 1998, available at www.fas.org/irp/world/para/docs/980223-fatwa.htm.

9. Khalid M. al-Tawil, 'The Internet in Saudi Arabia', King Fahd University of Petroleum and Minerals Working Paper (undated), available at www.faculty.kfupm.edu.sa/COE/sadiq/.../Internet%20in%20SA-update1.doc.

10. Emma Murphy, 'ICT and the Gulf Arab States: A Force for Democracy?', in Anoushiravan Ehteshami and Steven Wright (eds.), *Reform in the Middle East Oil Monarchies* (Reading: Ithaca Press, 2008), p. 183.

11. Michael Herb, 'Kuwait: The Obstacle of Parliamentary Politics', in Joshua Teitelbaum (ed.), *Political Liberalization in the Persian Gulf* (London: Hurst, 2009), p. 153.

12. Personal interviews with Bahraini activists in London, March and June 2011.

13. Ng Sue Chia, 'Social Media's Role in Revolt: A Technological or Social Phenomenon? Analysis', *Eurasia Review News and Analysis*, 22 March 2011.

14. Joel Migdal, *Shifting Sands: The United States in the Middle East* (New York: Columbia University Press, 2014), p. 156.

15. Klejda Mulaj, 'Violent Non-State Actors: Exploring their State Relations, Legitimation, and Operationality', in Klejda Mulaj (ed.), *Violent Non-State Actors in World Politics* (New York: Columbia University Press, 2010), p. 2.

16. Kristian Coates Ulrichsen, *Insecure Gulf: The End of Certainty and the Transition to the Post-Oil Era* (London: Hurst, 2011), p. 31.

17. Fifteen of the 9/11 hijackers were from Saudi Arabia along with two from the United Arab Emirates. The remaining two hijackers were from Egypt and Lebanon.

18. Lynn E. Davis, 'Globalization's Security Implications', RAND Issue Paper No. 3 (2003), p. 1.

19. Mary Kaldor, Helmut Anheier and Marlies Glasius, 'Global Civil Society in an Era of Regressive Globalization', in *Global Civil Society 2001* (Oxford: Oxford University Press, 2003), p. 7.

20. Marc Lynch, 'Globalization and Arab Security', in Jonathan Kirshner (ed.), *Globalization and National Security* (New York: Routledge, 2006), p. 191.

21. Thomas Hegghammer, 'Saudi Militants in Iraq: Backgrounds and Recruitment Patterns', *Norwegian Defence Research Establishment* (FFI), February 2007, p. 9.

22. Paul Rogers, 'Abqaiq's Warning', *Open Democracy*, 2 March 2006.

23. Ibid.

24. Ibid.

25. Daveed Gartenstein-Ross, 'Large-Scale Arrests in Saudi Arabia Illustrate Threat to the Oil Supply', *Long War Journal*, 24 March 2010.

26. Coates Ulrichsen, *Insecure Gulf*, p. 64.

27. Lawrence Potter, 'Introduction', in Lawrence Potter (ed.), *Sectarian Politics in the Persian Gulf* (London: Hurst, 2013), p. 28.

28. Toby Matthiesen, *Sectarian Gulf: Bahrain, Saudi Arabia, and the Arab Spring That Wasn't* (Stanford, CA: Stanford University Press, 2013), p. ix.

29. Justin Gengler, *Group Conflict and Political Mobilization in Bahrain and the Arab Gulf: Rethinking the Rentier State* (Bloomington, IN: Indiana University Press, 2015), p. 156.

30. Kristian Coates Ulrichsen, 'Basra, Southern Iraq and the Gulf: Challenges and Connections', LSE Kuwait Programme Working Paper No. 21 (2012), p. 16.

31. Furtig, *Conflict and Cooperation*, p. 638.

32. David Pollock, 'With Neighbours Like These: Iraq and the Arab States on Its Borders', Washington Institute for Near East Policy: Policy Focus 70, 2007, p. 16.

33. Thomas Hegghammer, '"Classical" and "Global" Jihadism in Saudi Arabia', in Bernard Haykel, Thomas Hegghammer and Stephane Lacroix (eds.), *Saudi Arabia in Transition: Insights on Social, Political, Economic and Religious Change* (Cambridge: Cambridge University Press, 2015), p. 217.

34. Anthony Cordesman and Khalid al-Rodhan, 'The Gulf Military Forces in an Era of Asymmetric War: Kuwait', Washington, DC: Center for Strategic and International Studies, 2006, p. 23.

35. Maurice Greenberg, William Wechsler, and Lee Wolowsky, 'Terrorist Financing: Report of an Independent Task Force. Sponsored by the Council on Foreign Relations', (New York: *Council on Foreign Relations*, 2002), p. 1.

36. Christopher Blanchard, *Saudi Arabia: Terrorist Financing Issues* (Washington, DC: CRS Report for Congress, 2007), p. 8.

37. Ibid., p. 9.

38. Kenneth Katzman, *Kuwait: Security, Reform, and U.S. Policy* (Washington, DC: CRS Report for Congress, 2011), p. 13.

39. Coates Ulrichsen, *Insecure Gulf*, p. 40.

40. Kristian Coates Ulrichsen, 'GCC-Iraq Relations', in Claire Spencer, Jane Kinninmont and Omar Sirri (eds.), *Iraq Ten Years On* (London: Chatham House, 2013), p. 45.

41. Toby Dodge, *Iraq: From War to a New Authoritarianism* (Abingdon: Routledge, 2012), p. 192; Patrick Cockburn, 'Isis Consolidates', *London Review of Books*, 36(16), 16–23 August 2014, p. 3.

42. Christoph Reuter, 'The Terror Strategist: Secret Files Reveal the Structure of Islamic State', *Der Spiegel Online*, 18 April 2015.

43. Cf. William McCants, *The ISIS Apocalypse: The History, Strategy, and Doomsday Vision of the Islamic State* (New York: St Martin's Press, 2015); Michael Weiss and Hassan Hassan, *ISIS: Inside the Army of Terror* (New York: Regan Arts, 2015); Charles Lister, *The Syrian Jihad: Al-Qaeda, the Islamic State and the Evolution of an Insurgency* (Oxford: Oxford University Press, 2016).

44. 'Jihadist Expansion in Iraq Puts Persian Gulf States in a Tight Spot', *Washington Post*, 13 June 2014.
45. Elizabeth Dickinson, 'Playing with Fire: Why Private Gulf Funding for Syria's Extremist Rebels Risks Igniting Sectarian Conflict at Home', Brookings Institution Analysis Paper No. 16, December 2013, p. 2.
46. Lori Plotkin Boghardt, 'Saudi Arabia's Old al-Qaeda Terrorists Form New Threat', Washington, DC: Washington Institute for Near East Policy (WINEP) *Policywatch*, 2370, 11 February 2015.
47. Shiv Malik, Ali Younis, Spencer Ackerman, and Mustafa Khalili, 'The Race to Save Peter Kassig', *The Guardian*, 18 December 2014.
48. Bill Law, 'Bahrain: The Islamic State Threat Within', *Middle East Eye*, 14 October 2014.
49. Plotkin Boghardt, *Saudi Arabia's Old al-Qaeda Terrorists Form New Threat.*
50. 'American Is Fatally Shot in Saudi Arabia', *New York Times*, 14 October 2014.
51. 'Saudi Probes Motive behind Attack on Canadian', *Al Arabiya*, 30 November 2014.
52. 'US Teacher Killed as Americans Targeted in Separate Abu Dhabi Attacks', *The Guardian*, 4 December 2014.
53. Jack Moore, 'ISIS Attack Saudi Border Post and Infiltrate Town', *Newsweek*, 28 January 2015.
54. Rori Donaghy, 'Islamic State Claims Deadly Suicide Attack on Mosque in Saudi Arabia's Qatif', *Middle East Eye*, 22 May 2015.
55. Toby Matthiesen, 'Mysticism, Migration and Clerical Networks: Ahmad al-Ahsa'i and the Shaykis of al-Ahsa, Kuwait and Basra', *Journal of Muslim Minority Affairs*, 2014, pp. 12–13.
56. 'Islamic State's Claimed Shooting Attack on Shia Mosque in Saudi Arabia Likely to Exacerbate Sectarian Divisions', *IHS Jane's Country Risk Daily Report*, 18 October 2015.
57. Elizabeth Dickinson, 'Kuwait, the Back Office of Logistical Support for Syria's Rebels', *The National*, 5 February 2013.
58. Dickinson, *Playing with Fire*, p. 2.
59. 'Kuwait, a U.S. Ally of Syria, Is Also the Leading Funder of Extremist Rebels', *Washington Post*, 25 April 2014.
60. 'Kuwait Justice Minister's Resignation Accepted', *Gulf News*, 12 May 2014.
61. Kristian Coates Ulrichsen, 'Qatar's Evolving Role in the Syrian Conflict', Norwegian Peacebuilding Resource Council (NOREF) Policy Brief, 22 January 2014, p. 3.
62. See, for example, Madawi al-Rasheed, *Contesting the Saudi State: Islamic Voices from a New Generation* (Cambridge: Cambridge University Press, 2007).
63. 'Saudi: Muslim Brotherhood a Terrorist Organization', *Al Arabiya*, 7 March 2014.
64. Yoel Guzansky, 'On the Road to Mecca? The Islamic State Threat to the Gulf', Institute for National Security Studies, INSS Insight No. 603, 8 September 2014.

65. Abdullah Al Shayji, 'The GCC–US Relationship: A GCC Perspective', *Middle East Policy Council Journal*, August 2014, http://mepc.org/journal/middle-east-policy-archives/gcc-us-relationship-gcc-perspective.

66. 'Leading Saudi Researcher Warns West of a Newly Assertive Saudi Arabia', *Gulf States Newsletter*, 35(901), 27 May 2011, p. 8.

67. 'Iran and P5+1 Sign Breakthrough Nuclear Deal', *Gulf States Newsletter*, 37(959), 28 November 2013, p. 3.

68. David Hearst, 'Has Iran Overreached Itself in Yemen?', *Middle East Eye*, 26 March 2015.

69. Frederic Wehrey, 'Into the Maelstrom: The Saudi-led Misadventure in Yemen', *Carnegie Endowment for International Peace Online Analysis*, 26 March 2015.

70. Rori Donaghy, 'Revealed: The Mercenaries Commanding UAE Forces in Yemen', *Middle East Eye*, 23 December 2015.

71. Author interviews, Washington DC, August 2015, March 2016, May 2016.

3. RENTING THE CASBAH: GULF STATES' FOREIGN POLICY TOWARDS NORTH AFRICA SINCE THE ARAB UPRISINGS

1. Morocco also saw limited protests, but not on the scale of Tunisia, Egypt, and Libya. Also, given their monarchical political system, all the GCC states want to ensure the survival of the Moroccan monarchy so as not to undermine the symbolically important notion that Arab monarchies are more 'resilient' and 'stable' than Arab republics in the wake of the Arab uprisings. Together with Jordan, Morocco had even been invited to join the GCC, although that proposal never seemed to be very serious on the part of the GCC, or very seriously considered by Morocco. Morocco also agreed to participate in a joint Arab military force announced in March 2015. Michael J. Willis, 'Evolution Not Revolution? Morocco and the Arab Spring', in Larbi Sadiki (ed.), *Routledge Handbook of the Arab Spring: Rethinking Democratization* (New York: Routledge, 2015), pp. 435–450.

2. Youcef Bouandel, 'Algeria: The Limits of Revolution and Democratization', in Sadiki (ed.), *Routledge Handbook of the Arab Spring*, pp. 451–462.

3. The chapter will not focus on the other two GCC countries, Bahrain and Oman, because they did not play a decisive role in North African affairs. As the two poorest GCC members, they do not have the resources to decisively influence events in North Africa. Indeed, Bahrain was more an arena of conflict rather than a proactive foreign policy player since 2011 and its foreign policy is now largely aligned with Saudi and UAE foreign policies. Oman has steered a staunchly independent path in its foreign policy and has broken with its GCC neighbours over the Iranian issue and many other issues, such as the GCC support for the Syrian uprising and the GCC intervention in Yemen. Oman's foreign policy is shaped by the idea that Oman should be a neutral broker in conflicts in the region, rather than taking sides. This was symbolised in Oman's hosting of the early parts of direct American–Iranian

nuclear negotiations. The Ibadi school of Islam, which is the dominant religious denomination in Oman, also has followers in North Africa, particularly in Algeria. Oman has also hosted parts of Muammar Gaddafi's family after they fled Libya in 2011. Its involvement in North Africa has, however, not been so decisive as that of the other Gulf countries discussed in this chapter and it will therefore only be referred to on the margins.

4. See, for example, Karen Young, 'The Emerging Interventionists of the GCC', LSE Middle East Centre, Working Paper Series, December 2013; Silvia Colombo, Kristian Coates Ulrichsen, Shafeeq Ghabra, Shadi Hamid and Eman Ragab, 'The GCC in the Mediterranean in light of the Arab Spring' (Washington, DC: German Marshall Fund of the United States, 2012), http://www.gmfus.org/publications/gcc-mediterranean-light-arab-spring; Carolyn Barnett, 'GCC-Maghreb Relations in a Changing Regional Order', CSIS Analysis Paper, August 2013, http://csis.org/files/publication/130814_Barnett_GCCMaghreb_Web_2.pdf
5. Anthony Barnett, *Dialogues in Arab Politics: Negotiations in Regional Order* (New York: Columbia University Press, 1998).
6. The UAE was also instrumental in putting together the conference in the first place. 'UAE to Build Egypt's New $45 billion Capital', *Albawaba*, 18 March 2015, http://www.albawaba.com/business/uae-build-egypts-new-45-billion-capital-670932; 'Gulf States Again Prove to be Egypt's Bulwark', *Gulf News*, 21 March 2015, http://gulfnews.com/business/economy/gulf-states-again-prove-to-be-egypt-s-bulwark-1.1475506. However, there were soon complications in the planning of the new capital and its future is uncertain. 'Egypt Admits "Complications" in Deal with UAE Firm for $45bn Project', *Reuters*, 9 June 2015, http://www.arabianbusiness.com/egypt-admits-complications-in-deal-with-uae-firm-for-45bn-project-595555.html#.VZZvuabH7II
7. 'Arab States Pledge Billions at Egypt Investment Meet', *The Peninsula*, 14 March 2015, http://thepeninsulaqatar.com/news/international/326853/arab-states-pledge-billions-at-egypt-investment-meet
8. Abdullah Baabood, 'Gulf Countries and Arab Transitions: Role, Support and Effects', *IEMed Mediterranean Yearbook 2014* (Barcelona: IEMed, 2014), pp. 42–47, http://www.iemed.org/observatori/arees-danalisi/arxius-adjunts/anuari/anuari-2014/Baabood_Arab_Spring_Gulf_role_support_IEMed_yearbook_2014_EN.pdf
9. Abdulkhaleq Abdulla, 'Contemporary Socio-Political Issues of the Arab Gulf Moment', London School of Economics: Kuwait Programme on Development, Governance and Globalisation in the Gulf States, Working Paper No. 11, September 2010.
10. Gabriele vom Bruck, "How the Past Casts its Shadows: Struggles for Ascendancy in Northern Yemen in the post-Salih Era" in: Gabriele vom Bruck and Charles Tripp (eds.), *Precarious Belonging: Ways of Being Shiʿi in Non-Shia Worlds* (forthcoming).

11. I have elaborated on this elsewhere: Toby Matthiesen, *Sectarian Gulf: Bahrain, Saudi Arabia, and the Arab Spring That Wasn't* (Stanford, CA: Stanford University Press, 2013).

12. The classic account of this is Malcolm Kerr, *The Arab Cold War: Gamal 'Abd al-Nasir and His Rivals, 1958–1970* (3rd edn, Oxford: Oxford University Press, 1971).

13. Much has been written on Qatari foreign policy towards the Arab uprisings, and about its relationship with the Muslim Brotherhood. See, for example, Mehran Kamrava, *Qatar: Small State, Big Politics* (Ithaca, NY: Cornell University Press, 2013), David Roberts, 'Qatar and the Muslim Brotherhood: Pragmatism or Preference?' *Middle East Policy*, 21, 2014, pp. 84–94, and Kristian Coates Ulrichsen, *Qatar and the Arab Spring* (London: Hurst, 2014).

14. Stéphane Lacroix, *Awakening Islam: The Politics of Religious Dissent in Contemporary Saudi Arabia* (Cambridge, MA: Harvard University Press, 2011).

15. For more on the relationship between the Saudi regime and Islamist forces, and how this shaped Saudi foreign policy towards the Arab uprisings and in particular the Egyptian revolution, see Toby Matthiesen, *The Domestic Sources of Saudi Foreign Policy: Islamists and the State in the Wake of the Arab Uprisings* (Washington DC: Brookings, 2015), https://www.academia.edu/ 15259726/The_domestic_sources_of_Saudi_foreign_policy_Islamists_and_the_state_in_the_wake_of_the_Arab_Uprisings

16. Interview with members of the Muslim Brotherhood, Bahrain, 2011, and with Saleh al-Bandar, Cambridge, 2014.

17. Nathan J. Brown, 'Pushing toward Party Politics? Kuwait's Islamic Constitutional Movement', Carnegie Endowment for International Peace, February 2007, http://carnegieendowment.org/2007/02/13/pushing-toward-party-politics-kuwait-s-islamic-constitutional-movement

18. Matthiesen, *Sectarian Gulf*, pp. 101–109.

19. Mazhar al-Zo'by and Birol Başkan, 'Discourse and Positionality in the Arab Spring: The Case of the Muslim Brotherhood in the UAE', *International Sociology*, Volume 30, Issue 4, July 2015, pp. 401–417. For more, see Kristin Smith Diwan, 'The Future of the Muslim Brotherhood in the Gulf', *Monkey Cage*, 10 February 2015, http://www.washingtonpost.com/blogs/monkey-cage/wp/2015/02/10/the-future-of-the-muslim-brotherhood-in-the-gulf; Guido Steinberg, 'The Gulf States and the Muslim Brotherhood', *POMEPS*, 21 March 2014, http://pomeps.org/2014/03/21/the-gulf-states-and-the-muslim-brotherhood

20. Abdullah Baabood, 'Islamism in the Gulf Region', in Khaled Hroub (ed.), *Political Islam: Context versus Ideology* (London: Saqi, 2011), pp. 127–160.

21. Marc Valeri, 'Identity Politics and Nation-Building under Sultan Qaboos', in L.G. Potter (ed.), *Sectarian Politics in the Gulf* (London: Hurst, 2013), pp. 179–206.

22. 'Gulf ambassadors Pulled from Qatar over "Interference"', *BBC*, 5 March 2014, http://www.bbc.co.uk/news/world-middle-east-26447914. Bahrain seems to have deemed Saudi Arabia's support as so important, that it even went as far as alienating a sizeable bloc of its Sunni constituency, the supporters of the Muslim Brotherhood.

23. This becomes evident in cables of the Saudi Ministry of Foreign Affairs leaked through WikiLeaks. For an overview, see Wael Eskandar, 'The Saudi Leaks and Egypt: A Recap', *Jadaliyya*, 2 July 2015, http://www.jadaliyya.com/pages/index/22034/the-saudi-leaks-and-egypt_a-recap

24. Khaled Abou el-Fadl, 'Failure of a Revolution', in Sadiki (ed.), *Routledge Handbook of the Arab Spring*, pp. 265f. For more on the Salafis in Egypt, see Stéphane Lacroix, 'Sheikhs and Politicians: Inside the New Egyptian Salafism', Brookings Policy Brief, 11 June 2012, http://www.brookings.edu/research/papers/2012/06/07-egyptian-salafism-lacroix

25. For the importance of Khaleeji capital in the political economy of the Middle East since the oil boom of the 1970s and the 'infitah' economic liberalisation policies of the late 1970s and 1980s, see Adam Hanieh, *Lineages of Revolt: Issues of Contemporary Capitalism in the Middle East* (Chicago: Haymarket Books, 2013). See also Clement Moore Henry and Robert Springborg, *Globalization and the Politics of Development in the Middle East* (2nd edn, Cambridge: Cambridge University Press, 2010).

26. 'Dislike for Qaddafi Gives Arabs a Point of Unity', *New York Times*, 21 March 2011, http://www.nytimes.com/2011/03/22/world/africa/22arab.html?_r=0

27. Christopher S. Chivvis, *Toppling Qaddafi: Libya and the Limits of Liberal Intervention* (Cambridge: Cambridge University Press, 2014), p. 55. In her memoir, Hillary Clinton justifies the continued cooperation with Bahrain after the crackdown by saying that she had to focus on building an international coalition against Gaddafi and that the UAE had threatened to pull out of that coalition had the United States taken a harsher stance towards the Bahraini regime and its crackdown on the protest movement. See Hillary Rodham Clinton, *Hard Choices* (New York: Simon & Schuster, 2014), pp. 355–359, 373.

28. Apart from Qatar and the UAE, Sweden and, to a lesser extent, Jordan and Morocco were the other non-NATO members that also participated in the NATO intervention. For more on NATO partners, see http://www.nato.int/cps/en/natohq/51288.htm

29. These four states became NATO partners as part of the Istanbul Cooperation Initiative (ICI) launched during NATO's 2004 Istanbul summit. For more on the GCC and NATO, see Matteo Legrenzi, *The GCC and International Relations of the Gulf: Diplomacy, Security and Economic Coordination in a Changing Middle East* (London: I.B. Tauris, 2011), pp. 139–148.

30. Jeffrey H. Michaels, 'Able but Not Willing: A Critical Assessment of NATO's Libya Intervention', in Kjell Engelbrekt, Marcus Mohlin and Charlotte Wagnsson

(eds.), *The NATO Intervention in Libya: Lessons Learned from the Campaign* (London: Routledge, 2014), pp. 17–40, 31.

31. Richard Northern and Jason Pack, 'The Role of Outside Actors', in Jason Pack (ed.), *The 2011 Libyan Uprisings and the Struggle for the Post-Qadhafi Future* (New York: Palgrave Macmillan, 2013), pp. 122–125. For more details on the negotiations that led to the participation of Arab countries in the alliance, see Chivvis, *Toppling Qaddafi*.

32. Marcus Mohlin, 'Cloak and Dagger in Libya: The Libyan "Thuwar" and the Role of Allied Special Forces', in Engelbrekt, Mohlin and Wagnsson (eds.), *The NATO Intervention in Libya*, pp. 206f, 215.

33. Michaels, 'Able but Not Willing: A Critical Assessment of NATO's Libya Intervention', pp. 17–40, 31. For Qatari and UAE Special Forces, see also Chivvis, *Toppling Qaddafi*, pp. 154–158.

34. Northern and Pack, 'The Role of Outside Actors', p. 125.

35. Ibid., pp. 124f.

36. Youssef Mohammed Sawani, 'Dynamics of Continuity and Change', in Pack (ed.), *The 2011 Libyan Uprisings and the Struggle for the Post-Qadhafi Future*, pp. 66, 76, 80. For more on the relationship between Belhaj, his Libyan Islamic Fighting Group and Qatar, see Noman Benotman, Jason Pack and James Brandon, 'Islamists', in Pack (ed.), *The 2011 Libyan Uprisings and the Struggle for the Post-Qadhafi Future*, pp. 191–228, 112–116.

37. Anas El Gomati, 'Libya's Islamists and the 17th February Revolution', in Sadiki (ed.), *Routledge Handbook of the Arab Spring*, pp. 118–132, 120–123.

38. Jonathan Schanzer, 'Turkey's Secret Proxy War in Libya?', *National Interest*, 17 March 2015, http://nationalinterest.org/feature/turkeys-secret-proxy-war-libya-12430

39. 'War in Libya: The Guardian Briefing', *The Guardian*, 29 August 2014, http://www.theguardian.com/world/2014/aug/29/-sp-briefing-war-in-libya. For more on alleged UAE involvement in Libya, see this interview with Abdul-Hakim Belhaj: 'Libya's Abdulhakim Belhadj: "We are working to find a solution to end this crisis"', *Euronews*, 3 February 2015, http://www.euronews.com/2015/02/03/libya-s-abdulhakim-belhadj-we-are-working-to-find-a-solution-to-end-this-crisis

40. 'Arab Nations Strike in Libya, Surprising U.S.', *New York Times*, 25 August 2014, http://www.nytimes.com/2014/08/26/world/africa/egypt-and-united-arab-emirates-said-to-have-secretly-carried-out-libya-airstrikes.html?smid=tw-share&_r=0

41. Interview with a political analyst from the Gulf, London, 2014.

42. 'Qatar's Influence in Tunisia', *Tunis Times*, 15 October 2013, http://www.thetunistimes.com/2013/10/qatars-influence-in-tunisia-91527

43. Youssef Cherif, 'Tunisia's Elections amid a Middle East Cold War', *Atlantic Council*, 22 October 2014, http://www.atlanticcouncil.org/blogs/menasource/tunisian-elections-amid-a-middle-eastern-cold-war

44. It was founded in 1982; see http://www.bte.com.tn/?cat=1&lang=en
45. 'UAE Sends Help for "the New Tunisia"', *The National*, 4 May 2012, http://www.thenational.ae/news/uae-news/uae-sends-help-for-the-new-tunisia
46. For the statements made at the summit, see http://www.lasportal.org/ar/summits/Pages/default.aspx?Stype=1&imgLib=ArabicSummit&year=2015#tab6
47. 'Arab League Unveils Joint Military Force amid Yemen Crisis', AP, 29 March 2015.
48. 'Egypt's Sisi Reassures Gulf Leaders after Alleged Derisive Audio Leaks', Reuters, 9 February 2015, http://www.reuters.com/article/2015/02/09/us-egypt-gulf-id USKBN0LD1H720150209
49. 'Putin Letter to Arab Summit Triggers Strong Saudi Attack', Reuters, 29 March 2015, http://in.reuters.com/article/2015/03/29/mideast-arabs-summit-putin-idINKBN0MP0HX20150329
50. 'Saudi Arabia Tells Citizens to Ignore Latest WikiLeaks Release', *The Guardian*, 21 June 2015, http://www.theguardian.com/world/2015/jun/21/saudi-arabia-ignore-wikileaks-release
51. 'Leaks Gain Credibility and Potential to Embarrass Egypt's Leaders', *New York Times*, 12 May 2015, http://mobile.nytimes.com/2015/05/13/world/middleeast/leaks-gain-credibility-and-potential-to-embarrass-egypts-leaders.html?_r=1&referrer=
52. A huge gas field between Egypt and Cyprus, whose discovery was announced in August 2015, may increase the revenues of the Egyptian state and make Egypt energy-independent. It remains to be seen, however, what impact this will have on Egypt's relationship with the Gulf. Yuri M. Zhukov, 'Egypt's Gift from God', *Foreign Affairs*, 23 September 2015, https://www.foreignaffairs.com/articles/cyprus/2015-09-23/egypts-gift-god
53. Saudi Arabia is even considering borrowing locally to fill the 2015 budget deficit. 'Saudi Arabia Seen Opting for Debt to Fill Fiscal Gap', *Zawya*, 21 June 2015, https://www.zawya.com/story/Saudi_Arabia_seen_opting_for_debt_to_fill_fiscal_gap-GN_21062015_220646
54. Glada Lahn and Paul Stevens, *Burning Oil to Keep Cool: The Hidden Energy Crisis in Saudi Arabia*, Chatham House Report, December 2011, http://www.chathamhouse.org/publications/papers/view/180825
55. 'Official: GCC Not Expected to Provide Egypt with Additional Aid during FY15/16', *Egypt Independent*, 28 June 2015, http://www.egyptindependent.com/news/official-gcc-not-expected-provide-egypt-additional-aid-during-fy1516

4. THE EMERGING ENERGY LANDSCAPE: ECONOMIC AND STRATEGIC IMPLICATIONS

1. International Energy Agency, *Energy Efficiency Market Report 2014* (Paris, 2014), p. 18.
2. Ibid., p. 18.

3. British Petroleum, *BP Energy Outlook 2035* (London, 2014), p. 9.
4. International Energy Agency, *World Energy Outlook*, p. 2
5. Ibid., p. 27.
6. Ibid., p. 4.
7. British Petroleum, *BP Energy Outlook 2035*, p. 39.
8. Ibid., p. 5.
9. Paul Stevens, 'The Shale Gas Revolution: Developments and Changes', Chatham House Report, http://www.chathamhouse.org, accessed 20 August 2012.
10. Energy Information Administration, *Review of Emerging Resources: U.S. Shale Gas and Shale Oil Plays* (Washington DC, 2011), p. 4.
11. Energy Information Administration, *Tight Oil Production Pushes U.S. Crude Supply to over 10% of World Total*, http://www.eia.gov/todayinenergy/detail.cfm?id=15571, accessed 26 March 2014.
12. Ibid.
13. Energy Information Administration, *Natural Gas*, http://www.eia.gov/dnav/ng/ng_shalegas_dcu_NUS_a.htm, accessed 1 December 2014.
14. Energy Information Administration, *Shale Gas Provides Largest Share of U.S. Natural Gas Production in 2013*, http://www.eia.gov/todayinenergy/detail.cfm?id=18951, accessed 25 November 2014.
15. British Petroleum, *Energy Outlook 2035*, p. 61.
16. Vipin Arora, 'Energy Production and Trade: An Overview of Some Macroeconomic Issues', Energy Information Administration, http://www.eia.gov, accessed 30 November 2014.
17. John Mitchell, *U.S. Energy: The New Reality*, http://www.chathamhouse.org, accessed 30 May 2013.
18. Energy Information Administration, *Analysis and Projections: Technically Recoverable Shale Oil and Shale Gas Resources: An Assessment of 137 Shale Formations in 41 Countries outside the United States*, http://www.eia.gov/analysis/studies/worldshalegas, accessed 1 December 2014.
19. Daniel Yergin, 'The Global Shakeout from Plunging Oil', *Wall Street Journal*, 30 November 2014.
20. Sarah A. Emerson and Andrew C. Winner, 'The Myth of Petroleum Independence and Foreign Policy Isolation', *Washington Quarterly*, 37(1), Spring 2014, p. 23.
21. Robert A. Manning, *The Shale Revolution and the New Geopolitics of Energy*, http://www.atlanticcouncil.org, accessed 10 November 2014.
22. Energy Information Administration, *World Oil Transit Chokepoints*, http://www.eia.gov, accessed 10 November 2014.
23. Colin H. Kahl and Marc Lynch, 'U.S. Strategy after the Arab Uprisings: Toward Progressive Engagement', *Washington Quarterly*, 36(2), Spring 2013, p. 48.
24. Bruce Jones, David Steven, and Emily O'Brien, *Fueling a New Order? The New Geopolitical and Security Consequences of Energy*, https://www.brookings.edu/

research/fueling-a-new-order-the-new-geopolitical-and-security-consequences-of-energy/, accessed 21 March 2014.

25. Energy Information Administration, *Country Analysis: China*, http://www.eia.gov, accessed 4 February 2014.

26. Daniel Yergin, 'US Energy Is Changing the World Again', *Financial Times*, 16 November 2012.

27. European Commission, *European Union Trade with GCC*, http://ec.europa.eu, accessed 15 February 2015.

28. See Gawdat Bahgat, *Alternative Energy in the Middle East* (London: Palgrave Macmillan, 2013).

29. International Monetary Fund, *Sovereign Wealth Fund: A Work Agenda* (Washington DC, 2008), p. 2.

30. For more details, see Reda Cherif and Fuad Hasanov, 'Soaring of the Gulf Falcons: Diversification in the GCC Oil Exporters in Seven Propositions', IMF Working Paper WP/14/177, Washington DC, February 2015.

31. 'IHS, Saudi Arabia Replaces India as Largest Defense Market for US', http://press.ihs.com/press-release/aerospace-defense-terrorism/saudi-arabia-replaces-india-largest-defence-market-us-ihs-study-says, ccessed 7 March 2015.

32. Tim Callen, Reda Cherif, Fuad Hasanov, Amgad Hegazy and Padamja Khandelwal, 'Economic Diversification in the GCC: Past, Present, and Future', IMF Staff Discussion Note, Washington, DC: IMF, December 2014, p. 4.

33. International Monetary Fund, *Regional Economic Outlook: Learning to Live with Cheaper Oil amid Weaker Demand*, Washington, DC, p. 2.

34. Rabah Arezki and Olivier Blanchard, *Seven Questions about the Recent Oil Price Slump* (Washington DC: IMF, January 2015), p. 10.

5. TOWARDS THE END OF THE OLIGARCHIC PACT? BUSINESS AND POLITICS IN ABU DHABI, BAHRAIN, AND OMAN

1. This research was supported by the UK Economic and Social Research Council [grant number ES/J012696/1].

2. Hazem Beblawi, 'The Rentier State in the Arab World', in Hazem Beblawi and Giacomo Luciani (eds.), *The Rentier State* (London: Croom Helm, 1987), p. 56.

3. Jill Crystal, *Oil and Politics in the Gulf: Rulers and Merchants in Kuwait and Qatar* (Cambridge: Cambridge University Press, 1995); Pete W. Moore, 'Rentier Fiscal Crisis and Regime Stability: State-Business Relations in the Gulf', *Studies in Comparative International Development*, 37, 2002, pp. 34–56; Pete W. Moore, *Doing Business in the Middle East: Politics and Economic Crisis in Jordan and Kuwait* (Cambridge: Cambridge University Press, 2004).

4. Giacomo Luciani, 'Linking Economic and Political Reform in the Middle East: The Role of the Bourgeoisie', in Oliver Schlumberger (ed.), *Debating Arab*

Authoritarianism. Dynamics and Durability in Non-Democratic Regimes (Stanford: Stanford University Press, 2007), pp. 161–176; Steffen Hertog, 'State and Private Sector in the GCC after the Arab Uprisings', *Journal of Arabian Studies*, 3, 2013, pp. 174–195; Steffen Hertog, Giacomo Luciani and Marc Valeri (eds.), *Business Politics in the Middle East* (London: Hurst, 2013).

5. Albadr S.S. Abu-Baker, 'Political Economy of State Formation: The United Arab Emirates in Comparative Perspective' (PhD diss., University of Michigan, 1995), p. 263.

6. Giacomo Luciani, 'Allocation vs. Production States: A Theoretical Framework', in Hazem Beblawi and Giacomo Luciani (eds.), *The Rentier State*, p. 69.

7. Nazih Ayubi, *Over-Stating the Arab State: Politics and Society in the Middle East* (London: I.B. Tauris, 1995), p. 323.

8. In Kuwait, the first concession agreement was signed in 1934 and oil was discovered four years later. Sheikh Sa'id of Dubai (r.1912–58) signed a concession agreement in 1937 but oil was actually discovered in the emirate in the 1960s.

9. In Dubai, it was agreed that the ruler's allowance was to be limited to one-eighth of the total revenue. See Rosemarie S. Zahlan, *The Origins of the United Arab Emirates* (London: Macmillan, 1978), p. 158.

10. Crystal, *Oil and Politics in the Gulf*, pp. 44–45.

11. Ibid., p. 110.

12. Khaldun al-Naqeeb, *Society and State in the Gulf and Arab Peninsula: A Different Perspective* (London: Centre for Arab Unity Studies, 1990), p. 115.

13. Crystal, *Oil and Politics in the Gulf*, pp. 7–8.

14. Ibid., pp. 8–9, 75.

15. The Hawala are Sunnis that migrated to Bahrain starting in the nineteenth century from the Iranian coast but claim Arab origins. An example of one of these merchant families historically close to the Al Khalifa is the Kanoo family, who moved to Bahrain from southern Persia in the mid-nineteenth century. Yusuf Kanoo, who began as a small merchant in 1890 trading with India, became in the 1920s and 1930s the largest banker on the island and the Bahrain agent of companies such as the Anglo-Persian Oil Company and Ford. In the 1950s and 1960s, the House of Kanoo evolved into a conglomerate of companies, with headquarters in Bahrain, Dammam, and Dubai. The Kanoo group of companies is currently one of the largest family-owned groups of companies in the Gulf. Khalid Kanoo, the current managing director of the Kanoo Group, was chairman of the Bahrain Chamber of Commerce until 2005.

16. Yitzhak Nakash, *Reaching for Power: The Shi'a in the Modern Arab World* (Princeton: Princeton University Press, 2006), p. 57.

17. Mahdi al-Tajir, *Bahrain 1920–1945: Britain, the Shaikh and the Administration* (London: Croom Helm, 1987), pp. 206, 258.

18. Mohamed G. al-Rumaihi, *Bahrain: Social and Political Change since the First World War* (London: Bowker, 1976), pp. 150–151.

19. Ibid.

20. The current Chamber's chairman is Khalid Almoayed, brother of Tareq Almoayed (the country's long-standing Information Minister and a senior adviser to Sheikh 'Isa in the 1990s) and chairman of AK Almoayed Group (AKAG), founded more than a hundred years ago as a Hawala–native family-run trading firm, supplying timber to the construction industry in Bahrain. Among the current board of directors of the BCCI are Mohammed bin Farooq Almoayyed, related to the head of the Chamber and vice-chairman of Almoayyed International Group; Mohamed Fakhro, son of former Minister of Commerce and Industry 'Adel Fakhro and of Mona Almoayyed, cousin of the Chamber's chairman; 'Afnan al-Zayani, chairman of Al Zayani Commercial Services S.P.C., sister of Minister of Commerce and Industry Zayed al-Zayani; Khalid al-Zayani, 'Afnan's brother, honorary chairman of Al-Zayani Investments holding and of the Bahrain British Business Forum; and 'Abd al-Hamid al-Kooheji, chairman of AJM Kooheji Group, founded in 1890 as a textile trading company and now distributor in Bahrain of Bridgestone and LG products.

21. Fred H. Lawson, *Bahrain: The Modernization of Autocracy* (Boulder, CO: Westview Press, 1989), p. 77.

22. Interior, Foreign Affairs and Defence, and the Prime Minister's office (when applicable), in contrast to technical ministries.

23. Abu-Baker, *Political Economy of State Formation*, p. 110.

24. Ibid., pp. 160, 206.

25. Since 1970, a clear distinction is established between the royal family—which is composed of Sultan Sa'id bin Sultan's (r.1804–56) descendants, bearing the name Al Sa'id—and all the other branches of the al-Busa'idi tribe, who kept the surname al-Busa'idi. Qaboos belongs to both the Al Sa'id family and the al-Busa'idi tribe.

26. Interviews, January 2003.

27. Crystal, *Oil and Politics in the Gulf*, p. 187.

28. For more details, see Marc Valeri, *Oman: Politics and Society in the Qaboos State* (London: Hurst, 2009), chapters 4 and 6.

29. Marc Owen Jones, 'Judge Orders Further Partial Release of Henderson Files', *Bahrain Watch*, 17 May 2015, https://bahrainwatch.org/blog/2015/05/17/judge-orders-further-partial-release-of-henderson-files/

30. Graham E. Fuller and Rend Rahim Francke. *The Arab Shi'a: The Forgotten Muslims* (New York: St Martin's Press, 1999), p. 125.

31. John E. Peterson, 'Bahrain: Reform, Promise and Reality', in Joshua Teitelbaum (ed.), *Political Liberalization in the Persian Gulf* (London: Hurst, 2009), p. 158.

32. *Wall Street Journal*, 12 June 1995.

33. Fuller and Francke, *The Arab Shi'a*, p. 128.

34. Cynthia O'Murchu and Simeon Kerr, 'Bahrain Land Deals Highlight Alchemy of Making Money from Sand', *Financial Times*, 10 December 2014.

35. Frederik Richter and Martin De Sa'Pinto, 'Special Report: In Bahrain, A Symbol at the Heart of Revolt', *Reuters*, 17 June 2011.

36. Since the 2008 financial crisis, 'Isam Jinahi has suffered tremendous economic losses and his influence in Bahrain has dramatically weakened. See ibid.

37. Hassan's brother 'Isam, chairman of Fakhro Group, was head of the Chamber of Commerce between 2005 and 2013. Hassan's nephew, Mohammed bin 'Adil, has been a BCCI board member since 2014. The Fakhro Group was founded in 1888. Yusef bin 'Abd al-Rahman (the minister's grandfather) and his five sons expanded the family business from the 1930s into a trade and economic empire spreading from Bahrain to India and Iraq.

38. The Bani Fatima are the six sons of Fatima bint Mubarak al-Kitbi, Shaikh Zayed bin Sultan's most prominent wife: Mohammed bin Zayed; Hamdan bin Zayed; Hazza' bin Zayed; Tahnoon bin Zayed; Mansour bin Zayed; and UAE Foreign Minister 'Abd Allah bin Zayed.

39. Effectively head of the intelligence services.

40. Its chairman, Khalifa bin Zayed; his son Mohammed bin Khalifa; Mohammed bin Zayed; his son Dhiyab bin Mohammed; Hazza' bin Zayed; Mansour bin Zayed; and Hamad bin Zayed.

41. Prominent examples include Khaldoon bin Khalifa al-Mubarak, board member of the Executive Council, managing director of Mubadala and chairman of the Executive Affairs Authority; Nasser bin Ahmed al-Suwaidi, board member of the Executive Council, chairman of the Abu Dhabi Energy Authority and of the National Bank of Abu Dhabi, and son of Ahmed bin Khalifa al-Suwaidi, former director of Abu Dhabi's Presidential Court and the UAE's first Foreign Minister (in the 1970s), and chairman of Al Suwaidi Engineering Group, one of the largest construction companies; Yousef bin Mana' al-'Utaiba, Ambassador to the USA from 2008, former senior adviser to Mohammed bin Zayed and son of Mana' bin Sa'id al-'Utaiba, former UAE Minister of Petroleum and Mineral Resources and former OPEC President; Abdullah bin Mohammed al-Hamed al-Qubaisi, Undersecretary at the Ministry of Foreign Affairs and son of Mohammed bin Butti al-Hamed, a former chairman of Abu Dhabi Municipality, three daughters of whom were married to sons of Sheikh Zayed (Hazza', Mansour, and Nahyan).

42. Sovereign Wealth Fund Institute, http://www.swfinstitute.org/fund-rankings/

43. Ibid.

44. *Gulf States Newsletter*, 1000 (17 September 2015): p. 43. Mubadala owns stakes in the Carlyle Group, a US private equity company, Mediobanco, Piaggio Aerospace, General Electric, etc.

45. IPIC owns 98 per cent of Aabar Investments, which has a 5 per cent stake in UniCredit, a 37 per cent stake in Virgin Galactic, and a 35 per cent stake in Arabtec.

46. EIA owns 60 per cent of Etisalat and 40 per cent of du.

pp. [91–99]

47. In addition to these high-profile roles, Mansour bin Zayed has developed his own business empire. He controls a number of holdings, including the Abu Dhabi United Investment and Development Group (which owns Manchester City Football Club) and Das Holding, which is particularly active in real estate, transport, and mass media.

48. Jean-François Seznec, 'The Sovereign Wealth Funds of the Persian Gulf', in Mehran Kamrava (ed.), *The Political Economy of the Persian Gulf* (London: Hurst, 2012), p. 79.

49. 'Abu Dhabi's Nexus of Economic Power, Part II: The Abu Dhabi Executive Council', WikiLeaks Cable from US Embassy in Abu Dhabi (03ABUDHA BI3208_a), 9 July 2003.

50. Calvin H. Allen and W. Lynn Rigsbee, *Oman under Qaboos: From Coup to Constitution, 1970–1996* (London: Frank Cass, 2000), p. 141.

51. Bank Muscat's main shareholder is the Royal Court Affairs, which is in charge of the Sultan's personal affairs (properties, personal economic interests, etc.).

52. Two of Khalid's brothers, Hamud (vice-chairman) and Qays, are members of the board of Bank Dhofar. Didic also owns Dhofar Insurance Company, Oman's largest insurer. Dhofar Insurance Company chairman is the Sultan's maternal uncle's son, Qays al-Ma'ashani.

53. See Marc Valeri, 'Simmering Unrest and Succession Challenges in Oman', Carnegie Endowment for International Peace, January 2015, http://carnegieendowment. org/2015/01/28/simmering-unrest-and-succession-challenges-in-oman

54. 'Oman's Sultan Qaboos Responds to Popular Protests with Successive Government Reshuffles', *Gulf States Newsletter*, 35(896), 11 March 2011, pp. 3–4.

55. Shaikha Ahmed Salman, 'BCCI's Call for Consolidated Efforts to Revive the Economy', 11 May 2011 Bahrain Chamber of Commerce and Industry, http://www.bcci.bh/en/ViewNews.aspx?nid=601&typeind=N

56. Sandeep Singh Grewal, 'Boycott Iranian Products', *Gulf Daily News*, 1 May 2011. BCCI treasurer 'Uthman Sharif said this call 'reflects an economic decision highlighting [the BCCI's] support to the Bahrain government and rulers'.

57. For more details on Suhar protests since 2011, see Marc Valeri, 'The Ṣuḥar Paradox: Social and Political Mobilisations in the Sultanate of Oman since 2011', *Arabian Humanities*, 4, 2015, https://cy.revues.org/2828

6. INDIA: A RISING POWER IN THE PERSIAN GULF?

1. Victor Mallet, 'Old Ties between India and the GCC are Renewed', *Financial Times*, 29 June 2014, http://www.ft.com/intl/cms/s/0/577314ce-f856-11e3-815f-00144feabdc0.html#axzz3Yu9IewY6

2. Neha Kohli, 'Indian Migrants in the Gulf Countries', in Rumel Dahiya (ed.), *Developments in the Gulf Region: Prospects and Challenges for India in the Next Two Decades*, Institute for Defence Studies and Analysis (IDSA), 2013, p. 117.

3. 'India's Highest Amount of Remittances Comes from the Gulf', *Economic Times*, 1 December 2014, http://articles.economictimes.indiatimes.com/2014–12–01/news/56614713_1_remittances-bangladesh-and-nepal-fdi; 'India's FDI Increased by 26% in 2014: UN', *Economic Times*, 30 January 2015, http://articles.economictimes.indiatimes.com/2015–01–30/news/58625677_1_2008-fdi-inflows-services-sector

4. 'India', US Energy Information Administration, 26 June 2014, http://www.eia.gov/countries/cab.cfm?fips=in

5. P.R. Kumaraswamy, 'Realism Replacing Rhetoric: Factors Shaping India's Middle East Policy', *Round Table*, 97(397), 2008, p. 575.

6. Victor Mallet, 'India's Reliance on Imported Energy Threatens Long-Term Recovery', *Financial Times*, 12 September 2013, http://www.ft.com/cms/s/0/c20792e2-1b84-11e3-b678-00144feab7de.html#axzz3XwqsW0uY

7. Oliver Stuenkel, 'Emerging India: A Farewell to Multilateralism?', *Indian Foreign Affairs Journal*, 8(4), 2013, p. 413.

8. 'South Asia and the Gulf Lead Rising Trend in Arms Imports, Russian Exports Grow, says SIPRI', Stockholm International Peace Research Institute (SIPRI), 17 March 2014, http://www.sipri.org/media/pressreleases/2014/AT_march_2014

9. Barack Obama, 'Remarks by the President to the Joint Session of the Indian Parliament in New Delhi, India', 8 November 2010, https://www.whitehouse.gov/the-press-office/2010/11/08/remarks-president-joint-session-indian-parliament-new-delhi-india

10. Charalampos Efstathopoulos, 'Reinterpreting India's Rise through the Middle Power Prism', *Asian Journal of Political Science*, 19(1), 2011, p. 76.

11. Carsten Holbraad, *Middle Powers in International Politics*, (London: St. Martin's Press, 1984), p. 3.

12. Jonathan H. Ping, *Middle Power Statecraft: Indonesia, Malaysia and the Asia-Pacific* (Aldershot: Ashgate Publishing, 2005), pp. 66–72.

13. Efstathopoulos, 'Reinterpreting India's Rise', p. 76.

14. Robert O. Keohane, 'Lilliputians' Dilemmas: Small States in International Politics', *International Organization*, 23(2), 1969, p. 296.

15. Efstathopoulos, 'Reinterpreting India's Rise', pp. 76–79.

16. See Kadira Pethiyagoda, 'The Influence of Dominant Cultural Values on India's Foreign Policy' (PhD thesis, University of Melbourne, 2013).

17. Joseph S. Nye, 'What China and Russia Don't Get About Soft Power', *Foreign Policy*, 29 April 2013, http://foreignpolicy.com/2013/04/29/what-china-and-russia-dont-get-about-soft-power/

18. India has been campaigning for a permanent seat on the UN Security Council, as well as an expanded role in institutions such as the International Monetary Fund (IMF) and the World Bank.

19. Sunil Khilnani, 'India as a Bridging Power', in *India as a New Global Leader*, The Foreign Policy Centre, 2005, http://fpc.org.uk/fsblob/377.pdf

20. Manjari Chatterjee Miller, 'India's Feeble Foreign Policy: A Would-Be Great Power Resists Its Own Rise', *Foreign Affairs*, May/June 2013, p. 14.

21. 'Can India Become a Great Power?' *The Economist*, 30 March 2013, http://www.economist.com/news/leaders/21574511-indias-lack-strategic-culture-hobbles-its-ambition-be-force-world-can-india

22. Stuenkel raises an interest point when he notes: 'These issues have immediate relevance for Indian multilateralism: widespread rural poverty is, until today, a determining factor in India's negotiation strategy in international institutions such as the WTO, or during climate talks.' See Stuenkel, 'Emerging India: A Farewell to Multilateralism', p. 414.

23. Chatterjee Miller, 'India's Feeble Foreign Policy', p. 14.

24. Chatterjee Miller claims: 'Officials who have worked with the foreign ministry and the prime minister's office told me that the disadvantage of the international discourse on India's rise was that the West, particularly the United States, might pressure India to step up its global commitments. India might have to abandon its status as a developing country and could be forced to make concessions on environmental issues, such as limiting its carbon emissions, and on trade, such as opening up the Indian market further to U.S. exports. India has not adequately thought through what its growing clout will mean in terms of assuming global leadership. This fact has had significant bearing on New Delhi's foreign policy.' See ibid., p. 18.

25. Efstathopoulos, 'Reinterpreting India's Rise', p. 84.

26. Khilnani, 'India as a Bridging Power', p. 8.

27. James Onley, 'Britain's Informal Empire in the Gulf, 1820–1971', *Journal of Social Affairs*, 22(87), 2005, pp. 30–1.

28. Ibid. p. 42.

29. Rahul Roy-Chaudhury, 'India: Gulf Security Partner in Waiting?', in Toby Dodge and Emile Hokayem (eds.), *Middle Eastern Security, the US Pivot and the Rise of ISIS, Adelphi*, 447–8, 2014, p. 225.

30. Manmohan Singh cited in Mushtaq Hussain, 'Gulf Cooperation Council (GCC)', in P.R. Kumaraswamy (ed.), *Persian Gulf 2013: India's Relations with the Region* (SAGE Publications India, 2014), p. 277.

31. Roy-Chaudhury, 'India: Gulf Security Partner in Waiting?', p. 227.

32. Ibid.

33. Ibid.

34. 'GCC Trade and Investment Flows', Economist Intelligence Unit, 2014, p. 4.

35. Ibid., pp. 11–12.

36. Ibid., p. 12.

37. Roy-Chaudhury, 'India: Gulf Security Partner in Waiting?', p. 229.

38. Biswajit Nag and Mohit Gupta, 'The Rise of Gulf Investment in India: Searching for Complementarity and Synergy', Middle East Institute, 9 October 2014,

"http://www.mei.edu/content/map/rise-gulf-investment-india-searching-com-plementarity-and-synergy"http://www.mei.edu/content/map/rise-gulf-investment-india-searching-complementarity-and-synergy
39. Roy-Chaudhury, 'India: Gulf Security Partner in Waiting?', p. 227.
40. 'India's Nondescript Foreign Policy Toward the Middle East', US Embassy in India, 12 December 2005, http://www.thehindu.com/news/the-india-cables/article1545798.ece. See also Girijesh Pant, 'Diaspora in Indian Politics and the 15th General Election', in Ajay K. Mehra (ed.) *Emerging Trends in Indian Politics: The Fifteenth General Election* (London: Routledge, 2013).
41. Roy-Chaudhury, 'India: Gulf Security Partner in Waiting?', pp. 227–228.
42. Ibid.
43. 'India's Highest Amount of Remittances Comes from the Gulf', *Economic Times*, 1 December 2014, "http://articles.economictimes.indiatimes.com/2014-12-01/news/56614713_1_remittances-bangladesh-and-nepal-fdi" http://articles.economictimes.indiatimes.com/2014-12-01/news/56614713_1_remittances-bangladesh-and-nepal-fdi; 'India's FDI Increased by 26% in 2014: UN', *Economic Times*, 30 January 2015, http://articles.economictimes.indiatimes.com/2015-01-30/news/58625677_1_2008-fdi-inflows-services-sector
44. Alyssa Ayres, 'India's Stakes in the Middle East', *Forbes*, 26 February 2014, http://www.forbes.com/sites/alyssaayres/2014/02/26/indias-stakes-in-the-middle-east/
45. Indian expatriates in the Gulf are predominantly composed of blue-collar labourers, but there has been a steady increase in the numbers of white-collar Indian expatriates, in sectors such as the media, health and education. See Arshiah Parween, '"Invisible" White-Collar Indians in the Gulf', *Middle East Institute*, 14 August 2013, http://www.mei.edu/content/'invisible'-white-collar-indians-gulf
46. Roy-Chaudhury, 'India: Gulf Security Partner in Waiting?', p. 229.
47. See 'India: Yemen Rescue Prompts Goodwill towards Pakistan', *BBC News*, 9 April 2015, http://www.bbc.com/news/blogs-news-from-elsewhere-32235807; 'India Ends Yemen Evacuation, Rescues People from 41 Countries', *Times of India*, 10 April 2015, http://timesofindia.indiatimes.com/india/India-ends-Yemen-evacuation-rescues-people-from-41-countries/articleshow/46875815.cms
48. Roy-Chaudhury, 'India: Gulf Security Partner in Waiting?', p. 228.
49. Toufic Haddad, 'Palestinian Forced Displacement from Kuwait: The Overdue Accounting', *Al Majdal* (44) 2010, http://www.badil.org/haq-alawda/item/1514-art07
50. 'Projected Population Change in Countries with Largest Muslim Populations in 2010', Pew Research Center, 2 April 2015, http://www.pewforum.org/2015/04/02/muslims/pf_15–04–02_projectionstables73/
51. 'The Future of World Religions: Population Growth Projections, 2010–2050', Pew Research Center, 2 April 2015, http://www.pewforum.org/2015/04/02/religious-projections-2010-2050/

52. Kumaraswamy, 'Realism Replacing Rhetoric', p. 576.
53. Manmohan Singh, 'Press Conference of Prime Minister Dr. Manmohan Singh, New York', 16 September 2005, http://www.mea.gov.in/media-briefings. htm?dtl/4302/Press+Conference+of+Prime+Minister+Dr+Manmohan+Sing h+New+York
54. Jaswant Singh cited in Siddharth Varadarajan, 'When Jaswant Took Indian Politics to Foreign Shores', *Hindu*, 16 September 2005 http://www.thehindu.com/ 2005/09/16/stories/2005091606041100.htm
55. Salman Khurshid, 'Middle East Security and Non-Proliferation', 8 December 2013, https://www.iiss.org/en/events/manama%20dialogue/archive/manama-dialogue-2013–4e92/plenary-5-fbc6/khurshid-632c
56. Roy-Chaudhury, 'India: Gulf Security Partner in Waiting?', pp. 236–237.
57. Khurshid, 'Middle East Security and Non-Proliferation'.
58. See 'Recommendations of the Group of Ministers: Reforming the National Security System', Government of India, February 2001, p. 10; 'Indian Maritime Doctrine (INBR 8)', Indian Navy, April 2004, p. 56.
59. Roy-Chaudhury, 'India: Gulf Security Partner in Waiting?', p. 231.
60. See Danielle Rajendram, 'India's New Asia-Pacific Strategy: Modi Acts East', Lowy Institute for International Policy, December 2014, http://www.lowyinstitute.org/ files/indias-new-asia-pacific-strategy-modi-acts-east.pdf
61. Efstathopoulos, 'Reinterpreting India's Rise', p. 87.
62. Saeed Shah, Jeremy Page, 'China Readies $46 Billion for Pakistan Trade Route', *Wall Street Journal*, 16 April 2015, http://www.wsj.com/articles/china-to-unveil-billions-of-dollars-in-pakistan-investment-1429214705
63. See S. Paul Kapu and Sumit Ganguly, 'The Transformation of U.S.–India Relations: An Explanation for the Rapprochement and Prospects for the Future', *Asian Survey*, 47(4), 2007.
64. 'Progress by Pak in Tackling Terror Not Quick as We Like: Obama', *Indian Express*, 7 November 2010, http://archive.indianexpress.com/news/progress-by-pak-in-tackling-terror-not-quick-as-we-like-obama/707820/0; 'Vision Statement for the U.S.–India Strategic Partnership: "Chalein Saath Saath: Forward Together We Go"', White House, 29 September 2014, https://www.whitehouse.gov/the-press-office/2014/09/29/vision-statement-us-india-strategic-partnership-chalein-saath-saath-forw
65. Munir Akram, 'India's Great Power Game', *Dawn*, 28 September 2014, http:// www.dawn.com/news/1134772/indias-great-power-game
66. C. Raja Mohan, 'Modi and the Middle East: Towards a Link West Policy', *Indian Express*, 5 October 2014, http://carnegieendowment.org/2014/10/05/modi-and-middle-east-towards-link-west-policy
67. Shivshankar Menon, 'India's Security Environment: Address to the Kerala State Planning Board', 19 March 2014, http://southasiamonitor.org/detail.php?type= emerging&nid=7606

68. Salman Khurshid cited in William Maclean, 'India Not Keen on U.S.-Style Gulf Security Role: Khurshid', *Reuters*, 8 December 2013, http://in.reuters.com/article/2013/12/08/gulf-security-india-khurshid-idINDEE9B700X20131208

69. Ibid.

70. Tanvi Madan, 'India's Relationship with Iran: It's Complicated', Brookings Institution, 28 February 2014, http://www.brookings.edu/blogs/markaz/posts/2014/02/28-iran-india-complicated-relationship-madan

7. THE RISE OF ISIS: IRAQ AND PERSIAN GULF SECURITY

1. Angus Mcdowall and Amena Bakr, 'Three Gulf Arab States Recall Envoys in Rift with Qatar', *Reuters*, 5 March 2014.

2. Alexey Khlevikov, 'The New Ideological Threat to the GCC: Implications for the Qatar-Saudi Rivalry', *Strategic Assessment*, 17(4), 2015, pp. 17–27.

3. Abd al-Jalil al-Marhoun, 'A New Paradigm for Gulf Security', *Al-Jazeera Center for Studies* (2010).

4. Bilal Saab, 'Why the Persian Gulf Isn't Ready for Joint Security', *Defense One* (2014).

5. Adviser to the GCC Sami al-Faraj, cited in Angus McDowall and William MacLean, 'Islamic State Blows Away Gulf Qualms about Joining U.S. Military Action', *Reuters*, 23 September 2015.

6. 'Al-Haramayn' refers to the two holy mosques in Mecca and Medina for which the Saudi royal family currently act as custodians. 'Saloul' is a derogatory way of referring to the Saudi royal family that compares them to the pagan family who guarded the holy Kaaba in pre-Islamic times. Ludovica Iaccino, 'Isis Leader Abu Bakr al-Baghdadi Threatens Saudi Arabia with "Volcanoes of Jihad"', *International Business Times*, 14 November 2014.

7. McDowall and MacLean, 'Islamic State Blows Away Gulf Qualms about Joining U.S. Military Action'.

8. Ahmed al-Omran, 'Saudis Link Deadly Attack to Islamic State', *Wall Street Journal*, 24 November 2014.

9. Frank Gardner, 'Islamic State Sets Sights on Saudi Arabia', *BBC News*, 14 November 2014.

10. Peter Neumann, 'Foreign Fighter Total in Syria/Iraq Now Exceeds 20,000; Surpasses Afghanistan Conflict in the 1980s', International Centre for the Study of Radicalisation and Political Violence, 26 January 2015.

11. Ibid.

12. McDowall and MacLean, 'Islamic State Blows Away Gulf Qualms about Joining U.S. Military Action'.

13. Nasser al-Haqbani, 'Arar Border Attack Carried Out by Saudi Isis Members: Sources', *Asharq al-Awsat*, 10 January 2015.

14. As Ross Harrison argues, responses such as these which fail to address the under-lying questions of political identity in the Arab world 'could mean leaving it to ISIS and the broader jihadist movement to answer'. Ross Harrison, 'Towards a Regional Strategy contra Isis', *Parameters*, 44(3), 2014, pp. 37–46.

15. Gregory Gause, 'Beyond Sectarianism: The New Middle East Cold War', Brookings Doha Center Analysis Paper 11 (2014), p. 2.

16. Angus McDowall and Amena Bakr, 'Saudi Arabia Confirms Role in Strikes against Islamic State in Syria', *Reuters*, 23 September 2014.

17. Gregory Gause argues that 'disagreements among Gulf States are more likely to arise in periods of relative stability than of instability'. Center for Strategic and International Studies, 'Will Unity Hold? The GCC and the Challenge of Joint Action', *Gulf Roundtable Series*, 2014.

18. Alexey Khlebnikov, 'The New Ideological Threat to the GCC: Implications for the Qatar-Saudi Rivalry', *Strategic Assessment*, 17(4), 2015.

19. Deborah Amos, 'Facing Threats from Isis and Iran, Gulf States Set to Join Forces', *NPR*, 8 December 2014.

20. Simeon Kerr, 'Gulf States Launch Joint Command to Counter Isis and Iran', *Financial Times*, 30 November 2014.

21. Emirates News Agency, 'Cabinet Okays GCC Joint Police HQ in Abu Dhabi', *Khaleej Times*, 20 April 2015.

22. Madawi al-Rasheed, 'Kuwaiti Activists Targeted under GCC Security Pact', *Al-Monitor*, 12 March 2015.

23. US Department of State, 'Foreign Ministers' Jeddah Communique on Terrorism', 11 September 2014.

24. Mick Krever, 'Qatar's Emir: We Don't Fund Terrorists', *CNN*, 25 September 2014.

25. US Department of State, 'Foreign Ministers' Jeddah Communique on Terrorism', 11 September 2014.

26. Jethro Mullen, 'U.S.-Led Airstrikes on Isis in Syria: Who's In, Who's Not', *CNN*, 2 October 2014.

27. Rajiv Chandrasekaran, 'In the UAE, the United States Has a Quiet, Potent Ally Nicknamed "Little Sparta"', *Washington Post*, 9 November 2014.

28. Craig Whitlock, 'U.S. Relies on Persian Gulf Bases for Airstrikes in Iraq', *Washington Post*, 26 August 2014.

29. Rick Gladstone, 'Saudi Arabia Donates $500 Million to Help Displaced Iraqis', *New York Times*, 1 July 2015.

30. United Nations Office for the Coordination of Humanitarian Affairs, 'UN Welcomes $10 Million Donation from Kuwait for Humanitarian Aid in Iraq', *Relief Web*, 9 July 2014.

31. 'Qatar Sends Aid to Iraqis in N. Cities, Jordanian Capital', Kuwait News Agency, 8 September 2014.

32. Elizabeth Dickinson, 'Playing with Fire: Why Private Gulf Financing for Syria's

Extremist Rebels Risk Igniting Sectarian Conflict at Home', Brookings Institution Analysis Paper, 2013, p. 1.

33. Ibid., p. 2.

34. US Department of the Treasury, 'Remarks of Undersecretary for Terrorism and Financial Intelligence David Cohen before the Center for a New American Security on "Confronting New Threats in Terrorist Financing"', 4 March 2014.

35. Dickinson, 'Playing with Fire', p. 9.

36. Simeon Kerr, 'Kuwait Clamps Down on Terror Financing', *Financial Times*, 9 September 2014.

37. William Mauldin, 'U.S. Calls Qatar, Kuwait over Terror Financing', *Wall Street Journal*, 23 October 2014.

38. Kerr, 'Kuwait Clamps Down on Terror Financing'.

39. 'U.S. Urges Stronger Fight against Isis Propaganda in Mideast', *CBS News*, 27 October 2014.

40. GCC support for UNSC Resolution 2170 was declared in the Final Communique of the GCC meeting on 30 August 2014. 'Excerpts from Final Communique after GCC Meeting', *Gulf News*, 30 August 2014.

41. United Nations Security Council, UNSC Resolution 2170.

42. US Department of State, 'Foreign Ministers' Jeddah Communique on Terrorism'.

43. Justine Drennan, 'Who Has Contributed What in the Coalition against the Islamic State', *Foreign Policy*, 12 November 2014.

44. Author interview with Fuad Hussein, 9 March 2015.

45. Ahmed Saad, 'Iraqi PM Maliki Says Saudi, Qatar Openly Funding Violence in Anbar', *Reuters*, 1 March 2014.

46. Awad Mustafa, 'GCC Nations Remain Vigilant, but Little Action Expected on Iraq', *Defense News*, 22 June 2014.

47. US Department of State, 'Readout of Secretary Kerry's Meetings with Syrian Opposition Council President Ahmad Jarba, Saudi King Abdullah bin Abdulaziz Al-Saud, and Call with Iraqi Kurdistan Regional President Masoud Barzani', 28 June 2014.

48. Nouf al-Sadiq, 'Gulf States Reactions to the New War in Iraq', *Atlantic Council*, 1 July 2014.

49. Mohamed Salman, 'Qatari: U.S. Intervention in Iraq Would Be Seen as War on Sunni Arabs', *McClatchy*, 16 June 2014.

50. Taimur Khan, 'GCC Ministers Denounce ISIL at Jeddah Meeting', *The National*, 30 August 2014.

51. 'Excerpts from Final Communique after GCC Meeting', *Gulf News*, 30 August 2014.

52. 'A Majority of Arabs Oppose ISIL, Support Air Strikes on the Ground', Arab Center for Research and Policy Studies, 13 November 2014.

53. 'Excerpts from Final Communique after GCC Meeting', *Gulf News*, 30 August 2014.

54. US Department of State, 'Foreign Ministers' Jeddah Communique on Terrorism'.
55. Azzaman, 'Iraq Seeks Saudi Help to Join Gulf Cooperation Council', *Oneiraqidinar. com*, 12 November 2014.
56. Hamza Mustafa, 'Iraq, Gulf States Close to Full Rapprochement: Iraqi President', *Asharq al-Awsat*, 12 February 2015.
57. 'Saudi Arabia Invites Iraq's Abadi to Visit in Big Sign of Thaw', *Reuters*, 23 March 2015.
58. Hamza Mustafa, 'Iraq, Gulf States Close to Full Rapprochement: Iraqi President', *Asharq al-Awsat*, 12 February 2015.
59. Nawaf al-Diqbasi, 'Iraqi President Welcomes One Year Pay Grace to Pay Damages to Kuwait', *Kuwait News Agency*, 11 February 2015.
60. Taimur Khan, 'GCC Ministers Denounce ISIL at Jeddah Meeting', *The National*, 30 August 2014.
61. Martin Chulov, 'Iran Sends Troops into Iraq to Aid Fight against Isis Militants', *The Guardian*, 14 June 2014.
62. Julian Borger, 'Iran Air Strikes against Isis Requested by Iraqi Government, Says Tehran', *The Guardian*, 6 December 2014.
63. Ned Parker, Babak Dehghanpisheh and Isabel Coles, 'Special Report: How Iran's Military Chiefs Operate in Iraq', *Reuters*, 24 February 2014.
64. Ibid.
65. Bita Bakhtiari, 'Iran Arms Exports to Iraq Tolerated in Fight against Isis, Says Report', *The Guardian*, 17 February 2015.
66. Eric Schmitt, 'Iran Sent Arms to Iraq to Fight Isis, U.S. Says', *New York Times*, 16 March 2015.
67. Author interview with senior Kurdish minister, 9 March 2015.
68. Author interview with Fuad Hussein, 9 March 2015.
69. Author interview with Hoshyar Zebari, 12 March 2015.
70. Ibid.
71. Author interview with senior Kurdish minister, 9 March 2015.
72. Ibid.
73. Author interview with Tariq al-Hashemi, 19 March 2015.
74. Ibid.
75. Author interview with Sheikh Jamaal al-Khamees, 3 March 2015.
76. Ibid.
77. Author interview with Sheikh Nawaf Hemoud Al Maghames, 18 March 2015.
78. Ahmed al-Omran and Felicia Schwartz, 'John Kerry Seeks to Calm Arab States Unsettled by Iran Talks', *Wall Street Journal*, 5 March 2015.
79. 'Arab Gulf States Reject Iran's Role in Iraq', *Al-Arabiya*, 12 March 2015.
80. Julien Barnes-Dacey, Ellie Geranmayeh and Daniel Levy, 'Encouraging Regional Ownership of the Fight against the Islamic State', in Julien Barnes-Dacey, Ellie Geranmayeh and Daniel Levy (eds.), *The Islamic State through the Regional Lens* (London: European Council on Foreign Relations, 2015), p. 12.

81. Ibid.

82. 'Why Saudi Arabia and Israel Oppose Iran Nuclear Deal', *Al-Jazeera*, 14 April 2015.

83. Every GCC country except Oman supported the Saudi-led strikes, in addition to Egypt, Morocco, Jordan, and Sudan. Nick Thompson, 'Operation Decisive Storm', *CNN*, 30 March 2015.

84. 'Saudi "Decisive Storm" Waged to Save Yemen', *Al-Arabiya*, 25 March 2015.

85. 'Saudi-Led Coalition Declares End to Yemen Air Strikes', *Al-Jazeera*, 22 April 2015.

86. Erika Solomon and Simeon Kerr, 'Syria's Rebels Heartened by Healing of Sunni Arab Rift', *Financial Times*, 13 April 2015.

87. Ryan Grim, Sophia Jones and Jessica Schulberg, 'Saudi Arabia, Turkey Discussing Unlikely Alliance to Oust Syria's Assad', *Huffington Post*, 12 April 2015.

8. A REGIONAL GREAT GAME? IRAN–SAUDI RELATIONS IN FLUX

1. Samuel P. Huntington, 'The Lonely Superpower', *Foreign Affairs*, 78, March/April 1999, https://www.foreignaffairs.com/articles/united-states/1999-03-01/lonely-superpower, accessed 3 December 2014.

2. Maxi Schoeman, 'South Africa as an Emerging Middle Power: 1994–2003', in John Daniel, Roger Southall and Adam Habib (eds.), *State of the Nation: South Africa 2003–2004* (Cape Town: HSRC Press, 2003), pp. 351–353.

3. Graham E. Fuller and John Arquilla, 'The Intractable Problem of Regional Powers', *Orbis*, 40, 1996, p. 610. For a succinct theoretical discussion of the role of regional conflicts in conflict management, see Fen Osler Hampson, 'A New Role for Middle Powers in Regional Conflict Resolution?', in Brian L. Job (ed.), *The Insecurity Dilemma: National Security of Third World States* (Boulder, CO: Lynne Rienner Publishers, 1992), pp. 191–208.

4. International Institute for Strategic Studies (IISS), *Military Balance 2015* (London: IISS, 2015), http://www.iiss.org/-/media/Images/Publications/The%20Military%20Balance/MilBal%202015/MB2015%20Defence%20budgets%20and%20expenditure.jpg, accessed June 2, 2015.

5. Stockholm International Peace Research Institute Database, http://www.sipri.org/research/armaments/milex/milex_database, accessed 8 June 2015.

6. For a brief overview of the comparative study of regional powers, see Damla Aras, 'Introduction: Coercion and Regional Powers', *Defence Studies*, 9, 2009, pp. 181–188.

7. Robin Wright, *The Last Great Revolution: Turmoil and Transformation in Iran* (Boston: Knopf, 2000).

8. Hossein Sadeghi and Hassan Ahmadian, 'Iran–Saudi Relations: Past Pattern, Future Outlook', *Iranian Review of Foreign Affairs*, 1, 2011, p. 120.

NOTES   pp. [129–133]

9. For a succinct overview of the hajj in Iranian–Saudi tensions, see Toby Matthiesen, *The Other Saudis: Shiism, Dissent and Sectarianism* (New York: Cambridge University Press, 2015), pp. 126–139. Also see Christin Marschall, *Iran's Persian Gulf Policy: From Khomeini to Khatami* (London: Routledge Curzon, 2003), pp. 45–61.

10. See Mehr News Agency, http://mehrnews.com/news/2538265, accessed 20 April 2015.

11. See Fars News Agency, http://www.farsnews.com/printable.php?nn=13940 129000050, accessed 18 April 2015.

12. See Mohammad Doroodian, 'Naqsh va Ta'seer Tahavolat-e Jang pas az Fath-e Khoramshahr bar Blooq va Takamol-e Nirooye Dafaiye Iran' (The Impact of the War on the Development and Progress of Iran's Defensive Forces after the Liberation of Khoramshahr), *Journal of Defence Policy*, 8, 2000, pp. 5–24. Also see Mohammad Doroodian, *Az Faw ta Chalamcheh* (From Faw to Chalamcheh) (Tehran: Pasdaran Center for War Studies and Research, 1995) and Mohammad Doroodian, *Payan-e Jang* (The End of the War) (Tehran: Pasdaran Center for War Studies and Research, 1999).

13. Kevjn Lim, 'National Security Decision-Making in Iran', *Comparative Strategy*, 34, 2015, pp. 149–168. Also, see J. Matthew McInnis, 'Iran's Strategic Thinking: Origins and Evolution', American Enterprise Institute, Washington DC, May 2015, pp. 1–24.

14. 'Saudi Arabia Welcomes Iran Nuclear Agreement', *Al-Jazeera*, http://www. aljazeera.com/news/middleeast/2013/11/saudi-arabia-welcomes-iran-nuclear-agreement-2013112513519366380.html, accessed 25 November 2013.

15. Mohammed bin Nawaf bin Abdulaziz Al-Saud, 'Saudi Arabia Will Go It Alone', *New York Times*, http://www.nytimes.com/2013/12/18/opinion/saudi-arabia-will-go-it-alone.html?_r=0, accessed 17 December 2013.

16. 'Iran's Arab Neighbors Keep Reservations Quiet over Nuclear Deal', *Reuters*, accessed 24 November 2013.

17. 'Geneva Nuclear Deal Will Strengthen Iran's Regional and Global Status', IR Diplomacy, http://www.irdiplomacy.ir/en/page/1925924/Geneva+Nuclear+D eal+Will+Strengthen+Iran%E2%80%99s+Regional+and+Global+Status.html, accessed 12 December 2013.

18. 'US Talks Belie Iran's Existing Sway through Much of the Arab World', *The National*, http://www.thenational.ae/opinion/comment/us-talks-belie-irans-existing-sway-through-much-of-the-arab-world, accessed 17 November 2014.

19. Faisal al-Yafai, 'Iran Will Not Become a Threat if It Acquires Nuclear Weapons. It is Already a Threat to the Gulf', *The National*, http://www.thenational.ae/opin ion/iran-will-not-become-a-threat-if-it-acquires-nuclear-weapons-it-is-already-a-threat-to-the-gulf, accessed 18 November 2014.

20. 'The Region Has Been Dancing to Tehran's Tune', *The National*, http://www.the-

national.ae/opinion/the-region-has-been-dancing-to-tehrans-tune, accessed 25 November 2014.

21. Tariq Al Homayed, 'Iran's Foreign Policy Is Shifting' *Asharq al-Awsat*, http://www.aawsat.net/2014/08/article55335965, accessed 29 August 2014.

22. 'Saudi Minister Blasts Iran's "Occupying Force" as Part of the Problem in Syria, Iraq, and Yemen', *National Post*, http://news.nationalpost.com/2014/10/13/saudi-minister-blasts-irans-occupying-forces-as-part-of-the-problem-in-syria-iraq-and-yemen, accessed 13 October 2014.

23. 'Gulf States "Offer Iran Uranium"', BBC News, http://news.bbc.co.uk/2/hi/middle_east/7073699.stm, accessed 1 November 2007.

24. 'GCC Must Join the Iran Talks, Prince Turki Says', *Khaleej Times*, http://www.khaleejtimes.com/kt-article-display-1.asp?xfile=data/middleeast/2013/December/middleeast_December70.xml&section=middleeast, accessed 9 December 2013.

25. For background on Iran–GCC relations, see Kaveh L. Afrasiabi, *After Khomeini: New Directions in Iran's Foreign Policy* (Boulder, CO: Westview Press, 1994). Also, Prasanta Kumar Pradhan, 'The GCC–Iran Conflict and Its Strategic Implication for the Gulf Region', *Strategic Analysis*, 35, 2011, pp. 265–276.

26. Abbas Maleki, 'Rouhani Stresses Regionalism in Iranian Foreign Policy', *Al-Monitor*, http://www.al-monitor.com/pulse/originals/2013/07/rouhani-stresses-regionalism-in-iranian-foreign-policy.html, accessed 13 July 2013. Also, Ahmad Sadeghi, 'Need for Intra-Regionalism in the Middle East: An Iranian Perspective', Tehran, Institute for Political and International Studies, http://www.ipis.ir/index.aspx?siteid=9&pageid=516&newsview=461, accessed 10 September 2014.

27. 'Iran Closes Hormuz Strait in Case of Evident Security Threat', IR Diplomacy, 10 July 2012, http://www.irdiplomacy.ir/en/page/1903933/Iran+Closes+Hormuz+Strait+In+Case+of+Evident+Security+Threat.html, accessed 10 July 2012.

28. Basma Mubarak Saeed, 'Oman, Iran Rapprochement and a GCC Union', Al-Jazeera Center for Studies, http://studies.aljazeera.net/en/reports/2014/01/20141218365065800.htm, accessed 8 May 2014.

29. Simeon Kerr and Najmeh Bozorgmehr, 'Iran's Hassan Rouhani Seals Gas Deal during Visit to Oman', *Financial Times*, http://www.ft.com/cms/s/0/8bdf1daa-aaba-11e3-be01-00144feab7de.html#axzz3dkBfSUK0, accessed 13 March 2014. Iran and Oman share a major gas field, most of it in Iranian waters, and the Iranians had earmarked $800 million for its development.

30. 'Kuwait Seeks to Import Gas from Iran', *Trade and Export*, http://www.tradeandexportme.com/2014/06/kuwait-seeks-to-import-gas-from-iran/, accessed 3 June 2014. For a broader yet succinct analysis of the causes and consequences of Iran's cold war with Saudi Arabia, see Robert Mason, *Foreign Policy in Iran and Saudi Arabia: Economics and Diplomacy in the Middle East* (London: I.B. Tauris, 2015), pp. 96–104.

31. UAE National Bureau of Statistics, http://www.uaestatistics.gov.ae/Reports ByDepartmentEnglish/tabid/104/Default.aspx?MenuId=1, accessed 2 March 2015.

32. 'Iran Nuclear Deal: Dubai Leader Backs Easing of Sanctions', *BBC News*, http://www.bbc.com/news/world-middle-east-25717804, accessed 13 January 2014.

33. Michael Wilner, 'Exclusive: Cornered but Unbound by Nuclear Pact, Israel Reconsiders Military Action against Iran', *Jerusalem Post*, http://www.jpost.com/International/Exclusive-Cornered-but-unbound-by-nuclear-pact-Israel-reconsiders-military-action-against-Iran-382541, accessed 22 November 2014.

34. See, for example, Niels Lesniewski, 'GOP Hawks Quick to Blast Iran Framework', *Roll Call*, http://blogs.rollcall.com/wgdb/gop-hawks-quick-to-blast-iran-framework/, accessed 2 April 2015; Colin Campbell, 'Republican Senator Compares Iran Deal to Nazi Appeasement', *Business Insider*, http://www.businessinsider.com/gop-senator-compares-iran-deal-to-nazi-appeasement-2015-4, accessed 2 April 2015, and Carol E. Lee, 'U.S. Group Urges Hardline on Key Areas in Iran Nuclear Deal', *Wall Street Journal*, http://www.wsj.com/articles/u-s-group-urges-hard-line-on-key-areas-in-iran-nuclear-deal-1435007155, accessed 22 June 2015. For a recent discussion of the emergence of a 'Saudi–Israeli axis' against Iran, see Eli Lake, 'Israelis and Saudis Reveal Secret Talks to Thwart Iran', BloombergView, http://www.bloombergview.com/articles/2015–06–04/israelis-and-saudis-reveal-secret-talks-to-thwart-iran, accessed 4 June 2015 and Amir Oren, '"Israel Can Help the Saudis Offset an Iranian Nuclear Bomb"', *Haaretz*, http://www.haaretz.com/opinion/.premium-1.655797, accessed 11 May 2015.

35. Kaveh Afrasiabi, 'Can the Nuclear Talks Survive the Gaza War?', *Eurasiareview*, http://www.eurasiareview.com/02082014-can-nuclear-talks-survive-gaza-war-oped/, accessed 2 August 2014.

36. Helene Cooper and Mark Landler, 'Interests of Saudi Arabia and Iran Collide, with the U.S. in the Middle', *New York Times*, http://www.nytimes.com/2011/03/18/world/18diplomacy.html?_r=0, accessed 17 March 2011.

37. David Ignatius, 'At an Impasse with Iran', *Washington Post*, http://www.washingtonpost.com/opinions/david-ignatius-at-an-impasse-with-iran/2014/11/25/fae90656–74dc-11e4-a755-e32227229e7b_story.html, accessed 25 November 2014.

38. 'Statement by the President on ISIL', The White House, http://www.whitehouse.gov/the-press-office/2014/09/10/statement-president-isil-1, accessed 10 September 2014.

39. Paul Richter and Ramin Mostaghim, 'Iran Backs Iraq's Effort to Form Unity Government, Diplomats Say', *Los Angeles Times*, http://www.latimes.com/world/middleeast/la-fg-us-iran-20140911-story.html, accessed 10 September 2014.

40. 'Exclusive: NBC News' Ann Curry Interviews Iranian President Hassan Rouhani', *NBC News*, http://www.nbcnews.com/news/world/exclusive-nbc-news-ann-

curry-interviews-iranian-president-hassan-rouhani-n205426, accessed 17 September 2014.

41. Quoted in Howard Portnoy, 'Who Is Responsible, and Not Responsible, for ISIS?' *The Examiner*, http://www.examiner.com/article/who-is-responsible-and-not-responsible-for-isis-1, accessed 8 September 2014.

42. 'Text of Speech by the President of Islamic Republic of Iran, Hassan Rouhani', United Nations, http://www.un.org/en/ga/69/meetings/gadebate/25sep/iran.shtml, accessed 25 September 2014.

43. Glen Carey and Mohammed Hatem, 'Gulf Arabs See Specter of Iran in Gains by Yemen's Houthis', BloombergBusiness, http://www.bloomberg.com/news/articles/2014–11–02/gulf-arabs-see-specter-of-iran-in-rise-of-yemen-s-shiite-rebels, accessed 3 November 2014. Other reports, however, emphasised Yemen as a point of 'common ground' by Tehran and Riyadh. See Alex Vatanka, 'Iran and Saudi Arabia Find Common Ground in Yemen', *Al-Monitor*, http://www.al-monitor.com/pulse/originals/2014/11/iran-yemen-saudi-arabia-houthi-islah.html, accessed 28 November 2014.

44. 'Saudi Prince Says Gulf States Must Balance Threat from Iran', *Al-Arabiya*, http://english.alarabiya.net/en/News/middle-east/2014/04/23/Saudi-prince-says-Gulf-states-must-balance-threat-from-Iran.html, accessed 23 April 2014.

45. Thomas W. Lippman, *Saudi Arabia on the Edge: The Uncertain Future of an American Ally* (Washington, DC: Potomac Books, 2012). According to Lippman, Saudi Arabia was unlikely to detach itself from its long-standing military and intelligence alliance with the Americans, who were the only power that could provide security for the kingdom.

46. Sahar Atrache, 'How Hezbollah Is Changing the War in Syria and Vice Versa', *Huffington Post*, http://www.huffingtonpost.com/sahar-atrache/hezbollah-war-syria_b_5455850.html, accessed 6 June 2014.

47. Phillip Smyth, 'Tehran, Washington and the UAE's New Terror List', *National Interest*, http://nationalinterest.org/feature/tehran-washington-the-uae%E2%80%99s-new-terror-list-11740, accessed 26 November 2014.

48. Robert F. Worth, 'Saudi Arabia Rejects U.N. Security Council Seat in Protest Move', *New York Times*, http://www.nytimes.com/2013/10/19/world/middleeast/saudi-arabia-rejects-security-council-seat.html?_r=0, accessed 18 October 2013.

49. For a recent collection of articles on the roots and forms of conflicts in contemporary Yemen, see the *Middle East Report*, 44, 2014, pp. 2–19.

50. Ali G. Scotten, 'Countering the Sunni-Shia Divide', New York, Foreign Policy Association, http://foreignpolicyblogs.com/2015/05/14/countering-the-sunni-shia-divide/, accessed 14 May 2015.

51. Ibid. Also see Henry Johnson, 'The Illusory Sectarian War in Yemen', LobeLog Foreign Policy, http://www.lobelog.com/the-illusory-sectarian-war-in-yemen/, accessed 12 June 2015.

52. Gareth Porter, 'Houthi Arms Bonanza Came from Saleh, Not Iran', *Middle East Eye*, http://www.middleeasteye.net/columns/houthi-arms-bonanza-came-saleh-not-iran-1224808066, accessed 23 April 2015.

53. Ali Watkins, Ryan Grim and Akbar Shahid Ahmed, 'Iran Warned Houthis against Yemen Takeover', *Huffington Post*, http://www.huffingtonpost.com/2015/04/20/iran-houthis-yemen_n_7101456.html, accessed 20 April 2015.

54. See, for example, Jamal Khashoggi, 'Let Us Use ISIS and Iran's Tool against Them', *Al Arabiya News*, http://english.alarabiya.net/en/views/news/middle-east/2015/05/12/Let-us-use-ISIS-and-Iran-s-tools-against-them.html, accessed 12 May 2015, and 'IRGC Deputy Top Commander Sees Yemen Invasion as Most Stupid Mistake of Saudi Arabia', Fars News Agency, http://english.farsnews.com/print.aspx?nn=13940317000891, accessed 7 June 2015. Also, see Roger Cohen, 'This Angry Arab Moment', *New York Times*, http://www.nytimes.com/2015/05/15/opinion/roger-cohen-this-angry-arab-moment.html, accessed 14 May 2015.

55. 'Deputy FM: Iran Ready to Send Aid to Entire Yemen, Riyadh Cannot Decide on Donor States', Fars News Agency, http://english.farsnews.com/newstext.aspx?nn=13940226000573, accessed 16 May 2015, and Parisa Hafezi, 'Iran Uses Maritime Confrontations to Project Power in Gulf', *Reuters*, http://www.reuters.com/article/2015/05/18/iran-saudi-gulf-idUSL5N0Y90CV20150518, accessed 18 May 2015.

56. Graham E. Fuller, 'Has Yemen Reshaped the Middle East Geopolitical Map?', *grahamfuller.com*, http://grahamefuller.com/has-yemen-reshaped-the-middle-east-geopolitical-map/, accessed 22 April 2015.

57. For a succinct analysis of the perils of the transfer of power in Saudi Arabia after King 'Abdullah's reign, see Paul Aarts and Carolien Roelants, *Saudi Arabia: A Kingdom in Peril* (London: Hurst & Company, 2015), pp. 125–134.

58. Quoted in Patrick Cockburn, 'Prince Mohammed bin Salman: Naïve, Arrogant Saudi Prince Is Playing with Fire', *The Independent*, http://www.independent.co.uk/news/world/middle-east/prince-mohammed-bin-salman-naive-arrogant-saudi-prince-is-playing-with-fire-a6804481.html, accessed 9 January 2016.

59. Toby Matthiesen, 'The World's Most Misunderstood Martyr', *Foreign Policy*, http://foreignpolicy.com/2016/01/08/the-worlds-most-misundestood-martyr/, accessed 8 January 2016.

60. Toby Craig Jones, 'Saudi Arabia's Dangerous Sectarian Game', *New York Times*, http://www.nytimes.com/2016/01/05/opinion/saudi-arabias-dangerous-sectarian-game.html?_r=0, accessed 4 January 2016.

61. For the full text of Foreign Minister Zarif's letters, see the Islamic Republic of Iran, Ministry of Foreign Affairs, http://en.mfa.ir/index.aspx?siteid=3&fkeyid=&siteid=3&fkeyid=&siteid=3&pageid=1997&newsview=374746, accessed 7 January 2016.

62. Mohammad Javad Zarif, 'Mohammad Javad Zarif: Saudi Arabia's Reckless

Extremism', *New York Times*, http://www.nytimes.com/2016/01/11/opinion/
mohammad-javad-zarif-saudi-arabias-reckless-extremism.html?_r=0, accessed
10 January 2016.

63. Reza Marashi, 'Ending the Iranian–Saudi Cold War', *Cairo Review of Global Affairs*,
http://www.aucegypt.edu/gapp/cairoreview/Pages/articleDetails.aspx?aid=830,
accessed 17 June 2015.

64. See Thomas Juneau and Sam Razavi, 'Introduction: Alone in the World', in Thomas
Juneau and Sam Razavi (eds.), *Iranian Foreign Policy since 2001: Alone in the World*
(New York: Routledge, 2013), pp. 1–17.

65. Marashi, 'Ending the Iranian–Saudi Cold War'.

66. Fars News Agency, http://www.farsnews.com/printable.php?nn=13940317
001091, accessed 7 June 2015.

9. THE POLITICS OF SUCCESSION IN SAUDI ARABIA: A STRUGGLE FOR PRIMOGENITURE

1. Justin Fox, 'Saudi Arabia's Royal Succession Takes a Leap Forward', *Bloomberg News*,
12 February 2015, http://www.chicagotribune.com/news/sns-wp-blm-news-bc-
saudi-comment11-20150211-story.html

2. Bruce Riedel, 'After Qabus, Who Will Be Oman's Next Sultan?', *Al-Monitor*,
25 January 2015, http://www.al-monitor.com/pulse/originals/2015/01/oman-
abdullah-Qabus-succession-power-yemen.html

3. Fox, 'Saudi Arabia's Royal Succession'.

4. For this speculation that is advanced without a shred of evidence, see Simon
Henderson, *After King Fahd: Succession in Saudi Arabia* (Washington. DC:
Washington Institute for Near East Policy, 1994), p. 11.

5. Fox, 'Saudi Arabia's Royal Succession'. The essay was reprinted in several outlets that
illustrated how prevalent the spread of rumours was in the Internet age and how it
significantly stifled academic work because scholars were tasked to refute such fare
before they could engage in methodical analyses. See, for example, Justin Fox,
'Running the Saudi Family Business', *Edge Financial Daily* [Selangor, Malaysia],
26 January 2015, p. 16, http://tefd.theedgemarkets.com/2015/FDsetia/
FDsetia_20150126fwl6yo.pdf, and *Japan Times*, 27 January 2015, http://www.
japantimes.co.jp/opinion/2015/01/27/commentary/world-commentary/running-
the-saudi-family-business/#.VRAihlwhzAM

6. For an assessment of King Fahd's reign, see Nasser Ibrahim Rashid and Esber
I. Shaheen, *King Fahd and Saudi Arabia's Great Evolution* (Joplin, MO: International
Institute of Technology Inc., 1987).

7. Joseph A. Kéchichian, *Legal and Political Reforms in Sa'udi Arabia* (London:
Routledge, 2013).

8. Simon Henderson, 'Saudi King in Hospital: Succession Crisis Looms', Washington

DC: Washington Institute for Near East Policy, 31 December 2014, http://www.
washingtoninstitute.org/policy-analysis/view/saudi-king-in-hospital-succession-
crisis-looms. After several newspapers repeated the Henderson-peddled dementia story, clarifications were issued, and apologies printed for the record. See Kevin
Sullivan and Liz Sly, 'Saudi King Abdullah's Death Sets Up Complex Succession
Process', *Washington Post*, 22 January 2015, http://www.washingtonpost.com/
world/middle_east/saudi-king-abdullahs-death-sets-up-complex-succession-pro-
cess/2015/01/22/340e0a9c-a28e-11e4–9f89–561284a573f8_story.html. See
also Tzvi Ben-Gedalyahu, 'Can Saudi King Salman Remember Where the Throne
Is Sitting?' *The JewishPress.Com*, 23 January 2015, http://www.jewishpress.com/
news/breaking-news/can-saudi-king-salman-remember-where-the-throne-is-sit-
ting/2015/01/23/. Although the *Washington Post* claimed Henderson was 'an
authority on Saudi Arabia and succession issues', it nevertheless posted a correction to its story online, and ran a rectification in the printed version of the publication on 31 January 2015. The correction read: 'This article has been amended to
correct an earlier, unverified characterization of King Salman's mental health. The
article's assertion that King Salman was "reportedly … suffering from dementia"
was too speculative and unsubstantiated to meet the Post's standards for publication. The Royal Court of Saudi Arabia, through its lawyers, has asserted to the Post
that King Salman is "most certainly not suffering from dementia or any other kind
of mental impairment"'. Henderson has yet to post a similar retraction anywhere.
9. Samuel Osborne, 'King Salman: The Man in Charge of the "Most Dangerous Man
    in the World"', *The Independent*, 23 January 2016, http://www.independent.co.
    uk/news/world/middle-east/saudi-arabia-king-salman-the-man-behind-the-most-
    dangerous-man-in-the-world-a6827716.html
10. Mohsen Milani, 'Saudi Arabia's Desperate Measures: The Domestic and Regional
    Fears Fueling Riyadh', *Foreign Affairs*, 10 January 2016, https://www.foreignaf-
    fairs.com/articles/saudi-arabia/2016–01–10/saudi-arabias-desperate-measures
11. For scholarly examinations of succession matters in the Arab world, see Joseph
    A. Kéchichian, *Power and Succession in Arab Monarchies: A Reference Guide*
    (Boulder, CO: Lynne Rienner Publishers, 2008); Anthony Billingsley, *Political
    Succession in the Arab World: Constitutions, Family Loyalties and Islam* (London:
    Routledge, 2010); and Stig Stenslie, *Regime Stability in Saudi Arabia: The Challenge
    of Succession* (London: Routledge, 2012). Several useful academic articles are also
    available, including Sean L. Yom and F. Gregory Gause III, 'Resilient Royals: How
    Arab Monarchies Hang On', *Journal of Democracy*, 23(4), October 2012,
    pp. 74–88; Russell E. Lucas, 'Monarchical Authoritarianism: Survival and Political
    Liberalization and a Middle Eastern Regime Type', *International Journal of Middle
    East Studies*, 36(1), February 2004, pp. 103–119; Mehran Kamrava, 'Royal
    Factionalism and Political Liberalization in Qatar', *Middle East Journal*, 63(3),
    Summer 2009, pp. 401–420; Zoltan Barany, 'Unrest and State Response in Arab

Monarchies', *Mediterranean Quarterly*, 24(2), 2013, pp. 5–38; Ludger Kuhnhardt, 'The Resilience of Arab Monarchy', *Policy Review*, 173, June–July 2012, http://www.hoover.org/research/resilience-arab-monarchy; and J. E. Peterson, 'The Nature of Succession in the Gulf', *Middle East Journal*, 55(4), Autumn 2001, pp. 580–601. For an update, see also Joseph A. Kéchichian, *Succession Challenges in the Arab Gulf Monarchies* (Seoul, Korea: ASAN Institute for Policy Studies, December 2015), http://en.asaninst.org/contents/succession-challenges-in-the-arab-gulf-monarchies/

12. David Andrew Weinberg, 'New Saudi King Won't Change a Thing', *National Interest*, 24 January 2015, http://nationalinterest.org/feature/new-saudi-king-won't-change-thing-12113
13. Caryle Murphy, 'In with the Old in the New Saudi Arabia', *Foreign Policy*, 26 February 2015, http://foreignpolicy.com/2015/02/25/in-with-the-old-in-the-new-saudi-arabia-king-salman
14. Ibid.
15. Princess Hassah bint Ahmad Al Sudayri, who married the founder twice, gave him seven sons: Fahd, Sultan, 'Abdul Rahman, Nayif, Turki, Salman and Ahmad. For details, see Joseph A. Kéchichian, *Succession in Saudi Arabia* (New York: Palgrave, 2001), pp. 6–8.
16. Hugh Miles, 'Saudi Arabia: Eight of King Salman's 11 Surviving Brothers Want to Oust Him', *The Independent*, 23 October 2015, http://www.independent.co.uk/news/world/middle-east/saudi-arabia-power-struggle-between-king-salman-and-mohammed-bin-salman-could-bring-down-the-a6706801.html
17. 'Power and Authority Sexually Transmitted among Najdi Bedouins', *Crescent International*, 30 April 2015, http://www.crescent-online.net/2015/05/power-and-authority-sexually-transmitted-among-najdi-bedouins-crescent-onlinenet-4953-articles.html. See also Yusuf Dhia-Allah, 'Salman Sweeps Away Abdullah Appointees', no date, http://www.latheeffarook.com/index.php/middleeast/1590-salman-sweeps-away-abdullah-appointees; and 'Are Saudi Arabia's "Sudairi Seven" Consolidating Power?', *Twenty Eleven Theme*, 29 April 2015, http://attwiw.com/2015/04/29/are-saudi-arabias-sudairi-seven-consolidating-power/
18. Prince Muqrin bin 'Abdul 'Aziz was born in 1945 in Riyadh and graduated from the Model Institute of the Capital in 1967. His education included attendance at the Royal Air Force College Cranwell, United Kingdom, and the positions he held included a stint with the Royal Saudi Air Force (RSAF) between 1965 and 1980; an appointment as Assistant to Air Operations Manager and Head of Plans and Operations Division in the RSAF in 1977; the Ha'il Province Governorship between 1980 and 1999; the Madinah Province Governorship between 1999 and 2005; and the chairmanship of the General Intelligence between 2005 and 2012. When Prince Muqrin was appointed secretary-general of the General Intelligence Presidency (GIP), which has its own forces, Heir Apparent Sultan was the defense

and aviation minister, with responsibility over all of that ministry's armed forces. Minister of the Interior Nayif exercised control over government internal security forces, the internal security service or secret police (Mabahith), and border forces. In April 2010, Prince Muqrin attended the Nuclear Security Summit in Washington DC, and pledged the kingdom's support for a zone free of weapons of mass destruction in the Middle East. In his remarks, Prince Muqrin argued that 'Israel's possession of nuclear weapons constitute[d] a fundamental obstacle to the achievement of security and stability in the Middle Eastern region'. With regard to Iran, he stated that Saudi Arabia 'welcome[d] the international endeavors to find a peaceful solution to this crisis through dialogue in such a way as to guarantee the right of Iran and other states in the region to the peaceful use of nuclear energy in accordance with the procedural safeguards, and under the supervision, of the International Atomic Energy Agency'. He warned of the dangers and ultimate futility of a nuclear arms race in the region and signalled support for recent changes in US nuclear policy. Regrettably, Prince Muqrin has been described as an 'unimportant man, both as the Governor of Ha'il and as head of the intelligence. He remained inconsequential after being sacked and there is nothing worth pointing out in his record.' It was also said that the then Heir Apparent was 'often preoccupied with women and alcohol, and has completely delegated his functions to his chief of staff, which led to catastrophic intelligence failures in Egypt, Iraq, Iran, and even in simpler issues such as the case of Princess Sara Bint Talal, who sought asylum in Britain'. One of the nice stories told about Muqrin is that while he was Governor of Ha'il Province (1980–99), on more than one occasion he was seen waiting at a red traffic light on his way to the Governor's office at eight o'clock in the morning. The Prince was appointed adviser and special envoy of King 'Abdullah in July 2012 and was named Second Deputy Prime Minister on 1 February 2013. This appointment surprised some analysts, after he had been relieved as chief of the General Intelligence Directorate in July 2012. While no explanation was given for the decision, some assumed he was not up to the task of undermining the pro-Iranian Assad regime in Syria. This assumption was probably mistaken since the monarch made such decisions although detractors added salt to festering wounds. For details on Prince Muqrin's short year-long stint as heir apparent, see Bruce Riedel, 'Yemen's War Shakes Up the Saudi Palace', *Markaz: Middle East Politics and Policy*, Brookings Institution, 29 April 2015, http://www.brookings.edu/blogs/markaz/posts/2015/04/29-yemen-war-shakes-up-saudi-palace-riedel Others speculated that Prince Muqrin was a mere place-holder for Prince Mit'ab bin 'Abdullah, allegedly after the latter's father made a 'deal' with his heir, to appoint the Commander of the National Guard as a potential successor. See S. Rob Sobhani, 'The Saudi Prince Who Could Be King: It's in America's Interest to Woo Saudi Arabia's Heir-Apparent', *Washington Times*, 12 November 2014, http://www.washingtontimes.com/news/2014/

nov/12/s-rob-sobhani-the-man-who-could-be-king/#ixzz3cC446RWm. It was critical to note that this view was not credible, notwithstanding customary speculations associated with the Al Sa'ud.

19. Two of the leading Saudi sources that discussed ruling family matters were the anonymous *al-mujtahid* [mujtahidmail@gmail.com] who boasted nearly 2 million Twitter followers at the following hashtag: @mujtahidd, and saudiwoman [http://saudiwoman.me] which is run by Eman al-Nafjan, who frequently responds to non-Arabs and non-Saudis giving expert advice or opinions about life and culture in the kingdom. There are dozens of such sites that provide additional insights.

20. For a colorful compilation, see Judith Miller, 'The Struggle Within', *New York Times*, 10 March 1991, http://www.nytimes.com/1991/03/10/magazine/the-struggle-within.html. See also Judith Miller, *God Has Ninety-Nine Names: Reporting from a Militant Middle East* (New York: Touchstone/Simon & Schuster, 1997), p. 491, note 54.

21. 'Saudi Attackers "Must Surrender"', *BBC News*, 27 June 2003, http://news.bbc.co.uk/go/pr/fr/-/2/hi/middle_east/3025848.stm

22. Although other grandsons of the founder, especially King Faisal's offspring, were entrusted with senior positions earlier, they were older that Prime Muhammad bin Nayif.

23. 'Al-Sa'udiyyah: Muhammad bin Nayif Walian lil-'Ahd ... wa Muhammad bin Salman Walian li-Wali al-'Ahd' [Muhammad bin Nayif Heir Apparent ... and Muhammad bin Salman heir to the heir apparent], *Al-Sharq al-Awsat*, 13302, 30 April 2015, pp. 1–2.

24. 'Saudi Aramco Gets New Supreme Council Headed by Deputy Crown Prince: Statement', *Reuters*, 1 May 2015, http://www.reuters.com/article/2015/05/01/saudi-oil-aramco-idUSL5N0XS0LR20150501. See also John Sawers, 'The House of Saud's Embryonic Embrace of Meritocracy', *Financial Times*, 1 May 2015, http://www.ft.com/intl/cms/s/0/27746568-ef52-11e4-87dc-00144feab7de.html#axzz3ZXDNBQ7z

25. 'Saudi Arabia's Monarchy: Nothing Succeeds Like Succession', *The Economist*, 29 April 2015, http://www.economist.com/node/21650011/

26. Prince Sa'ud al-Faisal, who was the world's longest-serving foreign minister by the time of his retirement, passed away in Los Angeles, California, on 9 July 2015. He was 75.

27. Ian Black, 'Saudi King's Son Drives Reforms and War in a Year of Anxiety and Change', *The Guardian*, 20 January 2016, http://www.theguardian.com/world/2016/jan/20/saudi-royals-best-of-the-worst-yemen-king-salman-saudi-arabia. See also Ashley Cowburn, 'Saudi Arabia's Foreign Affairs Minister Adel al-Jubeir Urges Britain to "Respect" the Kingdom's Use of the Death Penalty', *The Independent*, 16 January 2016, http://www.independent.co.uk/news/world/middle-east/saudi-arabia-s-foreign-affairs-minister-urges-britain-to-respect-kingdom-

s-death-penalty-two-weeks-a6815586.html; and Adel al-Jubeir, 'Can Iran Change', *New York Times*, 19 January 2016, http://www.nytimes.com/2016/01/19/opinion/saudi-arabia-can-iran-change.html

28. Unconfirmed reports tweeted by al-Mujtahid, for example, in mid-2015 claimed that Prince 'Abdul 'Aziz tendered his resignation but that this was not accepted. In the event, the number two person at the ministry apparently stayed away from his office, a news item that, once again, was impossible to verify independently.

29. 'Rumors Swirl around the Saudi Throne', *American Interest*, 18 January 2016, http://www.the-american-interest.com/2016/01/18/rumors-swirl-around-the-saudi-throne/

30. Ben Hubbard, 'King Salman Upends Status Quo in Region and the Royal Family', *New York Times*, 10 May 2015, http://www.nytimes.com/2015/05/11/world/middleeast/king-salman-upends-status-quo-in-region-and-the-royal-family.html; and Jajati K. Pattnaik, 'Challenges to Royal Legitimacy in Saudi Arabia', *Mainstream Weekly*, 53(21), 16 May 2015, http://www.mainstreamweekly.net/article5672.html

31. For details on some of these changes, see Joseph A. Kéchichian, *'Iffat Al-Thunayan: An Arabian Queen* (London: Sussex Academic Press, 2015), pp. 108–229.

32. In addition to the NSC, which was headed by Prince Bandar bin Sultan, the other ten councils and committees axed by the new monarch included: (1) the Civil Service Council, (2) the Higher Committee for Education Policy, (3) the Higher Committee for Administrative Organization, (4) the Higher Commission of the King Abdulaziz City for Science and Technology, (5) the Supreme Council for Education, (6) the Supreme Council for Disabled Affairs, (7) the Supreme Council of the King Abdullah City for Atomic and Renewable Energy, (8) the Supreme Council for Islamic Affairs, (9) the Supreme Council for Petroleum and Minerals, and (10) the Supreme Economic Council.

33. It was too soon to assess the committees' record although local papers provided extensive coverage of their weekly meetings.

34. Prince Turki al-Faisal, the chairman of the King Faisal Center for Research and Islamic Studies in Riyadh, coined the term Fahish (or Fahesh), which means obscene in Arabic, to refer to Da'ish, since the so-called Islamic State is neither Islamic nor a state. For background details on ISIS, see Patrick Cockburn, *The Rise of Islamic State: ISIS and the New Sunni Revolution* (London: Verso, 2015). See also Michael Weiss and Hassan Hassan, *ISIS: Inside the Army of Terror* (New York: Regan Arts, 2015).

35. 'Saudi Arabia: Young Prince in a Hurry', *The Economist*, 9 January 2016, http://www.economist.com/node/21685467/. See also 'Transcript: Interview with Muhammad bin Salman', *The Economist*, 9 January 2016, http://www.economist.com/node/21685432/. For a highly critical assessment, see Simon Henderson, 'The Next King of Saudi Arabia', *Policywatch* 2543, Washington, DC: Washington

Institute for Near East Policy, 8 January 2016, http://www.washingtoninstitute.
org/policy-analysis/view/the-next-king-of-saudi-arabia; and Bruce Reidel, 'Saudi
Executions Signal Royal Worries', *Al Monitor*, 4 January 2016, http://www.al-
monitor.com/pulse/originals/2016/01/saudi-arabia-iran-execution-nimr-al-nimr-
concerns-stability.html?utm_source=Al-Monitor+Newsletter+%5BEnglish%5
D&utm_campaign=ca91d3096f-January_04_2015&utm_medium=email&utm_
term=0_28264b27a0-ca91d3096f-93068653#. In what is sound bite rather than
scholarship, Riedel affirms that if one were 'to understand the Saudi royal family,
you don't go to the Kennedy School of Government, you read Shakespeare!'

36. The Royal Order that created CEDA fielded, in addition to the Minister of
Defence, the following: Walid bin Muhammad bin Salih al-Sama'ani (Justice),
veteran minister 'Ali al-Na'imi (Petroleum and Mineral Resources), 'Abdul 'Aziz
al-'Assaf (Finance), 'Abdullah bin 'Abdul Rahman al-Husayn (Water and
Electricity), 'Adil bin Muhammad bin 'Abdul Qadir Faqih (Labour), Shwaysh bin
Sa'ud bin Duwayhi al-Duwayhi (Housing), Bandar bin Muhammad Hajjar (Hajj),
Muhammad bin Sulayman al-Jasir (Economy and Planning), Tawfiq bin Fawzan
al-Rabi'ah (Commerce and Industry), 'Abdullah bin 'Abdul Rahman al-Muqbil
(Transport), Muhammad bin Ibrahim al-Suwayyil (Communications and
Information Technology), Majid bin 'Abdullah al-Qusaybi (Social Affairs), 'Abdul
Latif bin 'Abdul Malik bin 'Umar Al al-Shaykh (Municipal and Rural Affairs),
Ahmad bin 'Aqil al-Khatib (Health), Khalid bin 'Abdullah al-'Araj (Civil Service),
'Adel al-Turayfi (Culture and Information), 'Abdul Rahman bin 'Abdul Muhsin
al-Fadhli (Agriculture), 'Azzam bin Muhammad al-Dakhil (Education), and two
ministers of state, 'Isam bin Sa'ad bin Sa'id and Musa'id bin Muhammad al-Ayban.
This was the entire cabinet except for two full portfolios, namely Foreign Affairs
and the National Guard, which raised several critical questions as well. In addi-
tion to the retirement of Prince Sa'ud al-Faisal, Khalid bin 'Abdul 'Aziz al-Falih,
the chief executive of Saudi Aramco, became Minister of Health. Al-Falih replaced
Ahmad al-Khatib, who was dismissed after reports emerged that showed him in a
particularly egregious light, when he dismissed a citizen recording his grievances.
Ironically, the ruler further removed the Deputy Minister of Health, Mansur bin
Nasir al-Haways, as well as the Deputy Minister of Health for Planning and
Development, Muhammad bin Hamzah Khashim. The most surprising change
was that of Muhammad bin Sulayman al-Jasir, a former executive director at the
International Monetary Fund (IMF), who had been Minister of Economy and
Planning since December 2011. Moving into his job was 'Adil bin Muhammad
Faqih, previously Minister of Labour. Al-Jasir's replacement at the Labour Ministry
was Mufrij bin Sa'ad al-Haqbani. It was unclear who initiated these changes and
whether Prince Muhammad bin Salman, who presided over the first few CEDA
meetings, concluded that several new appointments were necessary. See
'Al-Sa'udiyyah: 'Ifa' Muqrin wa-Taayin Muhammad bin Nayif Walian lil-'Ahd wa

Muhammad bin Salman Walian li-Wali al-'Ahd' [Saudi Arabia: Muqrin Is Relieved and Muhammad bin Nayif Is Appointed Heir Apparent and Muhammad bin Salman Is Heir to the Heir Apparent], *Al-Hayat*, 19018, 30 April 2015, p. 2.

37. Dan Roberts and Kareem Shaheen, 'Saudi Arabia Launches Yemen Air Strikes as Alliance Builds against Houthi Rebels', *The Guardian*, 26 March 2015, http://www.theguardian.com/world/2015/mar/26/saudi-arabia-begins-airstrikes-against-houthi-in-yemen, and Nussaibah Younis, 'The Saudi–Iran Powerplay behind the Yemen Conflict', *The Guardian*, 29 March 2015, http://www.theguardian.com/commentisfree/2015/mar/29/iran-saudi-arabia-yemen-conflict

38. Simon Henderson, 'Saudi Arabia's Big Gamble', *Foreign Policy*, 26 March 2015, http://foreignpolicy.com/2015/03/26/saudi-arabias-big-gamble%E2%80%8B-yemen-airstrikes/

39. Ian Black, 'Iran's Advances Create Alarm in Saudi Arabia and the Gulf', *The Guardian*, 13 March 2015, http://www.theguardian.com/world/2015/mar/13/irans-advances-create-alarm-in-saudi-arabia-and-the-gulf. See also Ray Takeyh, 'The New Saudi Foreign Policy', *Council on Foreign Relations*, 17 April 2015, http://www.cfr.org/saudi-arabia/new-saudi-foreign-policy/p36456

40. Pamela Dockins, 'Kerry: US–Saudi Friendship Strong as Ever', Voice of America, 24 January 2016, http://www.voanews.com/content/us-gulf-allies-move-forward-on-syria/3159556.html

41. Office of the Press Secretary, 'Joint Statement on the Meeting between President Barack Obama and King Salman bin Abd al Aziz Al Saud', Washington DC: The White House, 4 September 2015, https://www.whitehouse.gov/the-press-office/2015/09/04/joint-statement-meeting-between-president-barack-obama-and-king-salman

42. See, for example, Christopher M. Davidson, *After the Sheikhs: The Coming Collapse of the Gulf Monarchies* (London: Hurst & Company, 2012). Interestingly, the anti-Al Sa'ud gloom and doom was not limited to Anglo-American news outlets, as the French jumped into the fray in early 2016 too with a slew of experts adding insult to injury. See, for example, Armin Arefi, 'Le Royaume qui fait trembler le monde', *Le Point*, 2263, 21 January 2016, pp. 26–45; and Christophe Boltanski, Sara Daniel and Sophie Fay, 'Nos amis les Saoud', *L'Obs* [Le Nouvel Observateur], 2672, 21 January 2016, pp. 18–27.

10. YOUTH, PROTEST AND THE NEW ELITE: DOMESTIC SECURITY AND DIGNITY IN KUWAIT

1. Ali M. al-Khouri, 'Population Growth and Government Modernization Effects: The Case of GCC Countries', *International Journal of Research in Management and Technology*, 1(2), 2012, p. 2.

2. Ibid., p. 3.

3. Alanoud Alsharekh, 'Reform and Rebirth in the Middle East', *Survival: Global Politics and Strategy*, 53(2), 2011, p. 53.

4. Dominic Dudley, 'The GCC Skills Gap', *MEED*, 11 March 2014, http://www.meed.com/sectors/economy/education/the-gcc-skills-gap/3190106.article.

5. Stephen Hertog, 'The GCC's National Employment Challenge', Monkey Cage Blog, *Washington Post*, 31 July 2014, https://www.washingtonpost.com/news/monkey-cage/wp/2014/07/31/the-gccs-national-employment-challenge/

6. Michael Herb, *The Wages of Oil: Parliaments and Economic Development in Kuwait and the UAE* (Ithaca, NY: Cornell University Press, 2014), p. 214.

7. Walid Jumblat's December 2012 Twitter feed, https://twitter.com/walid_jounblat

8. 'Corruption Scandal Widens, Deepening the Political Crisis', The Economist Intelligence Unit, 1 November 2011, http://country.eiu.com/article.aspx?article id=1678557752&Country=Kuwait&topic=Politics&subtopic=Recent+developments&subsubtopic=The+political+scene:+Corruption+scandal+widens,+deepening+the+political+crisis

9. Alanoud Alsharekh, 'Unprecedented Protests', *IISS Voices Blog*, 24 October 2012, https://www.iiss.org/en/iiss%20voices/blogsections/2012–6d11/october-2012–9f2f/protest-in-kuwait-e38c

10. Khalid Kamhawi, 'Jordan's Elections Cannot and Will Not be Democratic', *The Guardian*, 23 January 2013, http://www.theguardian.com/commentisfree/2013/jan/23/jordan-elections-democratic-boycotted

11. Suliman al-Atiqi, 'One Man One Vote', *Sada*, Carnegie Endowment for International Peace, 12 September 2013, http://carnegieendowment.org/sada/2013/09/12/one-man-one-vote/gmyf

12. There have been two instances in 1939 (under the rule of Sheikh Ahmad al-Jaber al-Sabah) and in 1989 (under the rule of Sheikh Jaber al-Ahmad al-Sabah) where tension between the Kuwaiti opposition and the ruling elite escalated into security crackdowns and arrests, but never on such a massive scale.

13. *Human Rights Watch World Report 2012: Kuwait*, http://www.hrw.org/world-report-2012/world-report-2012-kuwait

14. 'Kuwait police crackdown on stateless protests', *Al-Jazeera*, 14 January 2012, http://www.aljazeera.com/news/middleeast/2012/01/201211420266902157.html

15. Meshal al-Sabah, *Gender and Politics in Kuwait: Women and Political Participation in the Gulf* (London: I.B. Taurus, 2013), p. 117.

16. The Kuwaiti constitution does not stipulate that the Prime Minister be a member of the ruling family. Article 56 of the constitution simply state that the Emir appoints a Prime Minister after going through traditional consultations, without stating that the Prime Minister has to be a ruling family member, or male, even though that has been the tradition so far.

17. *The Progress of Democracy in the State of Kuwait*, 4th en, National Assembly of Kuwait, 2011, p. 22.

18. Mohammed al-Jassim, "ahd Jasim al Kabeer [Big Jassem's Era]", *Sabr*, 20 November 2011, http://www.sabr.cc/inner.aspx?id=16187

19. 'Kuwait Splits between Conflicts of Sheikhs and Sheikhs of Conflict', *Middle East Online*, 6 July 2011, http://www.middle-east-online.com/english/?id=46532

20. Mary Ann Tétreault, 'Kuwait's Annus Mirabilis', Middle East Research and Information Project, 7 September 2006, http://www.merip.org/mero/mero090706

21. 'Kuwait Development Plan: Opportunities and Uncertainties', presentation by Markaz Investment Group, at the French Kuwait Business Council Kuwait Plan Conference, June 2011, http://www.fbck.net/planevents.html

22. 2014 statistics, Central Bureau of Statistics, Kuwait, http://www.csb.gov.kw/Socan_Statistic_EN.aspx?ID=13

23. 'Kuwait Permit Peaceful Political Gatherings', *Human Rights Watch*, 11 December 2010, https://www.hrw.org/news/2010/12/11/kuwait-permit-peaceful-political-gatherings

24. Alsharekh, 'Unprecedented Protest in Kuwait'.

25. 'Three Kuwaiti Lawmakers File Request to Quiz Minister', *Gulf News*, 24 January 2011, http://m.gulfnews.com/news/gulf/kuwait/three-kuwaiti-lawmakers-file-request-to-quiz-minister-1.751428

26. Interview with Dahem al-Qahtani, 22 October 2015.

27. 'Insulted Kuwaiti Tribesmen Burn Down Tent of Election Candidate', *The National*, 31 January 2012, http://m.thenational.ae/news/world/middle-east/insulted-kuwaiti-tribesmen-burn-down-tent-of-election-candidate

28. 'Gang Gets Two Years for Storming Kuwait TV Studio', *Gulf News*, 2 October 2012, http://m.gulfnews.com/news/gulf/kuwait/gang-get-two-years-for-storming-kuwait-tv-studio-1.1083818

29. Gwenn Okruhlik, 'The Identity Politics of Kuwait's Election', *Foreign Policy*, 8 February 2012, http://foreignpolicy.com/2012/02/08/the-identity-politics-of-kuwaits-election/

30. Kristin Smith Diwan, 'The Politics of Transgression in Kuwait', *Foreign Policy*, 19 April 19, 2013, http://foreignpolicy.com/2013/04/19/the-politics-of-transgression-in-kuwait/

31. For a full list of the late emir's wives and 50 children, his Arabic Wikipedia page https://ar.wikipedia.org/wiki/#حجاب_الصلا_دمحالا_رباج.D8.B2.D9.88.D8.AC.D8.A7.D8.AA.D9.87

32. Toby Matthiesen, 'Shii Historians in a Wahabi State: Identity Entrepreneurs and the Politics of Local Historiography in Saudi Arabia', *International Journal of Middle East Studies*, 47, 2015, p. 25.

33. Richard Spencer, 'Kuwaiti Protesters Storm Parliament', *Telegraph*, 16 November 2011, http://www.telegraph.co.uk/news/worldnews/middleeast/kuwait/8895351/Kuwaiti-protesters-storm-parliament.html

34. Kuwait's Central Statistics Bureau, http://www.csb.gov.kw/Socan_Statistic.aspx?ID=12

35. Laurent A. Lambert, 'Water, State, Power and the Tribal Politics in the GCC: The Case of Kuwait and Abu Dhabi', Center for International and Regional Studies, Georgetown University School of Foreign Service in Qatar Occasional Papers, 15 (Doha, 2014), p. 26.

36. Mona Kareem, 'Identity Politics in Kuwait's Power Struggle', *Al-Akhbar*, 10 June 2013, http://english.al-akhbar.com/node/16069

37. Interview with Shamael al-Sharikh, member of the NYC project management office and head of the technical committee, 7 January 2015.

38. Former National Assembly member Dr Aseel al-Awadhi's November 2012 Twitter feed (https://twitter.com/AseelAlawadhi) has many references to this issue. Also see the late Dr Ahmad al-Baghdadi's numerous articles on how the interference of religious groups in the educational curriculum of Kuwait's public school system, especially in the teaching of human rights, will damage the future of Kuwait's educational system: *Al-Siyassa*, 16 December 2006 and 23 January 2007.

39. 'Kuwaiti MPs Push for Reinstating Co-education', *Gulf News*, 3 June 2013, http://gulfnews.com/news/gulf/kuwait/kuwaiti-mps-push-for-reinstating-co-education-1.1191933

40. 'Constitutional Court Rules That "Segregation" Is Co-education!', *Al-Rai*, 17 December 2015, http://www.alraimedia.com/ar/article/local/2015/12/17/643349/nr/kuwait

41. Interview with Minister Bader al-Issa, *Al-Qabbas*, 13 April 2015, http://alqabas.com.kw/Articles.aspx?ArticleID=1041207&CatID=0

42. Wendy Kristianasen, 'Kuwait's Islamists: Officially Unofficial', *Le Monde Diplomatique*, June 2002, https://mondediplo.com/2002/06/04kuwait

43. For more on the deterioration of the sports scene in Kuwait, see Abdallah Baabood, 'Sport and Identity in the Gulf', in Alanoud Alsharekh et al. (eds.), *Popular Culture and Political Identity in the Arab Gulf States*, SOAS Middle East Issues (London: Saqi Books, 2008), pp. 97–120.

44. See the al-Ruya school website, with the emphasis on Muslim teachers from abroad for an example of this new wave: http://english-schools.org/kuwait/al-ruya-bilin-gua-school.htm

45. Farah al-Nakib, 'Revisiting Hadar and Badu in Kuwait: Citizenship, Housing and the Construction of a Dichotomy', *International Journal of Middle Eastern Studies*, 46, 2014, pp. 5–30.

46. Comments made during the First International Conference of the Council of Arab and International Relations, Kuwait, 11 February 2013.

47. Although protesters and their leaders insisted that these protests were peaceful, some media sources have made references to the use of Molotov cocktails and other instances of destructive violence by young protesters. See, for example, the

coverage in the on 7 July 2014, http://news.kuwaittimes.net/amir-condemns-violation-law-pardons-prisoners-opposition-holds-protest-march-moi-issues-stern-warnings/

48. National Youth Project website, http://youth.org.kw/en/initiatives/housing-initiative.html

49. Sharifa Alshalfan, 'The Right to Housing in Kuwait: An Urban Injustice in a Socially Just System', Kuwait Programme on Development, Governance and Globalisation in the Gulf States, Working Paper No. 28, 2013.

50. Public Authority for Housing Welfare, Kuwait website, http://www.housing.gov.kw/

51. Kuwait's Municipality Council website, http://www.baladia.gov.kw/

52. 'Bugatti Veron', *7oqoqee Blogspot*, 27 April 2010, http://7oqoqee.blogspot.com/2010/04/blog-post_4313.html?m=1

53. 'fi istijwab min mi'hwar wa'hid ma' ra'ees al'hukooma' [A One Subject Interpolation with the Prime Minister], *Al-Qabbas*, 2 March 2009, http://www.alqabas.com.kw/Articles.aspx?ArticleID=477598&CatID=307

54. The Dubai School of Government Arab Social Media Report offers a detailed breakdown of penetration and adoption rates. See http://www.arabsocialmediareport.com/home/index.aspx

55. Alanoud Alsharekh, 'Social Media and the Arab Spring', Presentation for World Press Freedom Day, Reuters HQ, Canary Wharf, London, 3 May 2011, https://www.youtube.com/watch?v=4QVtO8hokcE

56. Alanoud Alsharekh, 'Unity and Disparity; Border Issues and Revolutions in the GCC', Global Perspectives Lecture Series, IISS, Manama, 7 March 2011, http://www.iiss.org/middle-east/global-perspectives-series/unity-and-disparity-border-issues-andrevolution-in-the-gcc/

57. Abdullatif Alomar, 'Could a Hashtag Send Twitter Users to Prison?', *Global Voice online*, 26 March 2012, http://globalvoicesonline.org/2012/03/26/kuwait-could-a-hash-tag-send-a-twitter-user-to-prison/

58. Courtney C. Radsch, 'Twitter vs. the Emir: Tweeting in Kuwait Becoming a Dangerous Pastime', *Huffington Post World Blog*, 8 February 2013, http://m.huffpost.com/us/entry/2620792

59. There have been many discussions of the 'random' or 'political' naturalisation of tribal Kuwaitis in the 1970s and 1980s, but none were more inflammatory than those presented by Nasser al-Fadhalah in 'AlHallah wa AlHall' (2010), which was banned in Kuwait.

60. 'Jalsa Khasa littasadee lil mudharat fi 'al-Sakaniyya' [A special session to put an end to demonstrations in tribal areas], *Al-Watan*, 12 December 2012, http://alwatan.kuwait.tt/articledetails.aspx?id=242460&yearquarter=20124

61. Elizabeth Dickinson, 'Kuwait Warns It Will Take All Necessary Measures to Break Up Protests', *The National*, 5 December 2012, http://www.thenational.ae/news/

world/middle-east/kuwait-warns-it-will-take-all-necessary-measures-to-break-up-protests

62. Camilla Hall, 'Kuwait Opposition Loses Momentum', *Financial Times*, 15 January 2013, http://m.ft.com/intl/cms/s/0/c5503ce6–5f29–11e2–8250–00144fe-ab49a.html.

63. 'Mulaifis Resignation Accepted', *Kuwait Times*, 26 May 2014, http://news.kuwait-times.net/mulaifis-resignation-accepted/

64. 'Kuwait Elections Boost Government Grip on Assembly', *Gulf News*, 27 June 2014, http//m.gulfnews.com/news/gulf/kuwait/kuwait-by-elections-boost-government-grip-on-assembly-1.1352943

65. Shafeeq al-Ghabra, 'Kuwait: At the Crossroads of Change or Political Stagnation', *Middle East Institute*, 20 May 2014, http://www.mei.edu/content/article/kuwait-crossroads-change-or-political-stagnation

66. Karen Young, 'The GCC in 2015: Domestic Security Trumps Regional Integration', *The Washington Institute–Policy Watch*, 15 December 2014, http://www.washingtoninstitute.org/policy-analysis/view/the-gcc-in-2015-domestic-security-trumps-regional-integration

68. The total number of revocations would be higher than this as families of the stripped citizen also lose their nationalities by association. The National Committee for Monitoring Violations places it at over 77 in a memo that was sent to human rights NGOs in Kuwait and abroad in early 2015.

69. 'Al Watan TV Closed', *Kuwait Times*, 4 June 2015, http://news.kuwaittimes.net/al-watan-tv-closed/

70. Adullatif al Duaij, 'Is Harak Dead?', *Kuwait Times* [trans from *Al-Qabbas*], 15 April 2015, http://news.kuwaittimes.net/pdf/2015/apr/15/p06.pdf

71. 'Kuwait Ruling Family Member Given a Suspended Jail Term', *Reuters*, 12 December 2015, http://uk.mobile.reuters.com/article/idUKKBN0TV0KE20151212?irpc=932

72. 'Al-Sadoon: We Will Not Deal with a Prime Minister Who Is Not Elected by the People', *Al-Rai*, 12 February 2013, http://www.alraimedia.com/Article.aspx?id=414205&date=13022013

73. 'Kuwait Charges Terror Cell Tied to Iran and Hezbollah', *Al-Jazeera*, 1 September 2015, http://www.aljazeera.com/news/2015/09/kuwait-charges-terror-cell-tied-iran-hezbollah-150901134517950.html

74. 'Kuwait Introduces Mandatory DNA Testing', *Independent Online*, 1 July 2015, http://www.iol.co.za/news/world/kuwait-introduces-mandatory-dna-testing-1.1879153#.VZwyns7Nbq0

75. 'Kuwait Electronic Crimes Law Threatens to Further Stifle Freedom of Expression', Amnesty International, 11 January 2016, https://www.amnesty.org/en/latest/news/2016/01/kuwait-electronic-crimes-law-threatens-to-further-stifle-freedom-of-expression/

76. Thomas Freidman, 'Iran and the Obama Doctrine', *New York Times*, 6 April 2015, http://www.nytimes.com/2015/04/06/opinion/thomas-friedman-the-obama-doctrine-and-iran-interview.html?_r=0

77. 'The Power of 1.8 Billion: Adolescents, Youth and the Transformation of the Future', *The State of the World Population 2014*, UNFPA, http://www.unfpa.org/sites/default/files/pub-pdf/EN-SWOP14-Report_FINAL-web.pdf

78. Interview with Shamael al-Sharikh, 7 January 2015.

79. Note provided by Adel Hamzia, Vice-Chairman of the Oxford Gulf and Arabian Peninsula Studies Forum (OxGAPS), 15 January 2015.

11. THE TRANSFORMATION OF UAE FOREIGN POLICY SINCE 2011

1. Robert Keohane, 'Lilliputians' Dilemmas: Small States in International Politics', in Christine Ingebritsen, Iver Neumann and Sieglinde Gstohl, *Small States in International Relations* (Seattle, WA: University of Washington Press, 2006).

2. Jeanne Hey, *Small States in World Politics: Explaining Foreign Policy Behavior* (Boulder, CO: Lynne Rienner, 2003), p. 2.

3. Robert Rothstein, *Alliances and Small Powers* (New York, NY: Columbia University Press, 1968).

4. Iver Neumann and Sieglinde Gstohl, 'Lilliputians in Gulliver's world', in Ingebritsen, Neumann and Gstohl, *Small States in International Relations*, p. 8.

5. Keohane, 'Lilliputians' Dilemmas', pp. 291–310.

6. Asbed Kotchikian, 'The Dialectics of Smallness: State-Making in the South Caucasus', Armenian International Policy Research Group, 2006, p. 8.

7. Khalid Almezaini, *The UAE and Foreign Policy: Foreign Aid, Identities and Interests* (Milton Park: Routledge, 2012), p. 35.

8. Ibid., p. 36.

9. Ibrahim Al Abed and Peter Hellyer, *United Arab Emirates: A New Perspective* (London: Trident Press, 1997), p. 177.

10. Kenneth Waltz, 'Structural Realism after the Cold War', *International Security*, 25(1), 2000, p. 39.

11. Michael Hudson, 'Letter from Abu Dhabi: Are the Gulf States Immune to Regional Changes?', *Middle East Insights*, 2012, p. 78.

12. Ingo Forstenlechner, Emilie Rutledge and Rashed al-Nuaimi, 'The UAE, the "Arab Spring" and Different Types of Dissent', *Middle East Policy*, 19(4), 2012.

13. Ibid.

14. Mahdi Darius Nazemroaya, 'How Saudi Attempts to Manipulate the Houthis and the Muslim Brotherhood Backfired in Yemen', *Global Research*, 11 April 2015, accessed 20 October 2015.

15. Forstenlechner, Rutledge, and Al-Nuaimi, 'The UAE, the "Arab Spring", and Different Types of Dissent'.

16. 'List of Groups Designated Terrorist Organizations by the UAE', *The National*, 16 November 2014.

17. Abdulkhaleq Abdulla, 'Why the UAE's Regional Activism?' *Gulf News*, 12 January 2015.

18. Ibid.

19. Ibid.

20. Peter Hellyer, 'The Evolution of UAE Foreign Policy', in Al Abed and Hellyer, *United Arab Emirates: A New Perspective*, pp. 161–178.

21. Joseph Nye, 'Limits of American Power', *Political Science Quarterly*, 117(4), 2013, pp. 545–559.

22. Ernest Wilson, 'Hard Power, Soft Power, Smart Power', *Annals of the American Academy of Political and Social Science*, 616(1), 2008.

23. Joseph Nye, *Hard and Soft Power in a Global Information Age* (London & New York: Routledge, 2004), p. 56.

24. Joseph Nye, 'Soft Power', *Foreign Policy*, 1990, pp. 153–171.

25. Ibid.

26. Ibid.

27. Wilson, 'Hard Power, Soft Power, Smart Power'.

28. Country Profile: United Arab Emirates (UAE), accessed 20 October 2015.

29. Sultan al-Qasimi, 'The Shifting Soft Power of the Arab World', *CNN*, 27 June 2014.

30. Mustafa, Awad, 'Saudi, UAE influence Grows with Purchases', *Defense News*, 22 March 2015.

31. Kareem Shaheen, 'UAE Fighter Jets on the Way to Libya' *The National*, 26 March 2011.

32. Alissa Fromkin, 'Alissa, Part Two: The UAE Military against Islamism', *International Affairs Review* (Elliot School of International Affairs at George Washington University), 20 February 2015.

33. Martin Steven Griffiths and Terry O'Callaghan, *International Relations: The Key Concepts* (London: Routledge, 2002), p. 292.

34. Daniel Wagner and Giorgio Cafiero, 'The United Arab Emirates: A Rising Military Power', *International Policy Digest*, 10 December 2014.

35. Robert Powell, *In the Shadow of Power: States and Strategies in International Politics* (Princeton, NJ: Princeton University Press, 1999).

36. Michael Stephens, 'A Big Rethink: Security in the GCC', *Al-Jazeera Online*, 2 March 2015.

37. Abdulmajeed al-Buluwi, 'UAE and Qatar Compete as Saudi Looks On', *Al Monitor*, 28 July 2014.

38. Ibid.

39. Brahim Saidy, 'GCC's Defense Cooperation: Moving towards Unity', Foreign Policy Research Institute, October 2014, accessed 5 July 2015.

40. Miriam Fendius Elman, 'The Foreign Policies of Small States: Challenging Neorealism in Its Own Backyard', *British Journal of Political* Science, 25(2), 1995, pp. 171–217.

INDEX

17 February Brigade: Qatari support for, 53–4

al-Abadi, Haider: 120–1; administration of, 123; criticisms of, 123
bin 'Abd Allah, 'Abd Al-Malik: family of, 87
'Abd al-Rahim, Khalid: Chairman of Cebarco, 89
bin 'Abdul 'Aziz, Prince Bandar bin Sultan: 148–9
Abdulla, Abdulkhaleq: 13, 197
'Abdullah of Saudi Arabia, King: 31, 52, 57, 117, 120, 149, 160–1; accession of (2005), 145; death of (2015), 40, 139, 143–6; reign of, 144–5
Abu-Baker, Albadr: 80, 85
Abu Dhabi Group: investments of, 91
Abu Dhabi Investment Authority (ADIA): personnel of, 90
Abu Dhabi Investment Council (ADIC): ownership of Union National Bank, 91; personnel of, 90
Abu Katif, Fawzi: head of 17 February Brigade, 53–4
Accountants' Association (Kuwait): 176
Afghanistan: 28, 110, 115, 196; Operation Enduring Freedom (2001–14), 53; Soviet Invasion of (1979–89), 115
Ahmadinejad, Mahmoud: 2; administration of, 14; direct cash payment to low-income families policy (2010), 6–7
'Ajman (tribe): 158, 174
al-Ajmi, Nayef: Kuwait Justice and Endowments Minister, 37; resignation of (2014), 37
Al-Alam al-Yowm: 184
al-Albani, Sheikh: 54
Algeria: 43–4, 74, 196; food subsidy protests in (1988), 8
'Ali Nayed, 'Aref: Libyan Ambassador to UAE, 54
Almazroui, Ayesha: 16
Alstom: 93
Amanpour, Christiane: 117
AMNAS: granted royal decree (2003), 93
Arab League: 58; Baghdad Summit (2012), 32; Doha Summit (2009), 52; Sharm el-Sheikh Summit (2015), 56–7
Arab Spring: 1–2, 4–5, 15, 17–18, 20–1, 23, 26, 40–1, 43–5, 58, 78,

255

96, 113–14, 140, 165–6, 169–70,
173, 178, 192, 194–6, 199; Bahraini
Uprising (2011), 30, 38, 50–2,
56, 87, 95; Egyptian Revolution
(2011), 26–7, 38, 45, 105, 163,
197, 200; Libyan Civil War (2011),
3, 43, 45, 47, 52–3, 105, 107, 197;
media coverage of, 26–7; Omani
Protests (2011), 50, 87, 179; Syrian
Civil War (2011–), 3, 17, 27, 33–4,
36, 56, 113, 124, 137; Tunisian
Revolution (2010–11), 43, 45, 47,
55–6, 197; use of social media in,
26, 179–80; Yemeni Revolution
(2011–12), 105
Arabic (language): 156
Arabism: 194
Aruilla, John: 128
Asad Investment Company: 92
Asala Party: 54
ASDA'A Burson-Marsteller: 7
Ashraq al-Awsat: 133, 158
al-Askar, 'Abdullah: Chairman of Saudi
Shura Council's Foreign Affairs
Committee, 132
al-Assad, Bashar: regime of, 12, 34, 47,
124, 137; supporters of, 125
al-Assad, Hafez: suppression of Muslim
Brotherhood under, 49
al-'Assaf, 'Abdul 'Aziz: Saudi Finance
Minister, 159
Association of Southeast Asian Nations
(ASEAN): 106, 111
al-Atiqi, Suliman: 169
Australia: 40, 101
Austria: Vienna, 135, 161
al-Awadhi, Dr Aseel: 176–7
al-Awda, Salman: 54
al-Ayban, Dr Musa'id bin Muhammad:
155
Ayubi, Nazhi: 81

Ba'ath Party (Iraq): 33, 188
al-Baghdadi, Abu Bakr: declaration of
ISIS Caliphate (2014), 33, 115; individuals pledging loyalty to, 35–6
Bahrain: 6, 19, 35, 45, 47, 51–2,
62, 78–80, 83–5, 87–9, 95, 97,
105–6, 117, 137, 146–7, 165, 175,
179, 189, 201; Amwaj Islands, 88;
Bahrain Chamber of Commerce and
Industry (BCCI), 83–4, 95; Bahrain
Financial Harbour, 88–9; Durrat
al-Bahrain, 88; gasoline prices in, 6;
GDP per capita, 5; government of,
184; Indian expatriate population of,
106; Majlis al-Shura, 89; Manama,
96, 163; Merchants' Association, 83;
National Assembly, 49; Northern
Town, 88; oil reserves of, 81; parlia-
mentary elections in (2006), 26; par-
ticipation in Istanbul Cooperation
Initiative, 53; Shi'a militancy in, 46;
Uprising (2011), 30, 38, 50–2, 56,
87, 95, 163; wealth redistribution in,
7; youth population of, 165–6
Bahrain Independent Commission on
Inquiry (BICI): findings of, 14
balance of threat theory: concept of, 13
Bank Alfalah: 91
Bank Dhofar: board of directors of, 93;
shareholders of, 94
Bank Muscat: personnel of, 94
al-Barrak, Musallam: 174, 182
Bayadir as-Salam: 177
Ibn Baz, Sheikh: 54
Beblawi, Hazem: 77
Bedouin (ethnic group): territory
inhabited by, 169–70, 174–5
Belhaj, Abdul-Hakim: 53–4; leader of
Tripoli Military Council, 53
Ben 'Ali, Zine El Abidine: removed
from power (2011), 55

Benedict XVI, Pope: 167
benzene: 8
Blackberry Messenger: 26
Bloomberg News: 143–4
Blue City (Omani construction proj-
    ect): investment in, 93
Bosnia-Herzegovina: 28
Bosnian War (1992–5): 53
Brazil: 101
British Broadcasting Corporation
    (BBC): 134, 182
British Petroleum (BP): 64
Brookings Institution: Intelligence
    Project, 143; personnel of, 143;
    papers produced by, 118
Al-Buluwi, Abdulmajeed: 203
al-Busaʿidi (tribe): clans of, 85
Bush, George W.: 2, 32; energy policy
    of, 62; foreign policy of, 31, 110,
    160, 195
Buzan, Barry: 11

Cable News Network (CNN): 117
Cameron, David: foreign policy of, 12
Camp David Summit (2015): key
    figures present at, 162
Canada: 101
Carnegie Endowment for International
    Peace: personnel of, 15
Carter, Jimmy: Carter Doctrine
    (1980), 9, 62
Cebarco: founding of (1992), 89;
    personnel of, 89
Charbel, Ghassan: 132–3
Chatterjee Miller, Manjari: 103
Chechnya: 28
China, People's Republic of: 18, 63,
    69–70, 101–2, 110–12; Beijing, 70;
    energy demand in, 64, 66; military
    of, 128; Xinjiang, 110
China-Pakistan Economic Corridor
    (CPEC): 110

Christianity: Coptic, 47
Chubin, Shahram: 15
Clinton, Bill: 161; administration of,
    25
Clinton, Hillary: meeting with UAE
    leaders (2011), 52; US Presidential
    electoral campaign of (2016), 8; US
    Secretary of State, 52
Cohen, David: US Treasury Undersec-
    retary for Terrorism and Financial
    Intelligence, 37, 118
Cold War: 11, 100, 194; end of, 10
colonialism: British, 191; French, 191
constructivism: 201; concept of, 10
Council on Foreign Relations: 31
Crystal, Jill: 78, 81–2

al-Dalal, Mohammd: 181
Davutoglu, Ahmet: Turkish Foreign
    Minister, 167
Der Spiegel: research into ISIS, 3
al-Dhari, Sheikh Harith: family of, 123
Dhofar International Development
    and International Company: person-
    nel of, 94
Dickinson, Elizabeth: 118
diesel: 8
Djibouti: 139
Dolphin Energy: personnel of, 91

Economist, The: 157
Efstathopoulos, Charalampos: 104
Egypt: 4, 46, 55–7, 71, 73, 167, 194,
    196, 199; Cairo, 27, 45, 48, 55,
    111, 147; Central Bank, 45; Coptic
    Christian population of, 47; food
    subsidy protests in (1977), 8; gov-
    ernment of, 160; Revolution (2011),
    26–7, 38, 45, 163, 197; Sharm el-
    Sheikh, 45, 56–7
Egypt Economic Development Con-
    ference (2015): 45

INDEX

reserves of, 67; Treasury Department, 32, 37; War of Independence (1775–83), 81; Washington DC, 25, 27, 31, 38–40, 61, 63, 68, 70, 73, 131, 133–6, 146, 152, 160, 163
University of Nizwa: board of trustees, 92
al-'Urayyid, Jawad: Bahraini Deputy Prime Minister without portfolio, 89; Bahraini Minister of State for Cabinet Affairs, 89; family of, 89
al-'Urayyid, Mansur: family of, 89
Ibn al-Uthaymin, Sheikh: 54

Venezuela: 74; oil reserves of, 105

W.J. Towell: 86
Wahhabism: 54, 148; spread of, 138
Walt, Stephen: role in development of balance of threat theory, 13
Walt, Kenneth: 195–6
War on Terror: 10–11
Washington Post: 118
Al-Watan: 184–5
Watan Party: electoral performance of (2012), 54
Weaver, Mary Ann: 26
Wendt, Alexander: 13
WhatsApp: 179
Wikipedia: 144
Wilayat al-Bahrain (Bahrain Province): Eastern Province Attack (2015), 36
Women's Cultural and Social Society: 176
World Trade Organization (WTO): 102

Yemen: 9, 29, 33, 45, 71, 100, 104–5, 124, 133, 137–8, 140–1, 160, 167, 188; Aden, 16, 40, 200; anti-fuel subsidy reduction protests in (1984), 8; Civil War (2015–), 1–2, 4, 13,

15–16, 36, 39–40, 46, 56–7, 113, 124–5, 127, 156–8, 186, 200, 203; evacuation of Indians from (2015) 107; Houthi movement in, 16, 39–40, 46, 57, 113, 124–5, 138–9, 156–8, 200; Revolution (2011–12), 105; Sana'a, 39–40; Zaidi population of, 138

Zarif, Javad: Iranian Foreign Minister, 140–1
al-Zarqawi, Abu Musab: 33
al-Zawawi, Qays: death of (1995), 86; family of, 86
al-Zawawi, 'Umar: Omani Special Adviser to the Sultan, 93
al-Zawawi, Yusuf: family of, 86
al-Zayani, 'Abd al-Rahamn: family of, 89
al-Zayani, Zayed: Bahraini Minister of Industry and Commerce, 89; family of, 89
bin Zayed, 'Abdullah: ministerial posts held by, 90, 197
bin Zayed, Crown Prince Mohammed: 197; Chairman of Abu Dhabi Executive Council, 89; Chairman of ADIC, 90; Chairman of Mubadala Development Company, 90
bin Zayed, Hamdan: ministerial and board posts held by, 90
bin Zayed, Khalifa: 146, 197; Chairman of ADIA, 90; family of, 91–2
bin Zayed, Lieutenant-General Saif: family of, 90; ministerial posts held by, 90
bin Zayed, Hazza': Vice-Chairman of Abu Dhabi Executive Council, 89–90
bin Zayed, 'Issa: 91; family of, 92
bin Zayed, Mansour: Chairman of